(44- 15029)

4-29-65

THE LAST YEARS OF THE PROTECTORATE

VOL. I. 1656–1657

4

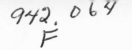
THE LAST YEARS

OF

THE PROTECTORATE

1656–1658

BY

CHARLES HARDING FIRTH, M.A.

VOL. I

1656–1657

NEW YORK

RUSSELL & RUSSELL · INC

1964

FIRST PUBLISHED IN 1909

REISSUED, 1964, BY RUSSELL & RUSSELL, INC.

L. C. CATALOG CARD NO: 64—15029

PRINTED IN THE UNITED STATES OF AMERICA

PREFACE

THESE volumes are intended to be a continuation of the 'History of the Commonwealth and Protectorate' which Dr. S. R. Gardiner left unfinished. The third volume of his book was published in 1901, just before he fell ill. The only portion of the projected fourth volume which he left in a sufficiently advanced state for publication was the chapter on the Parliamentary Elections of 1656, published separately in 1903. I cannot refrain from expressing once more the regret felt by all students of English history that Dr. Gardiner was not spared to complete the book to which he devoted so many years, and to give the world his final estimate of the aims and achievements of the Protector. A continuation by another hand has necessarily many defects. Though this was undertaken in accordance with Dr. Gardiner's wishes, I am conscious that I do not possess either the comprehensive knowledge or the perfect equipment which he brought to his task.

An explanation of this kind seemed necessary in order to show why these volumes begin, somewhat abruptly, with the meeting of Cromwell's second Parliament in September, 1656, and to account for the absence of any preliminary sketch of the position of English politics at that moment. The 'History of the Commonwealth and Protectorate' supplies the place of any such introduction, and a certain acquaintance with it is throughout assumed. The references made

to it in the following pages are to the original edition
in three volumes.

I feel it also necessary to apologise for the length of
this book.   During the later years of the Protectorate
the power of Cromwell at home and his influence abroad
reached their height; his field of action widened, and the
story becomes in consequence more complicated.   Some
episodes are, perhaps, treated in too much detail, but
it seemed to me as important to show the temper of the
time as to narrate the events.   I hope to continue this
narrative down to the Restoration of Charles II, and to
treat more fully in the next instalment the social and
economic condition of England during the rule of
Cromwell and his son.

Though this is not the place for an exhaustive
bibliography, it seems desirable to indicate some of the
manuscript sources used and to mention some of the
modern books bearing on the subject which have been
referred to.   Guizot's 'Histoire de la République
d'Angleterre et de Cromwell' appeared in 1854, Ranke's
'Englische Geschichte' between 1859 and 1868, the
fifth volume of Masson's 'Life of Milton' in 1877.   No
history of the Protectorate as a whole has been published
since, though there have been many biographies of
Cromwell, and many articles on different aspects of his
policy, while some new materials have been calendared
or made accessible.   Both in England and Germany the
character and career of Cromwell have attracted increasing attention.   Dr. Gardiner's lectures on 'Cromwell's
Place in History' appeared in 1897, his 'Cromwell'
in 1899; Lord Morley's 'Oliver Cromwell' was published in 1900, and the present writer's 'Cromwell and
the Rule of the Puritans' in the same year.   Moritz
Brosch published his 'Cromwell und die Puritanische
Revolution' in 1886, while Professor Alfred Stern's

excellent ' Geschichte der Revolution in England,'
first published in 1881, reached a second edition in 1898.
In 1907 Professor Wolfgang Michael of Freiburg published a life of Cromwell in two small volumes, containing
the result of fresh researches in foreign archives and a
very useful bibliographical appendix.   While Carlyle's
' Letters and Speeches of Oliver Cromwell ' still remains
an indispensable authority, his editorial methods and the
discovery of fresh letters and reports led to the demand
for a revised edition of his work.   Accordingly a new
collection of Cromwell's speeches, edited by Mr. C. L.
Stainer, was published in 1901, and three years later
Mrs. S. C. Lomas produced an edition of Carlyle's
book containing not only a corrected text of the speeches,
but a collection of over a hundred new letters derived
from various sources.   During the same period fresh
light has been thrown on Cromwell's foreign policy.
Guizot's account of the relations between England and
France has been supplemented by Chéruel's ' Histoire
de France sous le Ministère de Mazarin,' and by the
' Lettres de Mazarin ' edited by Chéruel in the series of
' Documents inédits sur l'histoire de France.' J. N.
Bowman's ' The Protestant Interest in Cromwell's
Foreign Relations,' 1900, and G. L. Beer's ' Cromwell's
Policy in its Economic Aspects,' 1902, are valuable
studies of particular sides of Cromwell's foreign policy,
to which may be added the dissertation by Mr. Guernsey
Jones on ' The Diplomatic Relations between Cromwell
and Charles X of Sweden,' 1897.   Carlbom's ' Sverige
och England,' 1900, narrates the negotiations between
the two powers from 1655 to August, 1657 ; a continuation, dealing with the later negotiations between Cromwell and Charles X, is promised but has not yet appeared.
The German policy of Cromwell is elucidated by the reports of Schlezer, the agent of the Elector of Brandenburg,

edited by Erdmannsdörffer in volume vii of the
collection of 'Urkunden und Actenstücke zur Geschichte
des Kurfürsten Friedrich Wilhelm von Brandenburg.'
Schlezer's reports throw some light on the domestic
history of the Protectorate, but unluckily the extracts
printed by the editor generally refer to external questions ; some additional extracts are given and more
promised by Professor Michael. The dispatches of
Bernardi, the Genoese agent, were printed in 1882 by C.
Prayer in volume xvi of 'Atti della Società Ligure di
Storia patria,' under the title of 'Oliviero Cromwell
dalla battaglia di Worcester alla sua morte.' Copies of
those of Giavarina, the Venetian agent, are in the
Record Office. These letters often supply information
which cannot be obtained from other sources, but they
should not be too implicitly credited.

Both for the domestic and foreign policy of the
Protector the most important source is the correspondence of Secretary Thurloe, contained in the seven folio
volumes published by Thomas Birch in 1742. The
originals of most of these papers were left to the
Bodleian Library in 1755 by Richard Rawlinson,
and are now numbered 'Rawlinson MSS.,' Class A.
vols. 1–67. A few of these MSS. are still unprinted,
and there are two small fragments of Thurloe's collection
outside Oxford. A small collection of letters relating
to foreign affairs during the period 1657–9, now at
Auckland, New Zealand, was printed in the 'English
Historical Review' in 1892 (vii. 720). A number of
letters, many of which are fragmentary or undated,
remained in the possession of Thomas Birch when the
rest were sold, and are now in the British Museum ('Add.
MSS.,' 4156–9, &c.). In 1899 the various versions of
the account of Cromwell's foreign policy drawn up by
Thurloe for the benefit of the government of Charles II

were collected and edited by S. von Bischoffshausen
as an appendix to 'Die Politik des Protector's Oliver
Cromwell in der Auffassung und Thätigkeit seines
Ministers des Staatsecretar's John Thurloe.'

The correspondence of Henry Cromwell in the
'Lansdowne MSS.' (vols. 821-3) is primarily valuable for
the history of Irish administration, but contains much
information of importance about political events in
England. Owing to the recent rearrangement of these
letters, I have frequently been obliged to refer to them
by dates instead of pages. For the history of Charles II
and the Royalist party in general the chief source is
the 'Clarendon MSS.' in the Bodleian Library. The
printed calendar at present ends with the year 1657,
but it is to be completed shortly, and fortunately rather
a large number of letters written during this period
were printed in the third volume of the 'Clarendon State
Papers' in 1786. They can be supplemented from the
'Nicholas Papers' and the 'Carte Papers,' especially from
the two volumes of 'Original Letters found among the
Duke of Ormond's Papers,' printed by Carte in 1739.
Mrs. Everett Green in her 'Calendar of the Domestic
State Papers' inserts a certain number of letters written
by Royalist exiles. The foreign papers of the period
preserved in the Record Office are scanty and for the
most part unimportant. The 'Domestic State Papers'
illustrate the details of administration, but throw little
light on larger questions of policy. On the ecclesiastical
affairs of the time Dr. W. A. Shaw's 'History of the
English Church during the Civil Wars and under
the Commonwealth,' 1900, is indispensable. For the
parliamentary history of the period, the Journals of
the House of Commons have been supplemented by
the discovery of the Journals of the 'Other House,'
which are printed in volume iv of the 'MSS. of the

House of Lords,' New Series, from the original in the
possession of Lady Tangye. Similarly, private letters,
newsletters, and the reports of foreign diplomatists
supplement, though only to a limited extent, the
debates recorded in ' The Diary of Thomas Burton,'
published in 1828. The series of newsletters written by
Dugdale and Charlton, calendared in the ' Fifth Report
of the Historical MSS. Commission,' and those addressed
by James Waynwright to Richard Bradshaw, calendared
in the ' Sixth Report,' are of some service for the years
1656–8, while those sent to the headquarters of the
army in Scotland from its agents in England, some of
which are printed in the third volume of the ' Clarke
Papers,' frequently contain political intelligence of
value. The ' Clarke Papers ' also contain some letters
of great interest relative to the services of the English
contingent in Flanders. Colonel Bourelly's ' Cromwell
et Mazarin,' published in 1886, is a history of the campaigns of 1657 and 1658 from French sources, and is
better described by its alternative title of ' Deux
Campagnes de Turenne en Flandre.' The organisation
of the English army in general is the subject of my
' Cromwell's Army,' published in 1902, and that of the
portion employed in these Flemish campaigns is treated
in a paper on ' Royalist and Cromwellian Armies in
Flanders ' printed in the ' Transactions of the Royal
Historical Society ' for 1903. On the organisation of
the English navy Mr. Oppenheim's ' History of the
Administration of the Royal Navy,' 1896, has thrown
new light, while Mr. Corbett's ' England in the Mediterranean,' 1904, brings out the significance of the
operations of the Protector's navy there, and their
connexion with European politics. Two letters of
Blake's, which I owe to the kindness of the Earl of Sandwich, and the discovery of Stayner's account of the

battle of Santa Cruz in the British Museum ('Add. MS.' 32093, f. 372), have enabled me to make the story of Blake's services clearer.

During the Protectorate the union of the three nations was completed, and the administration of Ireland and Scotland was organised on a civil instead of a military basis. The letters of Monck and others amongst the 'Clarke Papers' in Worcester College Library, and Monck's Order Book in the same collection, are the only new source of importance for the history of the English government of Scotland. A selection from these papers was edited by me in 1899 for the Scottish History Society. On the Irish history of the period Lord Fitzmaurice's 'Life of Sir William Petty,' 1895, 'Die Englische Kolonisation in Irland,' by Dr. M. Bonn, 1906, and Mr. Bagwell's 'Ireland under the Stuarts,' 1909, have all been of service, though the two former deal mainly with the land settlement, and the latter was published after my Irish chapter was written. Some new evidence is contained in the 'Report of the Historical MSS. Commission on the MSS. of the Earl of Egmont,' and in the 'Calendar of Irish State Papers,' edited by Mr. R. P. Mahaffy. That calendar, however, is restricted to the Irish papers in the English Record Office, and I have to thank Mr. Robert Dunlop for giving me the use of his transcripts of the domestic correspondence of the Commonwealth period at Dublin, which, though mostly belonging to the period before Henry Cromwell's government began, is essential to the understanding of the problems with which he had to deal. The publication of a calendar of these papers is much to be desired, and a selection from Henry Cromwell's correspondence in the 'Lansdowne MSS.' should be printed by one of the societies for publishing historical documents.

In short, during the last thirty years the labours of many historians have elucidated nearly all sides of the history of the period. The new evidence which has come to light during those years, though it includes no source of first-rate importance, completes, confirms, and corrects the evidence possessed by previous historians in such a way as to render possible a more exact narrative of events and a clearer understanding of their causes.

In conclusion I have to thank Mrs. S. R. Gardiner for placing Dr. Gardiner's notes at my disposal, and Dr. W. A. Shaw for his very valuable notes on the financial history of the Interregnum. I wish also to express my gratitude to Mrs. S. C. Lomas, Mr. H. W. C. Davis, and Miss D. K. Broster for corrections and suggestions of various kinds.

C. H. FIRTH.

OXFORD,
September 1, 1909.

CONTENTS

OF

THE FIRST VOLUME

CHAPTER I

CROMWELL'S SECOND PARLIAMENT

CHAPTER II

PARLIAMENT AND THE SPANISH WAR

CHAPTER III

CATHOLICS AND QUAKERS

CHAPTER VI

THE HUMBLE PETITION AND ADVICE

CHAPTER VII

'KILLING NO MURDER'

CHAPTER VIII

BLAKE AT SANTA CRUZ

THE FIRST VOLUME   xix

CHAPTER IX

THE CAMPAIGN IN FLANDERS

CHAPTER X

THE NORTHERN WAR

THE LAST YEARS OF THE PROTECTORATE

CHAPTER I

CROMWELL'S SECOND PARLIAMENT

THE meeting of Cromwell's second Parliament is the turning-point in the history of the Protectorate. Once more he attempted to reconcile force and law, military power and parliamentary government. Once more he sought to secure the consent of the nation to an authority founded on the usurpation of political power by the army. At the present moment his government was more nakedly the rule of the sword than it ever had been before. During the last twelve months the influence of soldiers upon its policy had steadily increased. A reconciliation between government and people was more difficult now than it had been in September 1654, when the Protector met his first Parliament. He had failed then, was he likely to succeed now ? Founded by the action of the officers of the army, the Protectorate could never lose its essentially military character; and yet it must lose its military appearance, and put on some semblance of constitutionalism, if it was to be regarded by the nation as more than a temporary dictatorship.

The events which immediately preceded and followed the opening of Parliament seemed to show that any such change was impossible. The army had almost become one of the estates of the realm, if there could be said to be any estates of the realm. On September 6, eleven days before Parliament met, a council of officers met at Whitehall, in which each regiment was represented by one of its field-officers. To this body Cromwell addressed a speech very like that which he made to the members of Parliament a few days later.[1] He told them that Charles II was raising an army in Flanders to invade England, that the King of Spain was assisting him, and that the Levellers had allied themselves with the Royalists and were plotting to seize a seaport where foreign forces might be landed, while the Fifth-Monarchy men were once more preparing to rise in arms. So long as the double danger of foreign invasion and domestic revolt hung like a black cloud on the horizon it was impossible for the Protector to break with the men whose fidelity was necessary to the very existence of his government. In the long run that consideration must determine his policy.

Parliament met on Wednesday, September 17. The members assembled in Westminster Abbey about ten o'clock in the morning. The Protector, with his household and chief officers of state, went in procession from Whitehall to the Abbey. Before his coach marched 300 officers on foot, and Major-General Lambert was seated in it with him. Behind, in other coaches, came the Secretary of State, the Keeper of the Great Seal, the judges and the councillors.[2] It appeared a military rather than a civil pageant, and the prominence of

---

[1] *Clarke Papers*, iii. 71.

[2] Prayer, *Oliviero Cromwell dalla battaglia di Worcester alla sua morte* (*dispatches of Francesco Bernardi*), 377 ; *Cromwelliana*, 158.

Lambert, the leader of the military party in the Protector's Council, had a sinister air.[1]

John Owen, who preached the opening sermon, took as his text the last verse of the 14th of Isaiah : ' What shall one then answer the messengers of the nation ? That the Lord hath founded Zion, and the poor of His people shall trust in it.' His discourse was a glorification of the religious blessings which the nation enjoyed under the Protector's rule. ' The people of God in this nation were despised, but are now in esteem ; they were under subjection to cruel taskmasters, some in prisons, some banished to the ends of the earth, merely for the worship of their God ; the consciences of all were enthralled while iniquity and superstition were established by law. But now the imprisoned are set at liberty ; the banished are recalled ; they that lay among the pots have got doves' wings ; conscience is no more enthralled ; their sacrifices are not mixed with their blood, nor do they meet with trembling to worship God. O ye messengers of the nations, this is what the Lord hath done ! ' [2]

After the service the members reassembled in the Painted Chamber, where the Protector addressed them. His speech was a powerful argument, but full, as usual, of digressions and repetitions.[3] He told them that he would not study the art of rhetoricians. His business was not to speak words, but things. He would begin, therefore, by setting forth the dangers in which the

---

[1] Gardiner, *Commonwealth and Protectorate*, iii. 181.

[2] Published under the title of *God's Work in founding Zion and the People's Duty thereupon.* See Orme's *Life of Owen*, 161, and *Thomason Tracts*, E. 891 (2).

[3] Carlyle's *Cromwell*, Speech v. Carlyle has taken liberties with the text, as the examination of it by Mrs. Lomas in her edition shows. The speech published seems to have been expurgated. ' Letters out of England the last week told us . . . that if my Lord Protector's speech be printed, some passages shall be left out, as not fit to be seen by the eyes of all the world, though very convenient for the ears of the parliament and of every true Englishman.'— Pell to Morland, October $\frac{16}{26}$. Vaughan, *Protectorate of Oliver Cromwell*, ii. 41.

nation stood; for to communicate this was the special end of their meeting.

'Abroad,' said Cromwell, 'your great enemy is the Spaniard. He is a natural enemy.' On religious grounds Spain was necessarily the enemy of Protestant England, 'by reason of that enmity which is in him against whatever is of God.' A long series of events had led up to this late breach. In the days of Queen Elizabeth 'of famous memory,' Spain had sought by all unworthy means to destroy her and to ruin these nations. King James made a peace, but England and the Protestant interest in general had suffered more damage by that peace than by all Spain's hostility. The Long Parliament sought an honest and honourable peace with Spain, but could not attain it. The present government had sought redress before resorting to war, but equally in vain. No satisfaction could be obtained, either for the denial of freedom of conscience to English traders, or for 'the blood of your poor people unjustly shed in the West Indies.' The truth was that no peace was possible with any popish state. Sign what you like with one of them, 'that peace is but to be kept so long as the Pope says Amen to it.' France was the sole exception to this rule. Of all European powers Spain was the most bigotedly Catholic; it was 'the head of the Papal interest, the head of the anti-christian interest.' Rarely had that interest been more dangerous than now. 'This Pope is a person all the world knows to be a person of zeal for his religion, and a man of contrivance and wisdom and policy; [1] and his designs are

---

[1] Alexander VII, Fabio Chigi, elected Pope in April 1655. He was personally hostile to Mazarin and thoroughly Spanish in his sympathies. Clarendon describes him as having expressed himself strongly in favour of the royal cause before he became Pope, but unwilling to do anything for it afterwards (*Rebellion*, xiv. 120). Ranke's account of Alexander VII hardly bears out Cromwell's estimate of his ability.

known to be nothing else but endeavours to unite all the
popish interests in all the Christian world, against this
nation above any, and against all the Protestant interest
in the world.' And besides this standing danger of a
union of Catholic powers headed by Spain, there was a
new source of danger in the late agreement between
Charles II and the Spaniard.

'He hath espoused Charles Stuart, with whom he
is fully at agreement; for whom he hath raised seven
or eight thousand men that are now quartered at
Bruges; [1] to whom Don John of Austria hath promised
as soon as the campaign is ended, which it is conceived
will be in about five or six weeks, he shall have four or
five thousand, and the Duke of Neuburg hath promised
good assistance according to his power, and other
popish states the like.' [2]

Spain, continued Cromwell, was also in league with
all the disaffected in England. Here the Protector
digressed into an account of all the plots against the
government during the last two years. He began by
referring to the Royalist rising in March 1655. The
government, he said, knew of the intended insurrection
beforehand, but could not persuade Parliament to
believe in its reality. Even now there were people who
minimised its importance and its danger. It was said:
'These were a company of mean fellows, not a lord,

---

[1] Though the different texts of the speech all agree in giving these figures
as 'seven or eight thousand,' it is probable that we should read 'seven or eight
hundred.' That was just about the number of men whom (according to the intelligence received by Cromwell's government) Charles II had actually raised.

[2] See Thurloe, v. 362, 391. The Duke, according to Clarendon, had con-
tracted a great friendship with Charles II in 1654 (*Rebellion*, xiv. 114).
Bordeaux in a letter to Mazarin says that Cromwell's statement met with little
credence. 'In regard there is very little advice conformable to this, many
believe that it is invented, and feigned to give an alarm and to keep the army
united in the present conjuncture' (Thurloe, v. 427). In a second letter,
addressed to Brienne, Bordeaux reported the Protector as saying that Spain
was to provide 5000 and Neuburg 4000.

nor a gentleman, nor a man of fortune amongst them ';
they were only ' a poor headstrong people.' He asserted,
on the other hand, that the plot was a 'general design,' in which the whole of the Royalist party were
concerned. ' We are able to make it appear that persons
that carried themselves the most demurely and fairly
of any men in England were engaged in this business.'
Other ' discontented spirits ' had been at work
then, and were at work still. These malcontents
might not all agree in their hearts with the Cavaliers,
but ' they must end at the interest of the Cavaliers in
the long run. That must be their support.' The
Protector divided the malcontents into three classes.
First came the Levellers proper, who had prepared in
1655 to join the Cavaliers in carrying on their design,
and had endeavoured to raise a revolt in the army in
Scotland. Allied with them were the discontented
republicans—a party that went ' under a finer name
or notion,' and called themselves ' Commonwealths-
men'—some of whom were 'men of fortune and great
estates.' Finally there were a set of men ' of notions
more seraphical,'· the Fifth-Monarchy men. All three
parties were working together to produce ' blood and
confusion ' in England, and one of them was in league
with Spain. The Protector acquitted the Commonwealths-men and the Fifth-Monarchy men of this
treason to their country : ' They stood at a distance ;
I think they did not participate.' The Levellers, however, had sent ' a fellow, a wretched creature, an apostate
from religion and all honesty, to Madrid to advise
with the King of Spain to lend forces to invade this
nation ;[1] promising satisfaction that they would comply
and concur with him to have both men and monies ;
undertaking both to engage the fleet to mutiny and also

[1] Colonel Sexby.

your army; if the Spaniard would say where he would
land, they would be ready to assist him.' A foreign
invasion and a new civil war, these were the ills which
Royalists and Levellers would bring upon England.
'Here is your danger, and here is a poor nation that
hath wallowed in its blood; though, thanks be to God,
we have had peace these four or five years, yet here is
the condition we stand in.'

These things justified the establishment of the new
militia and the appointment of the Major-Generals.
'When this insurrection was, and we saw it in all the
roots and grounds of it, we did find out a little poor
invention which I hear has been much regretted; I say
there was a little thing invented, which was the erecting
of your Major-Generals.' Their erection was 'justifiable
to necessity, and honest in every respect'; and the
decimation tax by which they were maintained was
strictly equitable. 'If there were need to have greater
forces to carry on this work, it was a most righteous
thing to put the charge upon that party which was
the cause of it.' Though it is probable that the scheme
was invented by Lambert rather than Cromwell, the
Protector made it his own by the emphasis with which
he defended it. He pronounced any man averse to it
'a man against the interest of England,' and declared
'if this were to be done again I would do it.'

After this declaration, which must have been
extremely unacceptable to most of his audience, the
Protector turned to discuss the measures necessary to
secure the nation from the dangers enumerated. One
was the energetic prosecution of the war with Spain.
'If you can come to prosecute it, prosecute it vigorously
or do not do it at all.' As to the ways and means, it
was true that the nation was overwhelmed in debt,
but the government had not managed the treasury

unthriftily. The assessment had been reduced from £120,000 to £60,000 per month. Great though the debt was, 'give me leave to tell you, you are not so much in debt as we found you.' The government not only permitted, but invited an inquiry into the state of the public finances.

After all, however, the best security against the danger which threatened England was not in forces or arms, but in a reformation of those things which were amiss. ' Be as politic and diligent and vigilant as you can be ; I think your reformation, if it be honest, and thorough, and just, will be your best security.' Religion, manners, laws, in all three reformation was needed. The Protector then sketched the religious policy he had pursued since the last Parliament, bringing out very clearly the two principles upon which it was based. One was the maintenance of liberty of conscience for all men who believed in Christ and lived peaceably. This liberty of conscience, said he, is 'undoubtedly the peculiar interest all this while contended for.' On the other hand no men were to be allowed to 'make religion a pretext for blood and arms,' and no sect was to be suffered to 'revile and reproach and provoke' another. He had endeavoured to be impartial between the different sects, 'to keep things equal,' and had been abused by some as too favourable to Presbytery, and by others as 'an inletter to all the sects and heresies of the nation'; but he was indifferent to such criticisms. 'I have borne my reproach, but I have, through God's mercy, not been unhappy in preventing any one religion to impose upon another.'

The second principle which had actuated his policy had been the maintenance of a National Church—'a public ministry' as Cromwell termed it. For that object tithes had been retained, and must be retained till

some other provision for the support of the clergy could
be devised. He called attention to the care taken
to secure a learned and pious clergy by instituting
the Triers and Ejectors, and to the success which had
attended their measures. ' This ministry of England
was never so upon the thriving hand since England
was, as it is at this day.'

Passing from religious to social reform, he urged
Parliament to take in hand the suppression of disorder,
debauchery, and immorality of every kind. ' Make it a
shame to see men bold in sin and profaneness, and God
will bless you.' Not only manners but laws needed
reforming, especially the criminal laws. There were
' wicked and abominable laws,' which Parliament
ought to remedy at the first opportunity.

In conclusion the Protector turned to answer the
criticisms of his republican opponents. Again he
repeated his defence of the Major-Generals. The
institution had not only preserved the peace of England
—' you had not had peace two months together without
it '—but it had also proved ' more effectual towards the
discountenancing of vice and the settling of religion,
than anything done these fifty years.' Necessity
justified it, and in sudden emergencies extraordinary
remedies might justifiably be applied. ' If nothing
should be done but what is according to law, the throat
of the nation may be cut while we send for some to
make a law.'[1] By the same argument he justified the

---

[1] This part of the Protector's speech was naturally exposed to criticism.
Two Royalist letters comment on it as follows :—

' And least any should be offended at some late proceedings, which might
seeme exorbitant because illegall, his Highnesse did take a greate deale of
paynes to remove such dissatisfactions : He told them that Necessity was the
greate standinge law of the world to which all other municipall lawes ought
to give place, that though Law, Liberty, Privilege, Property, etc. were pretty
words, and such thinges which in their season were very good and fitt to be
reguarded, yett they were not soe highly to be valued as to be sett in opposition

CHAP.
I
1656

imprisonment of Vane and some other malcontents. All had been found doing acts which tended to the disturbance of the public peace. No engagement to be faithful to the government had been pressed upon them, no bonds exacted. All they were asked to do was to live quietly in their own counties. 'Yet they would not so much as say, We will promise to live peaceably.'

Cromwell ended by adjuring Parliament to save the nation and the cause of European Protestantism. Let them quit themselves like men—Christian men. A neutral or a Laodicean spirit would not do the work that must be done. Men who thought that civil liberty should come before religious liberty, doubting, hesitating men under the bondage of scruples, carnal men merely having an outward profession of godliness—none of these could rise to such a spiritual heat as the work needed. Let them not dispute about unnecessary and unprofitable things that might divert them from carrying on the work. Union between Protector and Parliament, ' both united in faith and love to Jesus Christ

to the greate dispensations of Heaven, and to be made use of to cutt the throat of Providence, that lawes were to be adapted to providences, not providences to lawes ; that it was in compliance with the necessity of the times that he had done whatsoever was done contrary to law, and that as he had found by experience, that he could never have carried on the worke soe farre, if he had stucke at little punctilioes, so he did caution them above all thinges to preserve themselves from the bondage of nice scruples, and frankly to concurre in those thinges which the exigency of affaires required of them.'—John Fisher (i.e. W. Howard) to Sir E. Hyde, September 22, 1656. *Clarendon MSS.*

' Cromwell's speech to the Parliament was insolent beyond all show of prudence, telling them he only called them to raise him money, not at all to meddle with the government. That they would but break their own necks that strove to break his, and that he would be the last that should fall. That money he would not want while England had it, and that if he were forced to it he would send for the ships home and sell them, and let the nation defend themselves otherwise as well as they could, if they would not enable him to do it. One thing amongst the rest made his impudence most remarkable, which was his deriding the Government by a Commonwealth, and crying up Monarchy, which he said he never was against in his judgment, but was violenced by a giddy fantastical generation.'—Mr. Jennings to Hyde, October 24, 1656. *Clarendon State Papers*, iii. 309.

and to His peculiar interest in the world,' must be the
foundation of the work. Both must be ' knit together in one bond to promote the glory of God against the common enemy, to suppress everything that is evil, and encourage whatsoever is of godliness.' If they so united with him the nation would bless them, and the blessing of God would go with them. Let them read Luther's Psalm [1]—' a rare psalm for a Christian'—and, like Luther, take God for their refuge and their strength. Then they would have nothing to fear from their enemies. ' If Pope, and Spaniard, and Devil and all set themselves against us, though they should compass us about like bees, yet in the name of the Lord we should destroy them.' Then England would be secure from every danger. It would be with her as with the city of God in that Psalm: ' God is in the midst of her; she shall not be moved.'

After hearing the Protector's speech the members repaired to the House and proceeded to elect Sir Thomas Widdrington as their Speaker. Many, however, found themselves denied admission. The supporters of the government, alarmed by the election of some who were either adherents of the opposition or suspected of dis-affection to the Protectorate, had from the first suggested that a test should be imposed upon the persons elected before allowing them to take their seats. Major-General Kelsey had warned Secretary Thurloe that some such measure was absolutely necessary. ' I could wish,' he wrote, ' that all that sat in the House may be put to sign a recognition to own the government as it is in the Instrument, and not to meddle with what is past; for by this means many of your rigid fellows would be kept out; if not, so soon as the Parliament sits, you will have the counties thronging at the doors with

[1] Psalm xlvi.

petitions, which will put us into confusion.'[1] Such a
recognition had been imposed by the Protector in his
struggle with the Parliament of 1654, but this time the
government thought that a shorter way with the
opposition would be more effective. The influence of
Lambert and the military party in the Protector's
Council was doubtless responsible for the method
chosen, for the Protector himself appears to have left
them a free hand in the matter.[2] Accordingly, when the
returns from the different constituencies came in, the
Clerk of the Commonwealth in Chancery was ordered
to transmit the indentures to the Council.[3] That body
proceeded to examine the list, and to decide who should
be allowed to sit and who excluded. It then returned
the indentures to the clerk with instructions ' that he
should deliver tickets to such persons, and such only, as
being returned to serve in Parliament should be certified
to him from the Council as persons by them approved.'[4]
The clerk issued tickets certifying that such and such a
person had been returned to serve in Parliament for a
constituency named, and that he had been approved by
his Highness's Council.[5] Without this certificate no one
was allowed to enter the House. Three colonels, backed

[1] Thurloe, v. 384 ; cf. *Cal. State Papers Dom.*, 1656-7, p. 87.

[2] Thurloe, v. 424, 426 ; cf. Palgrave, *Oliver Cromwell*, 179, 183. In one
version of Cromwell's speech to the hundred officers on February 27, 1657,
about the question of kingship, he is represented as saying that the Parliament
was called at their desire and against his judgment, and that the exclusion of
the members elected was also the work of the officers.

' When they were chosen you garbled them, kept out and put in whom
you pleased by the Instrument, and I am sworn to make good all you doe,
right or wrong, and because 120 are excluded I must think them malignants
or scandalous whether they are soe or not.'—*Lansdowne MS.*, 821, f. 314.

[3] *Commons' Journals*, vii. 425, and Burton, *Diary*, i. clxxix.

[4] This procedure was specified in the Instrument, clause xxi. Tickets
had been issued to members in the Parliament of 1654. Burton, *Diary*, i. xvii.
Thurloe says on September 16 that the Council had decided to exclude about
one hundred members.—*State Papers*, v. 424.

[5] For a specimen see Whitelocke, *Memorials*, iv. 274 (ed. 1853).

by a guard of soldiers, kept the door, and examined the CHAP.
I tickets.[1]

1656
Sept.
18.

The excluded members were not minded to submit without a protest. On the morning of the second day Sir George Booth, one of the members for Cheshire, rose up and presented a letter to the Speaker. It was signed by seventy-nine members, and stated that they had been duly returned to serve in Parliament, but that when, in discharge of their trust, they attempted to enter the House, they were at the lobby door kept back by soldiers. Lest they should be wanting in their duty to the Speaker and their country, they represented these facts to him to be communicated to the House.[2]

The debate which followed lasted from Thursday, September 18, till the Monday following.[3] At first the decision seemed likely to be in favour of the excluded members. ' It was strongly urged that it was a breach of privilege of Parliament that any should be kept out of the House, and that none, sitting the Parliament, would be competent judges of any chosen by the people to be members but only the Parliament.'[4] Some

---

[1] *Clarke Papers*, iii. 74.

[2] *Commons' Journals*, vii. 424.

[3] From the journals it looks as if seventy-nine members signed the letters (*Commons' Journals*, vii. 425). Thurloe, however, says about fifty-six (v. 453).

[4] *Clarke Papers*, iii. 74. A Royalist gives the following account of the proceedings of the House :—

' The debate hereof was scarce entered upon when a paper was brought into the House by Sir George Booth from the secluded members, whoe are about 120. . . .

' The sight hereof diverted them from their former consultation and putt them upon the debate of their owne priviledges, which some thought soe highly affronted by this act of violence, that unlesse theire members were restored them they did not judge themselves a Parliament, nor in capacity to doe anything as a Parliament. Many questions grew from hence, and the debates were very strong and doubtfull, but allwayes before this day believed to encline in favor of the excluded members. 'Tis too long to have it in all the motions of it, but in short, this day contrary to all expectation it was voted that the admission or non-admission of the secluded members should be wholly left to his Highnesse and the Councill, to whom applications were to be made by those

CHAP.
I

1656

Sept.
22.

thought the privilege of Parliament ' so highly affronted by this act of violence that unless their members were restored to them they did not judge themselves a Parliament, nor in a capacity to do anything as a Parliament.'

The discussion was lengthy and bitter, and the House applied to the Council to know why the members in question were not admitted. On Monday Fiennes replied on behalf of the Council, pleading articles 21 and 17 of the Instrument. The 21st clause authorised the Council to examine and approve the returns ; the 17th specified that the men returned should be ' persons of integrity, fearing God and of good conversation.' [1]

This explanation only made the case of the government worse. The illegality of the Council's conduct was ' gross as a mountain, open, palpable.' A provision intended to secure that none but honest and godly men should be members of Parliament had been construed to mean that no opponents or critics of the government should sit in the House. What was designed as a moral test had been perverted into a political test.

Nevertheless, after a speech from Secretary Thurloe

that thought themselves unjustly secluded. There are that say, that this vote was surreptitiously gained in the absence of most of the members, there beinge not many above 150 in the House all that time, whereof 125 were for the vote, and 29 only against itt. Great disappointments are given hereby to the mal-contents, and great encouragements to the court party.'—John Fisher to Sir E. Hyde, September 22, 1656. *Clarendon State Papers*, iii. 287.

[1] ' That whereas by a clause in the Government it is ordained, That the Clerk of the Commonwealth, &c., as in the one-and-twentieth article ; and by another clause in the Government, it is ordained, That the persons who shall be elected to serve in Parliament, shall be such and no other than such, as are persons of known integrity, fearing God, and of good conversation :
' That the Council, in pursuance of their duty, and according to the trust reposed in them, have examined the said returns, and have not refused to approve any who have appeared to them to be persons of integrity, fearing God, and of good conversation ; and those who are not approved, his Highness hath given order to some persons to take care that they do not come into the House.'—*Commons' Journals*, vii. 426.

in defence of the government, the House surrendered its CHAP.
I
1656 right, and acquiesced in the subversion of the law. The resolution proposed by the government was: ' That the persons who have been returned from the several counties, cities, and boroughs to serve in this Parliament, and have not been approved, be referred to make their application to the Council for an approbation; and that the House do proceed with the great affairs of the nation.'

The opposition wished to postpone the vote. Eighty members (for whom Sir John Hobart and Colonel Purefoy were tellers) proposed to adjourn the debate till the next morning. A hundred and fifteen (for whom Major-General Desborough and Nathaniel Fiennes were tellers) voted against the adjournment.[1] It was evident that the government's resolution would be passed, and one of the leaders of the minority solemnly protested against the surrender of the privileges of Parliament which was contemplated. He then left the House, followed by many others of his party. When the final vote on the resolution was taken the majority had risen from 115 to 125, and the minority sunk from 80 to 29. About 40 who had voted in the first division had abstained from voting in the second, so that the number of the seceders was about 41.[2]

The supporters of the government exulted greatly

---

[1] *Commons' Journals*, vii. 426 ; a letter from Bordeaux to Mazarin, printed in Thurloe, *State Papers*, v. 427, contains some comments on the debate and its results.

[2] *Commons' Journals*, vii. 426. Many points about this division are notice-able. In the first place we have in the *Tanner MSS.* lii. 166, a list of the minority of twenty-nine. Neither Sir John Hobart nor Colonel Purefoy are amongst the number, and both had evidently left the House. The fact of the secession is distinctly stated both by Bordeaux and Giavarina in their dispatches. See Bordeaux to Brienne, $\frac{\text{September 25}}{\text{October 6}}$; Giavarina, $\frac{\text{September 26}}{\text{October 6}}$; *Venetian Transcripts, R.O.*

over this vote, which Thurloe described as 'a great providence of God.' [1] 'Truly,' wrote one of Monck's correspondents, ' we have great cause to bless the Lord this business is over, for it was very doubtful whilst it was debated what would be the result of the House, and had all that had been chosen been admitted of, I leave it to your Lordship to consider what obstructions we might have met with in owning the government, and doing good for the nations in the present juncture of times, when all our enemies are plotting against our peace and present government and to bring in Charles Stuart.' [2]

It was a high-handed measure which nothing but the necessity of the public safety could excuse. At one stroke the Protector and his Council had reduced Parliament by one-third of its members. Out of a total of 460 about 100 had been forcibly excluded, and some 50 or 60 more voluntarily abstained from taking their seats.[3]

The outrage, however, was not merely in the number of members kept out, but in the nature of the expedient employed for the purpose. It was an insult to stigmatise men like Haselrig, Maynard, Grimstone, Scot,

---

[1] Thurloe, writing to Henry Cromwell, says : ' Many are withdrawn from the House because they could not have their will in this vote.'—*State Papers*, v. 453.

[2] *Clarke Papers*, iii. 74.

[3] The Instrument fixed 400 members for England and thirty each for Scotland and Ireland. Thurloe speaks of 100 members as excluded (v. 453). A list amongst the papers of Secretary Nicholas gives ninety-nine names (*Cal. State Papers Dom.*, 1656–7, p. 113). Another, probably drawn up by John Hobart, who was one of the members, contains 105 names (*Tanner MSS.*, lii. 156). Add to these those who seceded of their own accord or abstained from taking their seats, and we get the higher totals given by other authorities, such as Bordeaux, who says 160 members were kept out, and a newsletter which gives the figure as 140 (Thurloe, v. 417 ; *Cal. State Papers Dom.*, 1656–7, p. 113). We have seen that there were about forty abstainers from the vote of September 22. The journals of the House contain a list of seventy-nine excluded members, three of whom are not given in Hobart's list.

and other republicans as not being ' persons of known CHAP.
I
1656
integrity, fearing God and of good conversation.'
Besides, if some of those excluded were notoriously
hostile to the Protector, others were obscure persons of
no political weight, who had not, so far as evidence is
available, taken any active part against the existing
government.[1] But obscurity proved no more a protection
than consistent republicanism. Royalist observers did
not hesitate to say that the Protector's information about
persons was bad, and that many of the excluded were
persons from whom the government had nothing to fear.[2]

An analysis of the constituencies represented by the
excluded members shows in what districts the strength
of the opposition lay, and testifies to a remarkable revulsion of feeling amongst the electorate. Over seventy
of the hundred members represented counties, and as a
rule counties which had been the strongest supporters

---

[1] Hobart's list contains the names of five Norfolk members who had signed
the test imposed by Cromwell in September 1654, and can hardly have been
very thorough-going opponents.—See Burton, *Diary*, i. xxxvi.

[2] This is the criticism of Captain Titus: ' You know that at the first
Cromwell excluded the House 140 of the members, and that since some eighty
have left it of their own accord. Amongst those that were excluded, it is
not a little satisfaction to me that Major-General Browne was one, whoe had
he beene admitted had, in such a house as Cromwell hath left it, been able to
doe verrie little good, but being rejected, I soe well understand the temper of
the man as to promise myself he will not neglect any opportunity that falls in
his way to resent the injury, and this he hath said himself, not with much com-
mendation to his prudence, though he had then the good fortune to be in
companie that were all of his mind. Booth of Cheshire, one of the most considerable of our partie, was likewise excluded. Rossiter was not, but refused
to take any ticket to goe into the House. But amongst many strange things
that Cromwell did that day I wonder what it was that he apprehended in my
Lord of Salisbury, that made him doe him the honour to keepe him out.
Those that well understood the temper of most of those that were chosen,
thinke Cromwell's information of persons was but bad, for they say he excluded
many of his friendes, at least that would not have had the courage to be
his enemies, and admitted many whom he hath noe other tye upon but their
owne feares; which he had of others and some of those too which have ventured
very farre in expressing theire dislike of his proceedings.'—*Clarendon MSS.*,
October 24, 1656.

of the Parliamentary cause during the Civil War. All
the five members for Hertfordshire were excluded, seven
out of the ten elected for Suffolk, six out of the ten of
Lincolnshire, five out of the ten of Norfolk, and five
out of the thirteen of Essex. The seven counties comprising the old Eastern Association were represented
by a total of fifty-seven members, of whom twenty-nine
belonged to the opposition. The same thing happened
in Sussex and Kent, where out of the nine members for
the first county five were excluded, and out of the eleven
for the second, seven. Yet these two counties had been
as unanimously opposed to the King's cause as the
Eastern Association. A similar phenomenon happened
in the West Riding of Yorkshire, which had been the
chief reliance of the Fairfaxes in the northern war :
four out of its six members were excluded.[1]

On the other hand the strength of the government
lay in the boroughs. Those included in the counties
comprising the old Eastern Association were represented
by twenty-five members of whom four only belonged to
the opposition. Nor was this only the case in the
smaller boroughs, which might be supposed to be more
easily influenced by the government than the larger
ones. In England there were twenty-two boroughs
returning two members apiece, and of the forty-four
chosen by them thirty-seven belonged to the government party and but seven to the opposition. On the
other hand four out of the six members chosen for
the city of London were amongst the excluded, while
the outlying districts of Southwark and Westminster
each returned two government candidates.[2] It seems

---

[1] Godwin makes a somewhat similar calculation, but it contains many
errors ; he professes to include the boroughs situated within the counties he
mentions, but fails to do so.—*History of the Commonwealth*, iv. 289.

[2] This computation is based on the list in the *Old Parliamentary History*,
which needs some correction. Mr. W. D. Pink is compiling an exact list of

clear that the Protectorate had the support of the chap.
middle classes, and of traders and manufacturers in I
general, although the rich merchants of the London 1656
companies were increasingly hostile to it.

For the moment the Protector's *coup d'état* was
effective. During the three months which followed
the vote of September 22 there was no mention of
the excluded members in the debates of Parliament.
'Some of them,' said a newsletter, 'are gone into the
country discontented, and will not apply themselves to
the Council; others are guilty and dare not.'[1] A few
convinced the Council that they were friendly to the
government, and were allowed to take their seats.

Some months later a feeble protest was made, but
proved fruitless. On December 20, when members
were beginning to go home to their families for Christmas, and the House had grown thin, it was proposed
that the roll should be called, and that all absent without leave should be fined. ' It is reported abroad,' said
the mover, ' that we are but a rag of a Parliament.
They say we are made up of none but soldiers and
courtiers, and I know not what friends to my Lord
Protector.' Lambert answered on behalf of the government that he desired to see the House as full as possible,
but that he hoped a distinction would be made between
those members approved by the Council and those
who had not been approved. Thomas Bampfield,
member for Exeter, promptly seized the opportunity
to raise the claim of the excluded members. ' I would
have these words left out, " such as are approved or
shall be approved." I hope the Council are by this
time satisfied of those that are left out, that they are

the members of this Parliament, which will make a more precise computation
possible.

[1] *Clarke Papers*, iii. 75.

now persons capable to sit. I know one person in town that was excepted, a very pious man, and there are others. I desire all may be called in now ; it is surely time ; to the end we may carry things on with more unanimity and general consent, especially when we come to tax the people.' Major Brooke, one of the members for Cheshire, seconded the motion, urging that the excluded members should no longer be restrained from taking their seats. Let ' all be admitted, or else all go home.' [1] No division took place, but on December 31 there was a call of the House at which 172 members were present. The names of the excluded members were omitted ; so Lambert Godfrey, one of the members for Kent, moved for their inclusion. ' I humbly move,' said he, ' that you would take an account of your own members, and know how and why they are detained. It is the common interest of the nation and the honour of your House.' Thistlethwaite, a member who like Godfrey had for some months absented himself from the House in order to show his abhorrence of the violence under which it laboured, eagerly supported Godfrey, and Bampfield again championed the cause of the excluded.[2] Again the debate ended without any result : ' the Speaker, being sick of the motion, left the chair,' and the opposition, content with its demonstration, did not go to a division.[3]

[1] Burton, *Diary*, i. 192–5 ; *Commons' Journals*, vii. 471, 477 ; *Clarke Papers*, iii. 85.

[2] On December 20 Godfrey had been twitted by Pickering with having been away for three or four months. Burton notes that Thistlethwaite first appeared at the call on December 31 (Burton, *Diary*, i. 194, 290). Thurloe, writing January 1, says : ' Yesterday the House was called, and upon the call several members did appear who had formerly withdrawn themselves upon some discontent, but now rest satisfied to act with us ' (Vaughan, *Protectorate of Oliver Cromwell*, ii. 77). Godfrey is always included in the list of the excluded members, but Thistlethwaite is not. John Goodwin, M.P. for East Grinstead, also took his seat about December 19.

[3] Burton, *Diary*, i. 287, 290–1.

But if within the walls of the House there was hardly a murmur, outside it the conduct of the government roused deep and general discontent, the more bitter because it was forcibly silenced. For the last year the press had been muzzled, and only two newspapers were now allowed to be issued : *The Public Intelligencer* appeared on Mondays, and *Mercurius Politicus* on Thursdays, but each was alike the organ of the government. Now Parliament was muzzled too, and freedom of speech had entirely ceased to exist for the opposition. By the imprisonment of some of their leaders and the exclusion of the rest the republicans were entirely debarred from giving utterance to their opinions in Parliament. Men who had fought by Cromwell's side in the struggle against Royalty were henceforth his irreconcilable adversaries, though they might have been merely critical or ill-affected before. What no King of England had ever dared to do the Protector and his Council had done. It was said that Cromwell's crime in excluding so many members was twenty-fold greater than that of Charles in going about to arrest five.[1] This feeling found expression in a

---

[1] 'Upon this breach made in the House, and giving up the rights and interests of the English nation in Parliament, to be judged without doors, by an inferior power, divers gentlemen then sitting in the House, who being endued with principles of justice and righteousness, and love to the nation's freedom, immediately withdrew ; and others would not enter into the House at all, but departed to their several habitations.

'Upon all which, it is proposed and queried :

'1. Whether since the Conquest there was ever such a blow given (by a people owning themselves a Parliament) to the interest and freedom of the English nation, as the suffering to be secluded from them (by an inferior power) so great a number of members chosen by the people to sit, as their representatives in Parliament ; without any cause shown for such a proceeding ?

'2. How this upstart Protector and his council of a little more than three years' standing, should come to be empowered to do those things, which a King and his council, of more than four hundred years' descent, could not, nor durst not do ? And whether the late, together with the former force, put upon the House, by excluding so many of their members, be not a crime twenty-fold beyond that of the late King's ; in going about to seclude the five members, so

CHAP.
I
1656

protest printed and privately circulated in the name of the excluded members. It denounced the Protector's exclusion of all ' who would not be frightened or flattered to betray their country, and give up their religion, lives, and estates, to be at his will, and to serve his lawless ambition.' It stigmatised the Protector himself as a man ' assuming an absolute arbitrary sovereignty as if he came down from the throne of God.' Only by some ' agreement with the body of the people in Parliament ' could the authority he claimed be legitimate. Till then he was ' the public capital enemy whom every man ought to destroy.' But no such agreement could be made with one part of the people's representatives whilst the other part was shut out. In conclusion they appealed to God and the good people of England to assist them, and promised to expose their lives and estates to the utmost hazard to prevent the ruin and confusion which threatened their country. To this manifesto the names of ninety-eight excluded members were appended, with or without their leave, and boxes containing a thousand copies or so were sent to sympathisers in London and the country for distribution. The pamphlet was suppressed by the government, but no attempt was made to prosecute any of those whose names were attached to it ; not that the government shrank from the odium that such a prosecution would entail, but because it

highly disresented in that day by the people, and afterwards attended with so great feud and bloodshed.

'3. Whether, till this unworthy generation, there ever were such a company of false-hearted, low-spirited, mercenary Englishmen sitting in that House before ; that would at once so easily give up the right, interest, and freedom of this nation, in suffering their fellow-members to be rent from them, and judged without doors ? as if there were a just power at present upon earth, higher and greater than the good people's representers in Parliament ; which, by all well-affected people, in the army and elsewhere, was so generally acknowledged the supreme authority.'—' Narrative of the Late Parliament,' *Harl. Miscell.*, iii. 450.

was well aware that the manifesto was the work of some zealous republican rather than of the miscellaneous band of malcontents whose views it was supposed to express.[1]

Bordeaux, the French ambassador, in one of his letters to Brienne, sums up the situation as it appeared to a well-informed and impartial observer.[2] ' Force alone can maintain the acts of this Parliament. The people is more angry at the exclusion of its representatives than at any other damage that it believes its liberties have received. Its discontent unites minds in favour of the King, and if he were lucky enough to land a body of foreign troops in any stronghold he would be received with as much joy as Henry VII was. But the Protector will be better prepared to resist such an attack than Richard III, from the great levies of men which he continues to make under pretext of the forces raised by the King in Flanders and Germany.' [3]

[1] The text of the declaration is printed in *Whitelocke's Memorials*, iv. 274, and in the *Old Parliamentary History*, xxi. 28. The declaration was printed in pamphlet form, and Thomason dates his copy October 7. It is E. 889. 8 in his collection. Its authenticity is called in question by Godwin, *History of the Commonwealth*, iv. 296. The chief evidence against it is the fact that Morley and Fagg, two of the signatories, repudiated all knowledge of it (Thurloe, v. 456, 490). On the same ground, Mr. R. H. Catterall in the *English Historical Review* for October 1901 (p. 737), also rejects it. The manifesto printed in Thurloe, v. 419, is the work of the same party, but obviously written about February 1655. Compare also Wildman's paper, *Whitelocke*, iv. 183. Another pamphlet of the same kind is ' *An Appeal from the Court to the Country made by a Member of Parliament lawfully chosen but secluded illegally by my Lord Protector*,' which Thomason dates October 27, E. 891. 3. It compares the conduct of the Protector with that of the King in demanding the five members in 1642, and pronounces it a greater violation of the constitution. Like the declaration it was probably printed abroad.

[2] Bordeaux to Brienne, $\frac{\text{September 25}}{\text{October 5}}$, *R.O. Transcripts*.

[3] On September 9, 1656, orders were given that one new regiment of foot, consisting of 1200 men, to be commanded by Colonel Gibbon, should be added to the army, and that nine of the existing regiments should be raised from 900 to 1200 men. This meant an addition of 3900 men to the establishment.

Cromwell was correct in warning Parliament that an invasion from Flanders was planned to take place during the coming winter. By the treaty between Charles II and the representatives of the King of Spain in Flanders, signed on April 12, 1657, and ratified by Philip IV on June 5, 4000 foot and 2000 horse were to be placed by Spain at the service of Charles for an expedition to England.[1] The Protector had received intelligence of the treaty from Mazarin, though the Cardinal had overstated the number of men promised, saying they were to be 6000 foot and 3000 horse.[2] Cromwell did not yet know the exact figures of the foreign forces promised the King, and Thurloe's spies could not supply them, though they sent exaggerated reports of the preparations which were being made. One stated that the Duke of Neuburg would provide 1000 foot, besides other great assistance, and that two Flemish nobles had promised to raise regiments of horse for Charles. Another related that 7000 or 8000 men were being raised in Germany in the name of the English King.[3]

Some foreign force, it was admitted, was necessary to the success of any attempt to overthrow the Protector's government. That eminent Royalist, Sir Marmaduke Langdale, writing a year earlier, asserted that, in spite of the general discontent, no party in England was willing to stir without aid from abroad. According to him foreign soldiers were not only indispensable, but they would be far better instruments for effecting a restoration than domestic malcontents. ' Certainly,' he wrote to Charles, ' strangers if they can possibly be

Besides this, militia regiments were to be raised in a number of counties.— *Clarke Papers*, iii. 72 ; Thurloe, v. 397, 424.

[1] *Cal. Clarendon Papers*, iii. 109, 136.

[2] Guizot, *Cromwell and the English Commonwealth*, ii. 554.

[3] Thurloe, v. 320, 362.

gotten are the most fit instruments for your Majesty to CHAP.
I
1656
act in England withal ; they are not interested in the
several factions of those that pretend to be for your
Majesty, neither have their hands been defiled with the
innocent blood shed in England. Those are not your
friends, or do not understand England, that will persuade
your Majesty that strangers will not be welcome to your
friends in England. For God's sake beware of letting
your own friends any more appear in arms, unless they
have either a foreign army to countenance them, or
some considerable party of the army to join with them,
or at the worst considerable ports to let in strangers.' [1]

In September 1656 Charles had not only the promise
of a foreign force for his invasion of England, but the
prospect of soon possessing a little army of his own to
act with it. By a further agreement with Spain he had
undertaken to summon all his subjects serving in the
French or other foreign armies, and to gather them
under his own banner in Flanders. The Spaniards
undertook to provide quarters in that country for
4000 men, and to contribute towards their pay and
equipment. In accordance with this agreement the
King during the summer of 1656 issued commissions for
the raising of four regiments of foot. One, composed
of Englishmen, was to be commanded by the Earl of
Rochester ; another, made up of Scots, by Lieutenant-
General Middleton, while the third and fourth were to
be Irish regiments under the Duke of Gloucester and
the Marquis of Ormond.[2] Recruits came in slowly at
first, and by the middle of September the King had not
more than 700 or 800 men, perhaps only 400 or 500.

[1] Langdale to Charles II, September 9, 1655. *Clarendon State Papers*, iii.
277.
[2] On the origin and history of these regiments, see a paper on ' Royalist and
Cromwellian Armies in Flanders, 1657–1662,' printed in the *Transactions of
the Royal Historical Society*, xvii. pp. 67–75, 1903.

During the autumn their numbers rapidly increased, and by Christmas he had at least 2000. Adding to these the 6000 of the Spanish contingent, Charles would have 8000 men at his disposal.

Eight thousand men, however, would not be enough to defeat the veteran soldiers of the Protector, unless they were supported by a general rising amongst the English Royalists or aided by a division in Cromwell's army. Some observers predicted that, at the first news of a foreign landing, the country would rally round the government. 'The nature of the English,' said a traveller to a German who questioned him about the prospects of the expedition, 'is that, if any strange army should set footing in any part of the dominions of the English, they will be as one man, and will rather lose life and goods than that any strange army should remain in any part of their dominions.'[1] Of all foreign armies one consisting of Spaniards and Irishmen was least likely to be welcomed as a deliverer in seventeenth-century England. Yet it was of these two elements that the invading army would be mainly composed; for the majority of Charles II's soldiers were Irish, and the bulk of the Spanish contingent was to consist of Irish regiments in the service of Spain. 'I am confident,' wrote Lockhart to Thurloe, 'all Englishmen (that can but pretend to the lowest principles of common honesty) will abhor conjunction with so barbarous a crew.'[2]

In spite of his reservation Lockhart was wrong. Amongst the Royalists and the Levellers a considerable number of persons were ready to facilitate the landing of the invaders and to co-operate with them when landed. The King's presence in Flanders, the rumour of his alliance with Spain, and the knowledge that he was raising forces, had filled the Cavaliers with excitement.

[1] Thurloe, vi. 255.   [2] Ib. v. 389.

In May, 1656, tickets bearing a message from the King were passed from hand to hand amongst them. They were couched in the legal phraseology common in the secret correspondence of the time : ' My lawyer tells me that my title is good and I intend shortly to visit my friends.' [1] The response to this call to action was a new crop of intrigues and conspiracies. Some of the older Royalists, dejected by repeated disappointments, and disillusioned as to the possibility of overthrowing a powerful government, were little inclined to stir. The council called ' The Sealed Knot,' which had managed the abortive insurrection of 1655, showed no eagerness to set in motion a fresh revolt. The disarming of the Royalist gentry effected by the Major-Generals, and the reinforcement of the standing army by the new county militia, had made the enterprise more desperate than it ever had been before. Nevertheless some individual members of the Knot threw themselves energetically into the plots, and young gentlemen who had grown up to manhood since the Civil War ended were full of zeal and hope. The most industrious plotters were Lord Willoughby, whose great object was to bring about an alliance between the Royalists and the Presbyterians, and Sir Robert Shirley, who endeavoured to form a similar connexion with the Anabaptists and the Levellers. Sir Thomas Peyton, John Mordaunt, brother to the Earl of Peterborough, and Colonel John Russell were also very active in ' the King's business.' Some of the conspirators talked vaguely of surprising Gloucester or Bristol, but it was agreed that Yarmouth or some port in the eastern counties would be more convenient and more valuable.[2]

The Protector's government was well aware of the ferment amongst the Royalists, and possessed a general

---

[1] Thurloe, v. 99.   [2] Cal. Clarendon Papers, iii. 142, 167.

CHAP. knowledge of their aims. Secretary Thurloe had
I
—␣— organised a very efficient system of espionage. As
1656
Postmaster-General he used his authority to intercept
or open all letters from abroad which seemed suspicious;
and his deputies in the country were instructed to keep
an eye on the movements of the Cavaliers, and to send
any letters written by suspected persons up to Whitehall. As Secretary of State he maintained a number
of correspondents abroad, who kept him informed not
only about European politics but about the political
gossip amongst the exiled Royalists in Flanders. In
England itself he had in his pay agents who were in
touch with all sections of the disaffected, so that in the
long run there was no conspiracy against the government which did not come to his knowledge, and as a
rule he was able to prevent any of the designs of its
enemies from being put into execution.[1] The next
generation admired the skill with which Thurloe kept
the Protector informed of the designs of foreign powers.
' Thereby,' said Colonel Birch in one of Charles II's
Parliaments, ' Cromwell carried the secrets of all the
princes of Europe at his girdle.' In reality the skill
with which he unravelled the schemes of domestic
plotters was far more remarkable than the exactness of
his information about foreign affairs. ' Really,' wrote
Henry Cromwell to Thurloe, ' it is a wonder you can
pick as many locks leading into the hearts of wicked
men as you do ; and it is a mercy we ought to own
that God has made your labours therein so successful.' [2]
The Secretary's task was facilitated by the faults of
the Royalists themselves. Subaltern conspirators over

---

[1] See 'Thurloe and the Post Office' (*English Historical Review*, 1898, p.
527) ; ' Mr. Secretary Thurloe' (*Macmillan's Magazine*, August 1894) ; and
Bischoffhausen's *Die Politik des Protektor's Oliver Cromwell in der Thätigkeit
seines Ministers John Thurloe :* Innsbruck, 1899, pp. 50-3.
[2] Thurloe, vii. 39.

their cups talked freely of the King's designs, and some- times drank in doubtful company. Even the gossip of underlings had its value to one who was able to sift and test it, and in 1656 Thurloe obtained in addition the services of a man high in the confidence of Charles II and trusted by the Royalists in general.

Sir Richard Willis was a member of the Sealed Knot. He had served in the French army before the Civil War, was knighted by Charles I during its progress, and became finally Governor of Newark. As his loyalty was unspotted and his military skill beyond a doubt, he enjoyed the confidence of all the leading Royalists, and took an active part from the first in the plots against the Protector's government. For this offence he twice suffered imprisonment, first in 1654, and again in 1655. Being merely a soldier of fortune Willis was permanently in extremities for want of money. When he was in prison he had to rely upon the assistance of his friends, and when he was at liberty his poverty was notorious. A friend, who could not believe that he was a traitor to their common cause, subsequently described his manner of life. He argued that a man who lived like Willis could not be suspected of any ill-gotten gains. 'To my certain knowledge he hath with great anxiety laboured under very small debts ever since we came together into England, being several times arrested and reduced to exigencies for small sums notwithstanding as much parsimony as any gentleman could use.' His only servant was as poverty-stricken as his master : ' one poor wretch, the most despicable creature I ever saw, who for 1s. 6d. per week and a few scraps, performed the whole service of his person and chamber.' Willis's sole luxury was a few fine clothes, ' which were managed with such dexterity in the first contrivance and frequent variations, beside that they were seldom on above four hours in a day, that it was a more thrifty ostentation than can be imagined by any who saw it not.' The closest scrutiny could detect no sign of anything questionable in his conduct. 'Several months,' said his friend, 'I have lain in the same lodgings, several years I have daily eaten with him, yet have I never seen an unknown face, letter, or note in his chamber; the visits or messages he received or made were never concealed from me, all his secret joys or griefs communicated.' [1] When this was written Willis had been for three years a traitor. Thurloe would never have dreamt of tempting such a pattern of frugality and loyalty, but Willis offered himself to Thurloe. He was weary of the fight with poverty, convinced that the struggle to restore the King was hopeless, and told himself that his treachery was almost a virtue because it would prevent useless bloodshed. Accordingly, some time during the summer of 1656, Willis entered into a contract with the Secretary by which he pledged himself to make such discoveries as should prevent any danger to the State, on condition that he should never be produced as a witness against any man, and that no man's life should be endangered by his evidence.[2] At a secret meeting which took

---

[1] Broderick to Hyde, September 19, 1659. *Clarendon State Papers*, iii. 563.

[2] The date when the treason of Willis began has been disputed, but there is no evidence that he had any communications with Thurloe before the summer of 1656. He was imprisoned for his share in promoting the insurrection of March 1655. He was released from imprisonment in December 1655, and obtained leave to go abroad (Thurloe, i. 757). There is an undated letter, addressed to Thurloe by a person signing himself Foster, which has been attributed to Willis (Thurloe, i. 757). The author offers to give information of plots against the government, stipulating that his name is to be known to the Protector alone, and stating that his object is 'rather to discover things than persons, plots than plotters.' These indications seem to point to Willis, who made, according to Clarendon, similar stipulations with Thurloe. 'He constantly gave Thurloe intelligence of all he knew, but it was with so great circumspection that he was never seen in his presence; in his contract he had promised to make such discoveries as should prevent any danger to the State, but that he would never endanger any man's life, nor be produced to give

place in August 1656 he gave Thurloe an account of CHAP.
I
1656 the intrigue which was in progress between the Royalists and the leaders of the Presbyterians. Some letters followed, but Willis usually preferred to communicate his information by word of mouth at some appointed rendezvous.[1]

Thurloe's acquisition of such an agent made the position of the Protector's government secure. Henceforth any general Royalist rising was impossible. When the Secretary combined what he learnt from Willis with the information he obtained from other sources he knew all that a statesman needs to know about any conspiracy. He could distinguish between the trivial and the important, between the real objects of the party leaders and the chimerical projects of irresponsible underlings. There were points upon which his knowledge was imperfect, and by-plots connected with the main plot of which he knew nothing : but he knew now

evidence against any ' (Clarendon, *Rebellion*, xvi. 28). On the other hand, the author of the letter proposes to give intelligence of the designs of Commonwealths-men and Levellers, which Willis was hardly in a position to do, and the style suggests Wildman rather than Willis. For that reason, writing in the *English Historical Review* in July 1889, in an article on Cromwell and the Insurrection of 1655, I took the view that the letter was not by Willis. The question of its authorship seems insoluble, but this uncertainty does not affect the question of the date when Willis entered into Thurloe's service.

[1] Amongst the unprinted portion of Thurloe's Papers now in the Bodleian Library there is a document endorsed by Thurloe, ' *Noates of a discourse with R. W., Aug.* 1656 ' (*Rawlinson MS.* A. xli. 576). Printed in the *Thurloe Papers* there is a letter of intelligence from Brussels dated September 3, 1656, which Mr. Macray attributes to Willis (v. 344). There are also a number of short letters signed Thomas Barrett (v. 595, 653, 657, 667), P. M. (v. 354, 602), or M. G. (v. 559), arranging meetings or giving information, which were written by Willis. The *Calendar of Domestic State Papers* for 1656–7 (p. 196) contains a letter from Thomas Barrett to Thurloe which belongs to this set. The fact that there are so few of Willis's communications amongst Thurloe's Papers is, no doubt, due to their abstraction in July 1659, in order that they might be used as proofs of his treason. The accusation against him was discredited when it was first made, on which, as convincing evidence, ' a great number of his letters were sent, whereof the character was well known ' (Clarendon, *Rebellion*, xvi. 30).

CHAP.
I
1656

with certainty how far it was safe to allow the conspirators to go, and against whom it was necessary to
direct his blows. When the critical moment came the
Royalist party was paralysed by the arrest of its leaders,
and no action followed the most carefully devised
designs. The maxim of Cromwell's government was
that prevention was better than punishment. The first
result of Willis's revelations was that, a week before
the meeting of Parliament, a proclamation was issued
ordering all officers who had fought for the King to
leave London. At the same time (September 9) Lord
Willoughby, Sir Robert Shirley, Colonel John Russell
and other active Royalists were arrested and committed to prison.[1]

So long as the coasts of England were properly
guarded the landing of a force from Flanders was
impossible ; and without such aid a Royalist insurrection
was hopeless. The scheme was tried in 1659 against the
weak Republic which succeeded the strong government of the Protector, and it ended in an ignominious
failure. It might succeed if the army which held down
England was itself divided, and for this reason the
attempt of the Republicans and the Levellers to under-
mine the power of the Protector by producing a schism
in the army was far more dangerous to the government
than the ceaseless plotting of the Cavaliers. In 1656
there were still amongst the officers of the army a large
number of advanced Republicans, and amongst the
rank and file a considerable number of men imbued
with Levelling principles. The imprisonment of Overton, the dismissal of Okey and Saunders, and the arrest,
in August 1656, of Rich and Alured, had deprived these
Republican officers of the leaders to whom they looked

[1] Thurloe, v. 407; *Public Intelligencer*, September 8–15, 1656; *Cal. Clarendon Papers*, iii. 175.

for political guidance.[1] On the other hand, Colonel CHAP.
I
Sexby, who since 1654 had been the recognised head of 1656
the Levellers, was still at large, and actively employed
in concerting the overthrow of the Protector.[2] He had
returned from Spain in 1655, and throughout 1656 he
was constantly negotiating with the ministers of Charles
II and the Spanish authorities in Flanders. Sexby
told the Spaniards that, if he was sufficiently supplied
with money, he could obtain possession of an English
port, create a revolt in Cromwell's army, and gather
20,000 men round him.[3] He felt confident that he
could bring about the downfall of the Protector. A
letter which he wrote to his old friend Wildman in May,
1656, was full of threats against ' the apostate ' and his
' janissaries.' ' His way,' predicted Sexby, ' within a
few months will be hedged up by that necessity his
own designs will bring upon himself ; being frustrated
there his soul, though as proud as Lucifer's, will fail
within him.'[4] Sexby was an adept in disguises, and
about June, 1656, he paid a visit to England in order to
renew his connexion with his partisans, and to lay the
groundwork of his plot.[5] After he returned to Flanders
he wrote again to Wildman, explaining that English
liberty could only be restored by the judicious expenditure of Spanish gold amongst the army. Instead of
appealing to principles it was necessary to appeal to
interests.[6] ' They are madmen, if not worse, that think

[1] *Commonwealth and Protectorate*, iii. 58; *Supplementary Chapter*, p. 16.
[2] Ib. iii. 458, 470.
[3] *Cal. Clarendon Papers*, iii. 75, 85, 91, 98, 102, 104, 106, 108, 116, 129,
141 ; Thurloe, vi. 83.
[4] Thurloe, v. 37.
[5] Ib. v. 100, 319, 362.
[6] According to Dyer, Sexby's servant, Sexby asked the Spanish government
for £200,000, which it is hardly necessary to say he did not obtain. However,
he was dismissed from Madrid with ' a purse of gold of about £800 sterling
value,' and also received ' several sums of money ' at Brussels from Fuen-
saldagua. ' This informant hath known him change 13,000 patacons at a time

either paper politics or great words can free us from our miseries. No, it's that must free us from it [that] hath brought it upon us ; the sword is that now enslaves us, and it's that must deliver us. That which kept it sharp, and the users of it so seemingly united, it's not love, nor fear, but money. . . . Money is the only thing that ties up this interest. They begin at a wrong end who think to untie this knot without this key.' . . . 'I shall ruin him from abroad in three or four years, as I have ordered, and am ordering my business, having money, which will not only gain the bodies but the souls of men.' [1]

Sexby's practical proposal was that Wildman, with some of this Spanish money, should gain over the governor and part of the garrison of Portsmouth.[2] On a convenient opportunity, such as the occurrence of a breach between Protector and Parliament, Portsmouth was to declare for liberty. ' I shall make such interest abroad as shall fill this perjured villain's hands, so that they shall not be able to gather much of the army to molest Portsmouth.' If the worst came to the worst the conspirators could save themselves. ' If the base spirit of slavery shall fall upon all our country terms may then be made for ourselves with this accursed villain.'

Sexby's plan for the surprise of Portsmouth was doomed to fail, although it was subsequently reported

into gold ' (Thurloe, vi. 831, 833). Some of the money which he sent to England was intercepted by the English government (Carte, *Original Letters*, ii. 103). The sum intercepted amounted to £800 (Thurloe, iv. 698). Lockhart states that on Sexby's return from his visit to England ' he got an order for 30,000 crowns, which with the 40,000 received formerly amounts to a sum they use not to disburse, except upon the hope of very considerable returns ' (ib. v. 319).

[1] *Rawlinson MS.*, A. 40, f. 661. One of the unpublished letters in Thurloe's collection.

[2] Sir Robert Shirley, who was in negotiation with the Levellers, was also concerned in the design against Portsmouth.

by a Royalist agent that a bargain had been made for the delivery of the place to the Levellers on payment of £15,000. Wildman, like Willis, had become one of Thurloe's intelligencers, and both Sexby's letters found their way to the Secretary's hands.[1] In addition to this, Lockhart informed his government in August, 1656, that Sexby had assured the Spaniards that he could get possession of a port not far from London, where their forces might safely be landed.[2] Thus forewarned, there can be little doubt that Portsmouth and other harbours were made secure against treachery or attack.

Yet though one part of Sexby's scheme was thus effectively frustrated, the most dangerous part of it was undetected. During his visit to England he had laid plans for the assassination of the Protector, and had enlisted agents amongst the many discharged soldiers who shared his political creed. They were told that if the Protector were taken off, ' all things would come to a confusion ; it being certain that the great ones would never agree who should succeed, but would fall together by the ears about it ; and then in that disorder the people would rise and so things might be brought to a commonwealth again.' [3]

---

[1] Wildman, no doubt, as Mr. Gardiner suggests, informed the Protector's government of the application of the Anabaptists to Charles II in June, 1656 (*Commonwealth and Protectorate, Supplementary Chapter*, p. 12). A letter informing against Howard, dated September 8, 1656, is amongst Thurloe's Papers. It looks as if it might be by Wildman (v. 393). Sexby's letter of May 28 to Wildman is also amongst Thurloe's Papers, with the endorsement : ' The letter was writt by Sexbye unto Major Wyldman and delivered to me G. C. the beginning of July 1656.' G. C. was probably George Cockaine, a Baptist minister who was one of Thurloe's spies. The unpublished letter of August 19, which is amongst Thurloe's MSS., no doubt reached his hands in the same way. A letter of intelligence dated February 25, 1657-8, is endorsed by Thurloe ' Wyldman ' (vi. 822) ; the letter printed vol. vii. 48, seems to be by the same author.

[2] Thurloe, v. 319, 776 ; *Cal. Clarendon Papers*, iii. 152, 192.

[3] Cecil's deposition, Thurloe, v. 774. The printed deposition says ' the great ones of the King,' but the meaning, of course, is the great ones of the army.

The leader of the plotters was one Miles Sindercombe, a Kentish man who had once been a quarter-
master in the regiment of Colonel Reynolds.[1] He was
one of the ringleaders of the mutiny of that regiment in
May, 1649, but succeeded in escaping, and subsequently
enlisted as a private in Colonel Thomlinson's regiment
of horse. There he was one of the principal agents in
the plot of 1654 for seizing General Monck and persuading the English army in Scotland to declare against
the Protector.[2] Thanks to his humble position the
importance of his share in the plot was not discovered
till he had been discharged from the army, so he again
evaded punishment. Sexby, who knew Sindercombe
of old, picked him out as a fit instrument for the execution of the design against the Protector's person, left
him a free hand in the choice of his partners, and supplied
him with ample funds. When the arch-conspirator
returned to Flanders he felt that he had left the work
in good hands, and boasted enigmatically to Wildman
that he had ' jackalls in the forest amongst the lions,'
and ' cubs, too, that have seasoned claws and teeth,'
to drive a certain beast out of his den. He gave
no details, but hinted that something important would
happen about the end of September. Owing to this
reticence, Wildman was not in a position to betray this
part of Sexby's designs to the government, even had
he desired to do so. All Thurloe knew was that the

[1] See *Mercurius Politicus*, February 5–12, 1657, p. 7587, and Gardiner,
Commonwealth and Protectorate, i. 54.

[2] This was the plot for which Colonel Robert Overton was so long imprisoned
(*Commonwealth and Protectorate*, iii. 71–6). Monck wrote to Cromwell on
January 25, 1655, that Sindercombe, ' late a private soldier in Col. Thomlinson's
own troop,' was able to give ' a particular information ' of the rise of the plot :
' Hee being (as I am credibly informed) one who was first employed as an agent
to severall regiments in Scotland, though till hee was gone I had noe such
intelligence concerning him, yet discharged him the troope as a busy and
suspisies person and one who was forward to promote such ill designes.'—
Firth, *Scotland and the Protectorate*, p. 243.

Spaniards and Levellers were concerting the Protector's assassination, and the Royalists were encouraging the proposal.[1] How, or by what instruments, the deed was to be effected was unknown to him.

Sindercombe was able to proceed unmolested to carry out his employer's orders. For that purpose he associated with himself another old soldier, John Cecil, and also obtained the assistance of a mysterious Royalist called Boyes.[2] The three conspirators decided to kill the Protector on September 17, at the opening of Parliament. They hired a room in the house of a tailor in King Street, Westminster, intending to shoot him from the window as he went by in his coach. But each of the three, though bent on taking Cromwell's life, was anxious not to risk his own; and 'it appearing that there was not any possible way of escaping out of the house they were discouraged from that enterprise.'[3] They therefore searched the neighbourhood till they found a house possessing several back-doors. It belonged to Colonel Mydhope, and stood next to the east door of Westminster Abbey and on the right hand of it, situated conveniently 'both for escaping after the fact and for all other purposes.'

[1] Thurloe, v. 344, 488, 511, 559, 602, 694.

[2] Thurloe, in the account of the plot which he subsequently gave to Parliament, describes Boyes as ' a considerable person of the late King's party.' He says that Boyes was not his true name, which apparently was still unknown in January, 1657 (Burton, *Diary*, i. 355). At Sindercombe's trial it was said that Boyes ' goes by several names and in several habits, sometimes as a poor priest in ragged clothes, sometimes well clad as a gentleman ' (*Mercurius Politicus*, 7599). Cecil said ' he was a man of somewhat low stature, and small boned, brownish hair curling to flaxen, sanguine complexion, and wore his beard long ' (Thurloe, v. 776). It is difficult to identify this mysterious person, but it may have been Major Wood. Cecil apparently seems to distinguish Boyes and Wood (ib. v. 777), but Wood was a spectator of their proceedings on September 17.

[3] ' A sempster's shop on the left hand of the street as we go to Westminster,' says Cecil (Thurloe, v. 777). The householder, whose name was Edward Hilton, was one of the witnesses at Sindercombe's trial.

Part of this house they hired, and resolved to shoot
Cromwell as he came out of the Abbey after the sermon
to proceed to the Palace and address the members,
who were to meet him in the Painted Chamber. On the
morning of the 17th, ' about sermon time,' while Dr.
Owen was enlarging on the spiritual benefits of Cromwell's rule, the three conspirators might have been seen
on their way from Hilton's to Mydhope's house, bearing
between them a viol case in which they had hidden a
blunderbuss and some pistols loaded with slugs. When
the sermon ended all three went into the yard of the
house next the Abbey; Sindercombe and Boyes remained
in the yard, Cecil stood on the wall, waiting for the
Protector. But once more caution resumed its sway.
' Finding so many people standing on both sides the
way as the Protector came by, and as he passed, they
durst not do anything for fear of being discovered before
they shot.'[1] So the Protector went by unscathed, and the
conspirators resolved to wait for a better opportunity.
' Never,' lamented Colonel Titus to Sir Edward Hyde,
' was anything more unhappily prevented than the
killing Cromwell the first day of the Parliament. . . .
All things were as well prepared as was imaginable.'[2]
Had Sexby been there, Titus believed that success
instead of failure would have been the result, and
the Protector's death would have been followed by a
general rising against the government.

As yet the negotiations between Charles II and the
Levellers had not resulted in an agreement. Sexby
demanded on behalf of his party constitutional changes
which neither the King nor his advisers would accept,
and it was difficult even to settle the terms upon which

[1] These particulars are derived from the depositions of Cecil (Thurloe, v. 775),
and in part from the trial of Sindercombe (*State Trials*, v. 842 ; *Mercurius
Politicus*, February 5–12, 1657, pp. 7588–7601).
[2] *Clarendon State Papers*, iii. 321.

the two parties were to co-operate when they took up arms.[1] The one thing on which the leaders of both were agreed was in thinking the 'removal' of Cromwell the essential preliminary to the success of the insurrection. The most respectable Royalists raised no objection when schemes for that purpose were proposed. 'No man,' declared Nicholas, 'that should effect so glorious a work can possibly fail of an ample and very honourable reward for it as well on earth as in heaven.'[2] Ormond had been cognisant of Dick Talbot's plan to assassinate Cromwell in November, 1655,[3] and Hyde was kept constantly informed by Titus of the progress of Sexby's design.[4] One of Thurloe's intelligencers related a conversation between the secretary of Don Alonzo de Cardenas and Sir Marmaduke Langdale. 'Said the secretary, "If Cromwell were out of the way all would be in confusion." "But how shall this be effected," said Sir Marmaduke ; " for he is a wary man, well guarded, resolute of himself and comes not much abroad ? " Saith the secretary, "He may be watched as he walks in the garden, and keys may be easily had to the gate."'[5]

The Protector was warned that plots of this kind were on foot. In his opening speech to Parliament he had alluded to former attempts of the kind with the contempt which a soldier naturally felt for skulking assassins. They were foolish designs, 'little fiddling things,' things 'which I would not remember as at all considerable to myself or to you.'[6] To his servants, however, they were a source of very great anxiety.

---

[1] Cf. *Clarendon State Papers*, iii. 289, 315.
[2] *Nicholas Papers*, iii. 265.
[3] Gardiner, *Commonwealth and Protectorate*, iii. 462.
[4] *Cal. Clarendon Papers*, iii. 324.
[5] Thurloe, v. 344.
[6] Speech, September 17, 1656.

From Paris Lockhart warned Thurloe of the plot against the Protector's life, and besought him to persuade Cromwell to be more careful. 'I pray God preserve him from their base and treacherous attempts, and give his friends hearts to beseech his Highness not to follow the counsels of his own courage, that can contemn all dangers, but to consider that in his life, as in a treasure, is bound up the mercy and happiness of all the good people in his dominions.' [1]

This was alike the strength and the weakness of the Protector's government : both friend and foe saw that it depended on one man's life, and had as yet no firm foundation.

[1] Thurloe, v. 488.   Lockhart to Thurloe, October $\frac{11}{21}$, 1656.

CHAPTER II

PARLIAMENT AND THE SPANISH WAR

PARLIAMENT, or rather those members who continued to sit in the House after the forcible exclusion of some and the voluntary retirement of others, proceeded at once to testify its loyalty to the Protector's government. The first step was to confirm the Protector's title. On September 18 Sir Charles Wolseley, member for Stafford-shire and one of the Protector's Council, introduced a bill for renouncing and annulling ' the pretended title of Charles Stuart.' It met with no opposition, was read a second time on the following day, and was passed on September 26. This was followed by a bill for the security of the Lord Protector's person, which was read a second time on September 26, and passed on October 9. By it any attempt to compass the death of the Protector, or to promote the claim of Charles II, was declared high treason. In each of the three nations a certain number of notables were named to be commissioners, from whom, when necessary, the Protector was to select a certain number to form a High Court of Justice for the trial of offenders under the Act. An oath was to be imposed upon the commissioners, and the measure was to remain in force until the end of the next Parliament.[1]   Thurloe, exulting over this proof of the good affections of the House, told Henry Cromwell that this High Court of Justice would be ' a

[1] *Commons' Journals*, vii. 424, 425, 427, 429, 436 ; Scobell, ii. 371–5.

CHAP.
II
1656

great terror to designing men,' and explained to another correspondent that it was thought 'more safe to try them this way than by the ordinary juries.' The trial of Penruddock and his followers had proved that it was possible to get jurymen to return a verdict against Royalists taken with arms in their hands, provided always that the jurymen were carefully selected. But the domestic enemies of the government were not limited to Cavaliers; and the case of Lilburne had shown that it was more difficult to persuade a jury to convict a Republican plotter. The government had now to guard itself against both classes.[1]

Parliament next turned to consider the question of the Spanish War. Men imbued with Cromwell's spirit might approve it from the religious point of view; but the crusading temper was rare amongst the merchants and lawyers who formed the bulk of the House. Hitherto the war with Spain, which, before it began, some of the Protector's counsellors had considered 'the most profitable of any in the world,' had ruined one branch of English trade, and had brought England little profit.[2] No treasure ships had yet been captured, and during the first months of the war the commerce of England suffered more than that of Spain. All through the first half of 1656 Flemish and Biscayan corsairs infested the North Sea and the Channel, capturing merchantmen, colliers, and fishing-boats within sight of the English shores. The captain of one Dunkirk privateer scornfully bade a captured crew to tell the Protector that whilst he was fetching gold from the West Indies they would fetch his coals from Newcastle.[3]

At first the English navy seemed unable to check

[1] Thurloe, v. 453, 454, 474 ; Vaughan, *Protectorate of O. Cromwell*, ii. 37.
[2] *Clarke Papers*, iii. 203.
[3] *Cal. State Papers Dom.*, 1655–6, p. 200.

these depredations. On paper its force was sufficient;
for in April, 1656, the ships set to guard the coast
were fifty in number, and they were manned by over 4000
men.[1] The government provided convoys for merchantmen and guards for fishing fleets, but these measures
proved ineffectual. The arrangements for convoy were
so irregular and unsystematic that merchants often
preferred to take the risk of capture rather than incur
the certain loss of delay. Moreover, the protection
which a single man-of-war could give to a dozen or a
score of merchantmen was very slight. The merchantmen lagged behind or failed to keep together, and
then some privateer would swoop down on the stragglers
and carry off his prizes under the nose of their guardian.
' This is the third time,' complained an angry captain
who had lost two of his charges in this way, ' that I have
fallen in with the enemy's men-of-war, but I cannot
catch any because they are too swift.' The most
formidable of the privateers were those from Dunkirk
and Ostend, ships built for speed, fresh from the
dockyard, and swarming with men. The Dunkirkers,
wrote another captain, were always ' tallowed and
fully manned,' while English men-of-war had weak
crews and foul bottoms. He went on to lament that
the forty-gun ship which he commanded had been
unable to take part in an engagement with a squadron
of privateers, ' not being able to sail through foulness,
though when clean she is inferior to few for sailing.' [2]

If it came to fighting, the larger Dunkirkers were
more than a match for some of the small craft employed by the government in convoy work. The
Cat pink, an eight-gun ship told off to protect the
fishing-boats of Hastings and Brighton, was taken, after
a good fight, by a Dunkirker carrying twenty-two guns

[1] *Cal. State Papers Dom.*, 1655–6, p. 248. [2] *Ib.* 257, 356.

and 180 men.[1] Small privateers were sometimes beaten off by a valiant merchantman; but the numbers of their crew generally ensured their victory if they could get close enough to board. However, Captain Wilson, in the *Anthony* of London, beat off an Ostender that boarded her thrice, and took six prisoners; while Captain Birkes in the *Recovery* of Bristol, with but nineteen seamen and thirteen passengers, captured a Royalist privateer called the *Royal James*, which carried sixteen guns and seventy-four men. To encourage such exploits the government gave the captured ship to the crew of the *Recovery ;* but the resistance of merchantmen was generally fruitless, and in many cases rich ships surrendered without firing a shot.[2]

As the summer of 1656 drew to its close the situation improved. The government resolved to appoint a special squadron to blockade Ostend and Dunkirk, in order to keep the corsairs at home. On the 28th of July eleven frigates took up their station off the Flemish coast; three set themselves before Dunkirk, five off Ostend, whilst the remaining three plied up and down the coast. ' They have each of them,' says a newspaper, ' a shallop armed after the Spanish or Flemish fashion, with a great gun at the forepart of them, quite covered with their sail, wherewith they are to fetch in and follow the enemies, where great ships cannot go.' The success of the new plan was immediate. Six weeks later the same paper announced that the coasts were clear from Dunkirkers and Ostenders, and that merchants could trade with freedom and safety.' [3]

---

[1] *Cal. State Papers Dom.*, 1655–6, p. 304.

[2] Ib. 1656–7, pp. 48, 106; 1655–6, p. 240. *Public Intelligencer*, July 28–August 4, 1656, p. 733.

[3] *Cal. State Papers Dom.*, 1655–6, p. 345. *Mercurius Politicus*, July 31–August 7, 1656, p. 7158; ib., September 4–11, p. 7223. Carte, *Original Letters*, ii. 112.

Besides these dangers to English trade, the breach
with Spain caused difficulties of another nature. The mere existence of a state of war led to complications with neutral powers. In spite of all the representations of Nieupoort, the Dutch ambassador, Cromwell resolutely upheld the right of search, and repudiated the Dutch doctrine that free ships made free goods. The sympathies of the Dutch were on the side of Spain, and it was continually asserted that they were harbouring Flemish privateers in their ports or transporting Spanish goods in their vessels. More than once attempts to exercise the right of search led to serious trouble; and peace or war often depended on the discretion of the naval officers of either state. In the spring of 1656 it became known that De Ruyter, who had been sent out to the Mediterranean to protect Dutch commerce from the Barbary pirates, was bringing home from Cadiz a quantity of silver which had crossed the Atlantic in two galleons which reached Spain just before Blake's arrival upon the Spanish coast. On April 19 De Ruyter was met in the Straits of Dover by an English man-of-war under Captain Whitehorn, who avowed his intention of carrying into port, for examination, the merchantmen which the Dutch fleet had convoyed from Cadiz. De Ruyter answered by declaring that he would resist any such attempt by force, and gave his word of honour that there were no Spanish ships or goods in his fleet. Whitehorn yielded and allowed him to pass, partly because his own force was too weak to engage, and partly because he could see no ship in De Ruyter's convoy which was obviously an Ostender or a Dunkirker.[1] More than once similar incidents recurred, and there was always

[1] Thurloe, iv. 698, 713, 730, 734, 748; *Cal. State Papers Dom.*, 1655–6, p. 284.

a risk that the attempted search of a Dutch vessel might lead to blows and shots. 'I do not like the carriage of the Hollanders,' wrote Thurloe to Admiral Montagu on August 28; 'our ships of war and theirs scarce ever meet in the Channel but they have some scuffle or other. The last week there came into Torbay some fifty merchantmen of theirs under three convoys, where they carried themselves so insolently, that there was little less than a fight between our and their men-of-war. . . . Certainly, if the greatest part of their strength were not in the Baltic Sea, I fear we should hear of them.'[1] Peace was preserved, though its preservation was due not merely to the complications which retained the Dutch fleet in the Baltic, but to the conciliatory policy of the Protector. Several times in the course of the summer Dutch merchantmen were carried into English ports, with the result that Cromwell, while refusing to acknowledge the justice of the complaints reiterated by Nieupoort, gave orders for their liberation.[2] To avoid war with Holland was the necessary condition of success in the struggle with Spain.

Hitherto the great fleet under Blake and Montagu, which had sailed from England at the close of March, 1656, had effected little against the Spaniards. It had started too late to intercept the plate fleet. After forcing the King of Portugal to ratify the treaty of 1654, the two admirals, at the end of June, 1656, returned to Cadiz Bay to resume the blockade of that port.[3] They found little to do there, for there was next to no Spanish trade to destroy. 'In the Dutch war,' wrote the English

---

[1] Carte, *Original Letters*, ii. 113 ; cf. Thurloe, v. 324, 358.
[2] Thurloe, v. 246, 499, 536, 571.
[3] Gardiner, *Commonwealth and Protectorate*, iii. 477.

ambassador at Lisbon, 'we were sure of an enemy that would fight, besides good prizes to help pay charges ; but the Spaniard will neither fight nor trade.' [1] There was nothing to be gained by keeping so many ships where there was so little to be done. Montagu emphatically recommended the division of the fleet. 'Indeed it is in my judgment a very bootless thing to lie here; the Spaniard prepares to set nothing out this year, unless it be four ships for the Indies, which they say must be gotten ready against October ; and he expects nothing home this twelve month ; and for trade, it would anger one to lie here and see the Dutch, Hamburgher, and Genoese, &c., come to and fro and trade with the Spaniard, which we cannot hinder, unless we should fight with all the world ; and to search them for contraband goods is to little purpose, though we do our best, for such goods are always stowed lowest, and to unlade a ship of any considerable burden is no small trouble, and requires no small time, and to be always doing is no pleasing employment ; and when one has rummaged a ship, and finds nothing, it begets a great deal of ill-will : in short it is the worst piece of work we meet with.

'I think a dozen or fifteen sail of nimble frigates kept in these seas constantly will secure your Straits trade, mischief the Spaniard most of all, and more probably light on his plate fleet than a greater number; and they will probably be always catching something or other to advantage, and the charge not so great to the nation at home ; and they have the benefit of Lisbon to careen and keep themselves always clean.' [2]

Blake agreed with Montagu, and on July 1 the two admirals informed the Protector that they intended to

---

[1] Thurloe, v. 216.   [2] June 30, 1656. Ib. v. 171.

divide the fleet. Part of it, under the command of Captain Stayner, was to be left to watch Cadiz; with the rest they meant to sail into the Mediterranean as far as Tripoli or Tunis. The corsairs of Tripoli had taken several rich merchantmen lately, and must be taught a lesson ; those of Sallee must also be visited and forced to come to terms.[1] Simultaneously orders reached the admirals from the Protector, directing that a squadron of the frigates or lighter ships should be sent home to guard the Channel, so the fleet was divided into three portions.[2] Ten ships returned to England, twelve with Vice-Admiral Stayner remained before Cadiz, while fourteen others accompanied Blake and Montagu. The expedition to Tripoli had to be abandoned, owing to a storm which scattered Blake's fleet, seriously damaged several ships, and delayed his sailing. But before proceeding against Sallee he thought it advisable to strike a parting blow at the Spaniards. A squadron of frigates under Captain Blagge of the *Fairfax* ranged the coasts of Galicia and Biscay, destroyed two Ostenders, and captured a few small prizes.[3] Five frigates were next dispatched to Malaga, partly ' to do what mischief they could there to provoke the Spaniard,' and partly in the hope of catching ' one Balthazar, a noted pirate ' who made that port his headquarters. The five frigates swooped down upon Malaga on July 10 ; Balthazar was not there; but they burnt nine ships, drove the Spaniards from the mole, spiked the cannons upon it, and poured a hail of shot into the town. A ballad, long popular in England, recorded this exploit, and dwelt with peculiar satisfaction on the fact that one well-aimed broadside battered down the steeple of the cathedral. A similar attempt upon Alicante was

[1] Thurloe, v. 171, 174.   [2] June 9, 1656. Ib. v. 101.
[3] Ib. v. 188, 195.

a failure, but the terror which these attacks caused hampered trade all along the coasts of Spain.[1] Meanwhile Blake watered his ships on the coast of Barbary, where he had some hopes of finding a convenient harbour, which might be occupied permanently and serve as a basis of operations. Bugia (or, as it is termed, Buzema) proved unsuitable, but it was thought that the King of Portugal might be induced to cede Tangiers, or that Oran might be captured from the Spaniards.[2] These projects were, however, for the present deferred, and when his frigates rejoined him Blake sailed for Sallee. There he began his negotia- tions by driving two pirate ships ashore and demanding from the governor the surrender of the twenty-four English captives whom he detained. The governor asked a ransom, which Blake refused to pay; yet it seemed likely that an agreement would be concluded, when a new dispute arose. There were two children, born of English parents, whom the governor refused to deliver up, and Blake insisted on requiring.[3] A rupture followed, and, leaving a couple of frigates to blockade the port, Blake returned to Cadiz. At the beginning of September he left Stayner with eight ships before Cadiz, and sailed with the rest of the squadron to the mouth of the Tagus, in order to revictual his ships from Lisbon. There, while lying at anchor in Oeiras Bay, he received the news of a victory gained by his subordinate in his absence.[4]

On September 9, Stayner, with the ships left to blockade Cadiz, had fallen in with one of the two annual

---

[1] Thurloe, v. 195, 233, 257, 337, 373.
'"Come," then says our captain, "let's fire at the church!"
And down came their belfry, which grieved them much.'
'The Famous Fight at Malago,' *Naval Songs and Ballads*, 1908, p. 47.
[2] Thurloe, v. 195, 257.   [3] Ib. i. 729 ; v. 285.
[4] Ib. i. 729, 730.

plate fleets from America.[1] It was that known as the fleet of the Tierra Firme, or the Spanish Main, which had escaped one English commander only to fall into the jaws of another. During July and August Vice-Admiral Goodson, who commanded the squadron sent by Cromwell to the West Indies, had been cruising off Havana, hoping to intercept this particular fleet. At last he learnt that it had sailed for Spain on July 14, four days before he had taken up his station off the port. The fleet of the Tierra Firme consisted of seven ships: two galleons and two store ships armed for war belonged to the Spanish government, and the other three were merchant ships owned by private persons.[2] For two months they had waited at Havana expecting a squadron of men-of-war to convoy them home, but Blake's blockade of Cadiz prevented this, and at last, 'upon consideration of the King of Spain's necessities for money,' they resolved to sail alone. After a voyage of fifty-eight days they sighted the Spanish shore, and thought themselves in safety. On their way they captured a Portuguese ship, and asked their prisoners anxiously where the English fleet was.

---

[1] Stayner's victory is announced in a letter from him to the generals dated September 9 (Thurloe, v. 399), and in an unpublished letter of September 14, which is in the *Rawlinson MSS.*, A. liv. 133. See also a letter from Montagu to Thurloe, September 19 (Thurloe, v. 433), and one from an anonymous intelligencer in Spain (ib. v. 523). The official account is a compilation from these various sources : *A True Narrative of the Success which it hath pleased God to give to some Part of the Fleet of this Commonwealth upon the Spanish Coast against the King of Spain's West India Fleet*, folio, October 4, 1656.

[2] English lists of the Spanish fleet are printed in Thurloe, v. 400, 434, and a Spanish list in Duro's *Armada Espanola*, v. 22–4. Both agree as to the number of vessels ; Duro also gives their armament. The largest, the admiral's ship, had twenty-six bronze guns and a crew of 400 men; two others had, one twenty-four bronze guns and 200 men, the other thirty bronze and iron guns and 200 men. It appears from this that in armament the Spanish ships were inferior to Stayner's. The Spaniards captured a small prize on this voyage, so that they were eight in number when Stayner fell in with them.

The answer they received was that the Spaniards had beaten them off the coast a month before, so that all fears of danger were allayed, and they bore up confidently for Cadiz. On the evening of September 8, Captain Stayner, who had been driven out of Cadiz Bay by a gale, spied the Spanish ships five or six leagues to the westward of Cadiz, and at once gave chase. The unsuspecting Spaniards took Stayner's six ships for fishing-boats, and kept company with them all night, hanging out lights and firing guns, as it was their custom to do. Next morning, when Stayner bore up to engage, it was too late to escape. To a spectator his ships looked small compared to the bulky galleons, but they seemed ' all fire and sail.' [1] Half his squadron was too far to the leeward to take part in the engagement, but the three which did engage were his strongest ships. These were the *Speaker*, a second-rate carrying sixty-four guns, commanded by Stayner himself, the *Plymouth*, of fifty-four, and the *Bridgwater*, of fifty-two guns. When the fight ended, only two of the Spaniards had escaped. The Spanish admiral's ship succeeded in reaching Cadiz.[2] Stayner captured the galleon of the Rear-Admiral Don Juan de Hoyos, said to contain two million pieces of eight,[3] and Captain John Harman, of the *Tredagh*, took a richly laden merchantman.[4]

---

[1] Thurloe, v. 579.

[2] Don Marcus del Porto, the commander of the fleet, had removed his flag into one of the smaller ships. ' As for the Admirall, which gott into Cadiz,' writes Stayner, ' she was, as the prisoners inform me, nothing considerable, for she was only made Admirall to have preserved the gallioon I tooke, and that she might have gotten clere away, it being their custome to make their least considerable ship carry the flag' (*Rawlinson MS.*, A. liv. 133). At first the ship was reported to have run ashore and sunk (Thurloe, v. 434; but see p. 524).

[3] This was the biggest ship, and had been the flagship till two days previously, according to Stayner. The armament, according to Duro, consisted of 400 men and twenty-six bronze guns.

[4] A ship of Cartagena, commanded by Juan de la Torre (Thurloe, v. 434). It had twenty-six guns, according to Duro.

CHAP.
II
1656

Captain Rodriguez Calderon's ship was also taken, but caught fire accidentally, and went to the bottom with a cargo worth 600,000 pieces of eight.[1] The galleon of the Spanish vice-admiral fought for six hours before it struck; then it was fired—according to English accounts by the Spaniards themselves—and all but ninety of its crew sank with it.[2] Amongst the survivors was a boy of sixteen—'a most pregnant, ingenious, learned youth,' said Montagu, ' whose story is the saddest that I have heard or read of to my remembrance.' He was the eldest son of the Marquis de Baydes, the governor of Peru, who had embarked upon the galleon all the fortune he had gained in the colonies and the whole of his family.[3] ' In the fire,' relates Montagu, ' the marquis's lady and one of the daughters fell down in a swoon and were burned. The marquis himself had opportunity to have escaped, but seeing his lady and his daughter, whom he loved exceedingly, in that case, said he would die where they had died, and embracing his lady was burned also with them.' [4] The younger children were saved, but only to find themselves without father, mother, or means.

When the battle ended, out of the eight Spanish ships only the smallest of the King's ships and two merchantmen of little value had escaped ; the rest were either sunk or captured. From the nature of the fight the loss of the vanquished was far greater than the gain of the victors, and it was at first estimated that

[1] A ship of thirty guns and 200 men, according to Duro, containing, according to Stayner, a cargo worth 600,000 pieces of eight.

[2] A ship of twenty-four guns and 200 men, according to Duro, commanded, according to Stayner, by ' Don Francisco de Esquevel, a Biscainer,' and containing not less than 1,100,000 pieces of eight.

[3] Don Francisco Lopez de Zuniga, Marquis de Baydes, Governor of Chili, who repulsed an attack of the Dutch upon it in 1641 ; subsequently Governor of Peru.

[4] Thurloe, v. 433 ; cf. Waller, *Poems*, ed. Drury, p. 154.

the loss of Spain amounted to nine million pieces of CHAP.
II
eight, whilst the captured silver and merchandise were 1656
said to be worth half that sum.

The news of Stayner's victory reached England on
Wednesday, October 1.   On the morning of September
30, Parliament had commenced the discussion of the
Spanish War, and Lord Commissioner Fiennes, on
behalf of the Protector, had stated the grounds upon
which the government had proceeded in appealing to
arms.   The debate closed on the morning of October 1
with the resolution : ' That the Parliament doth declare
the war against the Spaniard was undertaken upon just
and necessary grounds, and for the good of the people
of this Commonwealth: and the Parliament doth approve
thereof, and will by God's blessing assist his Highness
therein.'[1]   Whatever might be thought outside the
walls of the House, no dissentient voice was raised
within it.   ' So much reason,' wrote one of its members,
' was shown to have a war with that old enemy, both to
our nation and religion, that I think his Highness hath
done good service therein, if the Parliament will back
him with moneys.   To me it is sufficient that the war
is against the Spaniard, because I am satisfied he
watcheth for nothing less than an opportunity to tread
us to dirt, and say he doth God good service, as did the
Irish.   The Lord grant we may not be too wise in
saving our purses, and afterwards it be said, "it is
too late."[2]   Some three hours after the House rose,
Captain Robert Storey, of the *Hampshire* frigate,
arrived with letters from Blake and Montagu.   Next
morning Thurloe laid them before the House, which Oct. 2
appointed the following day for a thanksgiving in
London, and ordered that the 5th of November

<hr>

[1] *Commons' Journals*, vii. 431.
[2] *Clarke Papers*, iii. 75.

should be observed for the same purpose throughout the three nations.'[1]

This great and unexpected victory came at the right moment; for though the war might be unanimously judged necessary and just, it had hitherto been unsuccessful. The official narrative published by the House, while exalting the mercy of God in giving His servants so glorious a triumph, dwelt with special emphasis upon its opportuneness. ' This mercy,' it said, ' is the more magnified by the suitableness and seasonableness of it when God's people were laid low in their own thoughts and expectations, and lower in the eyes and hearts of some that were lookers on.'[2] Thankful as well as exultant, the members of the House turned to discuss how money was to be raised to carry on the war. At intervals throughout October the question was taken up and debated.[3] On October 17 Colonel Sydenham laid before the House a statement of the public debts for which funds must be provided. They amounted, for the sea forces, the land forces, and the ordinary civil charges of the government, to £865,000. Besides this there was an old debt of £260,000 charged upon the excise. Moveover, a committee estimated that the cost of carrying on the Spanish War would be near a million per annum.[4] The government made no proposals as to the way in which the required sum should be raised ; the problem was left to the House, and the inexperienced financiers who filled its benches found themselves unable to solve it. Thurloe wrote to Henry Cromwell on October 28, saying that there had been some debates about raising money for the Spanish War, and that the

[1] *Commons' Journals*, vii. 432 ; Thurloe, v. 471 ; *Clarke Papers*, iii. 75 ; *Mercurius Politicus*, October 2–9.

[2] See *Cal. State Papers Dom.*, 1656–7, p. 126.

[3] *Commons' Journals*, vii. 433, 438, 440, 442–5.

[4] Ib. vii. 440 ; *Clarke Papers*, iii. 76.

House ' expressed a good readiness ' thereto. ' Only,'
he added, ' they are willing to try if anything can be
done this way without taxing the people too high.' [1]
With this object the House considered suggestion
after suggestion. Inquiries were ordered into the
arrears of the excise, of the London assessment, and of
the arrears due from the prize office. Something, it
was thought, might be made out of the forests, and
something more wrung from the estates of papists and
the sequestrated lands of Cavaliers. It was suggested
that the revenue derived from the excise on ale and
beer might be increased, and that the duty on Spanish
wines might be made higher. A scheme was proposed
for the amalgamation of the customs and the excise,
and for setting both to farm.[2] Practical men saw
plainly that these expedients would never suffice, and
that the only effective measure would be to increase
the monthly property tax, but no one was bold enough
to propose so unpopular a plan. ' Most of the last
week,' wrote Thurloe on November 11, ' hath been
spent in considering ways to raise money, being loath,
exceeding loath, to raise the tax ; but I believe we shall
be compelled to it at last, when we are weary of seeking
money by other means without fruit.' [3]

There was also another motive which made members
of Parliament reluctant to vote new taxes. They
waited to learn the precise value of the prizes captured
by Stayner. Five million pieces of eight would amount
to £600,000, and if it were true that the cargo of the
galleons was worth so much, it might be unnecessary

---

[1] Thurloe, v. 524. The Secretary adds: ' Little fruit hath been hitherto of
attempts of this nature,' and predicts that it will be necessary to add somewhat
to the monthly tax.

[2] *Commons' Journals*, vii. 440–5, 450–5, 470–3. Burton, *Diary*, i. 179. Cf.
Clarke Papers, iii. 76, 77.

[3] Thurloe, v. 584.

to lay fresh burdens on the English people.   Perhaps
the war might be made to support itself.

The question was soon answered.   On August 28
the Protector had sent fresh orders to Blake, saying
that as the Spaniards kept their ports and intended to
set no fleet to sea, it would be better to send the great
ships home before the storms of winter began.[1]   Twenty
of the smaller ships were to remain with Blake, and
Montagu with the rest was to return to England.
Blake received these orders about the end of September,
removed his flag from the *Naseby* to the *Swiftsure*, and
sent Montagu home in the *Naseby* with the heavier
ships and the prizes.[2]   Montagu arrived at Portsmouth
about October 28, and a week later took his place in
Nov. 4 the House and received its thanks for his services.[3]
The Spanish treasure, packed in ammunition wagons,
was conveyed by road to London, and stored in the
Tower.   Colonel White, who was in charge of it, reported
to the House on November 11 that there were two hundred and twenty-five chests of silver, worth about as
many thousand pounds, and cochineal to the value of
perhaps another twenty thousand.   The disappointment at White's report was universal ; it was not half
the amount which people had been led to expect, nor
was the explanation of the decrease of a nature to
diminish the dissatisfaction.   The prize itself, wrote
Thurloe to Henry Cromwell, was even richer than it
was at first reported to be, for it was worth near a
million sterling.   All, however, except a quarter or a
third of it had been plundered or embezzled by its
captors.   'A private captain, they say, hath got to his
own share £60,000, and many private mariners £10,000

[1] Thurloe, v. 363.   [2] Ib. v. 452.
[3] Ib. v. 509, 524, 528, 535 ; *Commons' Journals*, vii. 450 ; Carte, *Original
Letters*, ii. 114.

a man; and this is so universal amongst the seamen CHAP.
II
1656
and taken in the heat of fight, that it is not possible to
get it again, or any part of it.' Rumour no doubt
exaggerated both the defalcations and the original value
of the prizes, but the fact remained that the cost of the
war could not be defrayed from this source.[1]

Obliged once more to approach the question of
fresh taxation, Parliament again hesitated to face the
problem. After White had made his report it was
moved that the monthly assessments should be increased;
but the subject was shelved by appointing a committee
to consider the augmentation of the customs and
excise duties. Four days later it was resolved that the
rates upon Spanish wine and Spanish raisins should
be raised, and during the next six weeks there were
some desultory discussions about finance, but nothing
was done.[2] On December 20, in a discussion about
the state of public business, a motion was made that
the House should adjourn for two or three months. The
weather, it was said, was cold, the days were short, all
members had business at home, and about a hundred had
left for the country during the last week. The supporters
of the government indignantly replied that the House
ought not to adjourn till it had made provision for the
war it had voted. 'We had better never have met
than to adjourn now,' declared Captain Fiennes. 'We
cannot kill the King of Spain, nor take Spain or Flanders
by a vote. There must be monies provided and bills
passed.' The motion for adjournment was dropped
without a division, and a call of the House was
ordered to take place on December 31. At the
same time two days a week were set aside for ' the

---

[1] Thurloe, v. 542, 557, 569; *Clarke Papers*, iii. 82; *Cal. State Papers Dom.*,
1656-7, pp. 143, 148, 152; see also Giavarina's Dispatch of November 17,
R.O. Transcripts.

[2] *Commons' Journals*, vii. 452, 453.

CHAP.'. business of monies.' Yet no immediate result followed
II
—⁓— these votes.[1]
1656
The delay of Parliament to vote supplies was not
entirely caused by aversion to fresh taxation, still less
was it a sign of hostility to the Protector's government.
Much was due to the disorderly way in which public
business was conducted. The House had not been idle.
On November 27, five public and six private bills had
received the Protector's assent. 'Though you have
sat but a little time,' said Cromwell to the assembled
members, ' you have made many good laws, the effect
whereof the people of this Commonwealth will with
comfort find hereafter.'[2]   The fault of the House was
misdirected industry rather than laziness. In its zeal
it had taken in hand more schemes of legislation than
it could properly consider.

It was actively engaged in the task of social reform.
How to suppress superfluous and disorderly alehouses,
to regulate the wages of servants and labourers, to
relieve prisoners for debt, to ' set the poor on work,'
to revive the sumptuary laws, and to put a stop to
excessive apparel and ' undecent fashions ' amongst
women, were some of the problems which it undertook
to deal with. The subject it had most at heart was the
reform of the Law, and the establishment of cheaper
local tribunals. On November 3 Major-General Lambert brought in a bill for the setting up courts of law
and equity at York. Another member introduced a
bill for the probate of wills, which established registry
offices for the purpose in every county, and a third a
similar one for the registration of all incumbrances on
real estate. ' It is a more weighty business than I
could have imagined,' said a news-writer of the last

---

[1] Burton, *Diary*, i. 191 ; *Commons' Journals*, vii. 471.
[2] *Commons' Journals*, vii. 460; *Clarke Papers*, iii. 83.

bill, ' but I believe it will be pressed so far as shall be
practicable.' ' The lawyers,' said another letter, were
startled ' to see the administration of law like to be
carried into provinces,' and there was clearly some
controversy between the military reformers of the law
and its practitioners, in which reflexions were cast
upon ' the gentlemen of the long robe' for their obstruc-
tiveness.[1]

Every day some new matter came before the House,
and so many things were discussed that nothing was
determined. As Colonel Sydenham said, ' one business
jostled out another.' At the same time private petitions
and private bills occupied the attention of Parliament
to an extent unknown in modern times. Divorce cases,
disputed wills, naturalisation bills, the grievances of
individuals, and a hundred cases that should have been
settled in Westminster Hall, consumed time which ought
to have been devoted to public affairs. ' It is private
business jostles all out,' said Captain Fiennes in answer
to Sydenham.[2]

In addition to all this, constitutional questions of the
first magnitude had arisen since the session began.
Until some of these were settled to its satisfaction the
House was not inclined to relax its hold upon the purse
of the nation.

One of these constitutional questions concerned the
powers of Parliament itself. The House did not know
how long it had to live. The Instrument of Government divided Parliaments into two classes. There
were ordinary Parliaments, which were to be called
together every third year, and to sit for five months,
and which could not be dissolved till those five months

---

[1] See *Clarke Papers*, iii. 75, 76, 80 ; *Commons' Journals*, vii. 430, 431, 433,
439, 447, 449, 462.
[2] Burton, *Diary*, i. 190, 191.

CHAP.
II
1656

were over.[1]   There were extraordinary Parliaments to
be summoned by the Protector and Council at any
time when the necessities of the State seemed to require
it, and to be summoned forthwith in case of war with
any foreign state.   The duration of these extraordinary
Parliaments was not specified, but during the first
three months of their sitting they were not to be prorogued or dissolved without their own consent.[2]   Now
Cromwell's first Parliament, which met in September,
1654, was one of these ordinary Parliaments, while his
second, which met in September, 1656, was an extraordinary Parliament called in consequence of the war
with Spain.   The general belief among its members
was that it was only meant to sit for the specified
three months, and would be dissolved directly that
term ended.   On November 25 it was moved in the
House ' that in respect they had but sixteen days to
sit, and many bills were under consideration which could
not be finished without a longer time of sitting,' the
Protector should be asked to extend the session, but
this motion was dropped and does not appear in the
journals of the House.[3]   On December 9, in its anxiety
to finish off some of its business, the House sat very
late, ' almost till nine o'clock, it being the last night of
the natural life of the Parliament.'   When the House
met on Wednesday, December 10, it fully expected to
be either prorogued or dissolved; for three lunar months
had now elapsed since the opening of the session.   ' This
is the last day of sitting, for aught I know,' said one of
the members in the course of the morning's debate ; but,
as no message from the Protector came, business went
on as usual ; and without any definite announcement on

---

[1] Articles vii, viii of the Instrument of Government.
[2] Article xxiii of the Instrument.
[3] *Clarke Papers*, iii. 83.   *Commons' Journals*, vii. 458.

the part of the government the existence of the Parliament was indefinitely prolonged.[1] By delaying to vote the new taxes necessitated by the war the House had forced the hand of the government, and the Protector could not afford to dissolve it, even supposing he wished to do so.

In addition to the delay and the uncertainty which this doubt about its duration produced in Parliament, there was another question of still greater importance which also hampered the progress of business. In public the members might discuss all kinds of social reforms; in private what occupied their minds was the question of the succession to the Protectorate. The topic continually recurs in the dispatches of observant foreign ambassadors and in the letters of private persons, and it was more than once raised in the debates of the House itself. For that reason, when Sir Christopher Pack, on February 23, 1657, introduced a definite proposal for making Cromwell King and revising the constitution, less surprise was felt than historians in general have supposed. No one was unprepared for it, and least of all the members of the House to which it was proposed.[2]

There was nothing new in the proposal that the title of King should be conferred upon Cromwell. It had been made several times since the expulsion of the Long Parliament had rendered the revival of a monarchy feasible; but the suggestion had invariably been discountenanced by Cromwell himself, nor had it ever been discussed very seriously or with much publicity. At the beginning of December, 1653, Lambert and the officers who drew up the first sketch of the Instrument of

[1] Burton, *Diary*, i. 92, 97, 105 ; *Clarke Papers*, iii. 84.

[2] This question is discussed in detail and with copious extracts from dispatches and pamphlets in an article on ' Cromwell and the Crown,' published in the *English Historical Review*, in July, 1906, vol. xvii. p. 429.

Government had offered Cromwell the title of King, and he had refused it. A year later, about December 23, 1654, during the sittings of the first Parliament called by the Protector, Augustine Garland, an obscure regicide, moved to have the Protector crowned ; but though the motion was seconded by Sir Anthony Ashley Cooper, it dropped after a brief debate. Later still, in the summer of 1655, a petition which received many signatures was circulated in the City, asking Cromwell to take the title of King or Emperor, and to assume the legislative power. In this instance the petition was suppressed by the Council of State, and its promoter reprimanded.[1]

There was also nothing new in the suggestion that the Protectorate should be made an hereditary instead of an elective office. Article xxxii of the Instrument of Government declared that upon the death of the Lord Protector ' another fit person shall be forthwith elected to succeed him in the government, which election shall be by the Council.' An attempt had been made to alter this in the Parliament of 1654, and the question had been three days debated (October 16–18, 1654). Major-General Lambert ' made a long speech to persuade the Parliament that it was necessary to make the charge of Protector hereditary,' but a large majority of the House were in favour of keeping it elective, and the friends and relations of the Protector voted with the majority.[2] The Protector himself was hostile to the change proposed. In his speech at the dissolution of the same Parliament, on January 22, 1655, he went out of his way to protest against the idea that the government should be made a patrimony.

[1] Gardiner, *History of the Commonwealth and Protectorate*, ii. 271 ; iii. 67, 156. *Clarke Papers*, iii. 16, 43, 48.

[2] Gardiner, *Commonwealth and Protectorate*, iii. 40. Burton, *Diary*, i. p. li. Thurloe, i. 681–5. *Report on the MSS. of the Earl of Egmont*, i. 562.

His judgment, he said, was 'against making it hereditary, to have men chosen for their love for God and to truth and justice, and not to have it hereditary.' If the offer that the government should be hereditary in his family had been made to him, he declared that he would have rejected it.[1]

Thus, on both the forms in which the question of the restoration of monarchical government was raised, on the question whether the title of the chief magistrate should be King or Protector, and on the question whether the chief magistracy should be elective or hereditary, the Parliament of 1654 had negatived any attempt to alter the stipulations of the Instrument of Government. By 1656, however, the position of affairs had altered. The arbitrary expedients to which Cromwell had resorted after the breach with his first Parliament had produced a wide-spread reaction against military rule, even amongst the supporters of Cromwell. They desired the re-establishment of constitutional government, and therefore that of the only form of constitutional government with which they were familiar. ' Were this nation polled,' said a pamphleteer, ' not one in twenty but would desire their old government again.' [2] This desire for the restoration of monarchy took originally the form of a demand that the Protectorate should be made hereditary; and the question of the precise title to be borne by the supreme magistrate was, at first, of subordinate importance, though it afterwards became the chief question at issue between the two parties.

Now, as soon as Cromwell's second Parliament met, the desire for the restoration of monarchy showed itself.

---

[1] Carlyle's *Cromwell*, Speech iv.
[2] *A Copy of a Letter written to an Officer of the Army by a true Commonwealth's Man*, &c., British Museum, E. 870 (5). Published in March, 1656.

Ten days after its meeting, Giavarina, the Venetian ambassador, wrote to his government saying that Cromwell's elevation to the rank of King was being seriously discussed in political circles, and that the event was expected to take place in a few days.[1] However, for some time nothing was said about the matter in the House itself. Suddenly, on October 28, an Irish member, Major-General William Jephson, who sat for Youghal, raised the question of the succession and boldly proposed to amend the thirty-second article of the Instrument of Government so as to make the Protectorate hereditary instead of elective.[2]

Jephson did not persist in his proposal, which was perhaps meant merely to sound the feelings of the members, but the matter was not allowed to drop. According to the foreign ambassadors in London, Giavarina the Venetian ambassador, Bernardi the Genoese, and Bordeaux the representative of France, the question of the succession was several times discussed in the House during the month of November, both incidentally in the course of debates on other subjects, and purposely by means of motions directly raising the subject. More than once, say they, a day was named for the formal discussion of the matter. All three agree that the Protector himself disapproved the proposition, and privately interposed to prevent its further discussion. Each of them regarded the Protector's disapproval as mere dissembling, holding that neither he nor any other man alive could be really averse to a scheme which

---

[1] Giavarina, $\frac{\text{September 26}}{\text{October 6}}$, 1656. *Venetian Transcripts, R.O.*

[2] *Clarke Papers*, iii. 77. Thurloe, v. 525. Bordeaux, $\frac{\text{October 30}}{\text{November 9}}$, *French Transcripts, R.O.* Burton, *Diary*, iii. 160. Ludlow, *Memoirs*, ed. 1894, ii. 20.

would establish his own greatness and that of his
family.[1]

This momentous discussion went on entirely behind
the scenes. The world in general knew nothing of it.
There is no trace of it in the journals of Parliament, and
not a word about it in the newspapers. We learn of it
solely from the dispatches of foreign ambassadors and
from a few incidental references in private letters.[2] As
might have been expected, the officers of the army were
from the first hostile to the idea. About the middle of
November there was a meeting of some thirty officers at
Wallingford House, in which it was resolved to oppose
any change with regard to the succession. Those
officers who were members of Parliament—and there
were many such—though they could not formally debate
the question in the House itself, argued it out at length
in the committee rooms and the lobby. Colonel John
Bridge, an Irish member, describes one of these informal
debates in a letter to Henry Cromwell. Going into the
Speaker's Chamber on November 21, he found Major-
General Berry, member for Worcestershire, earnestly
contending with another member about the succession.
Bridge interposed, upon which Berry left his original prey
and assailed him. They fell to it hammer and tongs,
and after a while Major-General Desborough, member
for Somersetshire, came in and parted them by carrying
Berry away. As he went off, Berry turned back, and
sourly bade Bridge to put ' his scattered notions ' into
writing, and then he would undertake to answer them.
Bridge did so at once. His argument was that, while
every man in the nation had the same right to succeed
on the Lord Protector's death, there would infallibly be

---

[1] *English Historical Review*, xvii. 435; *Prayer, Oliviero Cromwell dalla
battaglia di Worcester alla sua morte*, 1882, pp. 388, 441.

[2] *Sixth Report, Historical MSS. Comm.*, p. 441. *Carte MSS.*, ccxxviii. p. 79.

a contest upon every change. The great officers of the army would compete with each other, and instead of dividing up the realm amongst them, as Alexander's captains did, they would doubtless come to blows. The one that was worsted would probably call in the help of the Royalists, and come to an agreement with the exiled King. When the nation found that each change of governor brought a new civil war, it would conclude ' that it 's better to settle upon the old bottom, and better that some particular men suffer than that the whole be ruined.' The result would be the restoration of the old monarchy without any security for the interests of those who had fought against it. Having drawn up his paper, Bridge returned to the House, and upon his way fell across Major-General Desborough in the smoking room (' the tobacco room ') and showed him what he had written. Desborough read it and confessed that Bridge's reasons were not easily answered, but talked about the inconvenience of suddenly converting an elective into an hereditary government. To this Bridge answered that the inconvenience of such a change and the danger of a competition after Cromwell's death might be avoided by a simple expedient. Let the Protector be given power to nominate his next successor; in that way the great objection would be removed, for he would doubtless nominate the fittest person. Desborough liked the expedient suggested. ' He replied he was very free to that, and so,' adds Bridge, ' are all the officers of the army and others I speak with, which are not a few.' [1]

We see from this not only that the question of the succession was actively discussed in November, 1656, and that the officers of the army were divided upon it,

---

[1] *Lansdowne MS.*, 821, p. 89. The letter is printed at length in the *English Historical Review*, xvii. 438.

but also that the very compromise which was adopted in the end was put forward by the supporters of the change and won a certain amount of support amongst its opponents.

Opposition was to be expected not merely from the army but from the Republican party in general. Though their leaders had been excluded from Parliament, they still exerted considerable influence upon public opinion. On the other hand, their influence was diminished by the fact that they were divided. The orthodox Republicans were entirely retrospective in their ideas. Men like Bradshaw, Haselrig, and Ludlow looked back to the government which had existed between 1649 and 1653 as the model of what a Republican government should be. They demanded the restoration of the Long Parliament as the supreme authority of the State, and the removal of all the checks which the army had sought to impose upon its sovereignty. As events showed, three years later these political ideals were absolutely incompatible with the political ideals of the officers of the army. No lasting union between these two sections of the opposition was possible. A second section of the Republican party, represented by the Fifth-Monarchy men and the extreme sectaries, looked back to the Little Parliament of 1653—the Barebones Parliament—as the model to be imitated. They wanted a republic in which dominion should be founded on grace; in which the government should be vested in the saints, that is, in the representatives of the various Independent sects elected by the congregations, or, in the phrase of the time, the gathered churches. But this section of the Republican party was weak in numbers and influence, and discredited by the failure of the experiment made in 1653.

There was also a third section of the Republican party, smaller in numbers than either of the others, indeed at present a mere group, only in process of formation, but destined to become more important two or three years later. This was the group of speculative Republicans who desired neither a parliamentary nor a theocratic republic, but a commonwealth with a constitution derived from Greek or Italian models. Their representative in the literature of the time is Harrington; and it was not by a merely accidental coincidence that his chief work was published at the very moment when this controversy about the succession and the form of government was beginning. The ' Commonwealth of Oceana ' is advertised, as newly published, in *Mercurius Politicus* for October 29 to November 6, 1656.[1] If we neglect the romantic form in which Harrington cast his speculations, and look only at the ideas the book sets forth, it is clear that he was separated by a wide gulf from the rest of the Republican opposition. The lawyers and parliamentarians, who have been termed the orthodox Republicans, imagined that a republic could be made by the simple process of, so to speak, decapitating a monarchy, that is, cutting off the crown and the House of Lords, and leaving everything else as it was. Harrington, on the other hand, saw plainly that a republic without republican institutions could not be lasting, and that the permanence of a free state could only be secured by adapting the machinery of the government to the form of the state. ' A parliament consisting of a single assembly elected by the people and invested with the whole power of the government ' seemed to him ' so strange a thing that neither ancient nor modern prudence can show any example of

---

[1] It is said to be ' Sold by Livewell Chapman, at the Crown in Pope's Head Alley.' Chapman was the chief printer of opposition pamphlets, &c.

the like.' The only precedents he could recall were the Thirty Tyrants of Athens or the Roman Decemvirs. ' A council without a balance,' such as the Long Parliament had been from 1649 to 1653, was, he asserted, ' not a commonwealth but an oligarchy.' To this extent Harrington agreed with the views of the army rather than those of ordinary republicans, and he was more in harmony with Cromwell than with Bradshaw and Haselrig.[1]

A second principle in Harrington's political speculations was that there must be a certain harmony between the structure of society and the form of government, and that the social institutions of a state must correspond in some way with its political institutions. Hence the theory of the ' balance of property,' as he termed it. According to him the nature of the government was really determined by the distribution of landed property in the particular state. If one man was sole landlord of a country, or of the greater part of it, you had an absolute monarchy as the result. If the greater part of the land was in the possession of a few, of the nobles and clergy for instance, you had a mixed monarchy. If the whole people were landowners, or held the land so divided amongst them that no one man or number of men could overbalance them, then that state must be a commonwealth, unless force was employed to prevent the natural result from taking place. Applying this principle to England, Harrington argued that, if a lasting commonwealth was to be established in England, property in land must be more equally distributed; and in order to bring this about, no one must be allowed to own land of a greater value than a certain amount, primogeniture must be abolished, and estates must be equally divided amongst children at the

[1] Harrington, *Works*, ed. Toland, 1700, pp. 76, 77.

parent's death.[1] Here he was anticipating the theorists of the French revolution, and advocating the principle which its legislators embodied in the Code Napoleon. Other political thinkers, in Harrington's day, had made similar proposals, especially amongst the Levellers, but the difference was that Harrington dreamt of effecting the reforms he proposed and creating his ideal commonwealth not by means of a democracy, but by means of an autocracy. Instead of appealing to the people he appealed to one man, and, unless we suppose his appeal to the Protector to be a mere rhetorical device, urged Cromwell to establish a republic organised according to certain fundamental principles laid down in 'Oceana.' In that book Olphaus Megaletor—Oliver the great-hearted—is urged to emulate the glory of Moses, and to give England a new code of laws as his prototype did to the Hebrew people. Or let him take Lycurgus as his model, and remember the famous saying of Machiavelli : 'Thrice happy is that people which chances to have a man able to give them such a government at once as may without alteration secure them of their liberties.'[2]

There was no reason, Harrington declared, why a properly constituted commonwealth should not last for ever. In his view the State was not, as we hold it to be, an organism which is constantly growing and developing, but an artificial creation, which if sufficiently well constructed in the beginning ought never to need alteration afterwards. He pictured Cromwell, like Lycurgus, establishing this ideal constitution in England, and seeing that his work was good, and resolving to make it immortal and immutable. Lycurgus, says Plutarch, 'when he saw that his government had taken root and was in the very plantation strong enough to stand by

---

[1] Harrington, *Works*, pp. 102–11.   [2] Ib. p. 77.

itself, he conceived such a delight within him as God is described by Plato to have done when he finished the creation of the world, and saw his own orbs move below him : for in the art of man (being the imitation of nature, which is the art of God) there is nothing so like the first call of beautiful order out of chaos and confusion, as the architecture of a well-ordered commonwealth.' Thereupon Lycurgus, in order that his work might be everlasting, assembled the people and made them swear that they would observe his laws without change or alteration until he returned from Delphi, and having reached Delphi, in order that his citizens might be inviolably bound by their oath, resolved never to return again, and so taking no manner of food soon after died there.[1] Harrington did not propose that Cromwell should take any such drastic method of rendering his Commonwealth permanent, but he suggested that after he had established it he should abdicate. The book closes with a picture of the Lord Archon, Olphaus Megaletor, solemnly resigning his power to the senate and retiring into private life, of the grateful people unanimously summoning him to resume the authority which he had laid down, and of his living many years in great glory and felicity as the chief magistrate of a free state.

It is said that the 'Commonwealth of Oceana' was at first regarded as a dangerous book, and that it was seized while it was in the press and threatened with suppression, but that Harrington by the intercession of Mrs. Claypole obtained the Protector's permission to print it.[2] It was even dedicated to Cromwell, though no one was less likely to adopt its proposals. Cromwell had no great belief in paper constitutions, and his experience of the Instrument of Government had increased his

[1] Harrington, *Works*, ed. Toland, p. 211.
[2] Ib. p. xix.

doubts. The examples held up for his imitation were not convincing. He had great respect for Moses, but Whitehall could not be made into Sinai, and though he knew little about Lycurgus he knew that England was not Lacedæmon. Of all the dreams of ideal republics he had met, and he had come across many, this was surely the most fantastic and unpractical. Tradition says that the Protector read Harrington's book, and briefly remarked that the gentleman would like to trepan him out of his power, but what he had got by the sword he would not quit for a little paper shot. Cromwell had become Protector, not in the expectation of doing much good but in the hope of preventing evil, of preventing England from relapsing into disorder and anarchy. While he was not anxious to increase his power, and so discouraged the movement for making himself King, he was quite determined not to resign his power to Parliament or any other body of men. He would stay where the Providence of God had put him. And, being an experienced statesman, he foresaw that all this underground agitation about the question of the succession and this rising excitement amongst the officers of the army and the Republicans portended something.   There was a deceptive stillness in the air, but the uneasy heaving of the waters showed that a storm was coming.

CHAPTER III

CATHOLICS AND QUAKERS

ONE of the perennial difficulties of the Protectorate was the difference of opinion which existed between the Protector and the Puritan party in general on the question of religious liberty. Those members of Parliament who, after the purgation which opened the session, still continued to sit at Westminster, were firm supporters of Cromwell's government, as they had shown by their approval of the Spanish War and their votes for the defence of his person and title. But in general they were Presbyterians rather than Independents, and even most of the Independents amongst them were less tolerant than the Protector himself.

This was shown in two instances, in one of which the divergence of views between Cromwell and his party threatened seriously to embarrass his foreign policy, whilst in the other it seemed likely to produce a serious constitutional dispute.

By the Instrument of Government Catholics were denied the free exercise of their religion in England, though they had been more leniently treated by Cromwell's government than by the Long Parliament.[1] Some of them hoped for the toleration of their creed now that Cromwell had allied himself with France. They felt secure against any recrudescence of persecution, because any rigorous treatment of the English Catholics would

---

[1] Gardiner, *Commonwealth and Protectorate*, iii. 224.

endanger the French alliance. On the other hand, the outbreak of the war with Spain had roused once more the mingled feeling of hostility and suspicion which had led to the enactment of so many penal laws. The Protector himself, by representing the war as part of a world-wide struggle with Popery, had stimulated and strengthened this feeling. He had suggested a political reason for suspecting the English Catholics by representing them as the natural and Sept. perpetual enemies of their country. ' The Spaniard,' 17 he had told the assembled members of Parliament when the session began, ' hath an interest in your bowels. The Papists in England have been accounted Spaniolised ever since I was born. They never regarded France ; they never regarded any Papist state ; Spain was their patron.' [1]

Under these circumstances it was natural that Parliament should show its Protestant zeal by reviving the disused penal laws and inventing additions to them. It was still more natural that it should attempt to defray some part of the cost of the war by increased taxation of the friends of Spain. A bill against recusants, which was brought in on November 29, 1656, passed its second reading on December 3, and its third on June 26, 1657.[2] The preamble recited that popish recusants had greatly increased of late, that this increase was occasioned by the neglect to put the laws against them into execution, and that thereby great danger to the public peace might follow. In future the justices in their quarter sessions and the judges at assizes were to summon all suspected Papists to appear before them and to take an oath of abjuration. Such persons were not only to abjure the Pope's authority and his deposing

---

[1] Carlyle's *Cromwell*, Speech v.
[2] *Commons' Journals*, vii. 461, 577.

power, but to renounce belief in transubstantiation, CHAP.
purgatory and other theological doctrines. Those who ‾III‾
declined the oath were to be adjudged recusants, and 1656-7
to forfeit two-thirds of their estates to the Lord
Protector. Stringent provisions were inserted to prevent recusants from evading the penalty by settling
their estates on their wives or children ; and any man
marrying a recusant was to be adjudged one himself.
No person once sequestered for recusancy was to be
allowed to take the oath without proving constant
attendance, for six months previously, at some church
or Christian meeting allowed by public authority.
Finally, any English subject who attended mass at the
chapel of a foreign ambassador was to be fined a hundred
pounds.[1]

This was a reactionary measure. The fine of two-
thirds of the estate was the traditional penalty imposed
on recusants since the time of Queen Elizabeth, but the
oath of abjuration was a larger and more comprehensive
version of that imposed by the Long Parliament in 1643.
The clause requiring attendance at a Protestant place
of worship as a test of sincerity was another retro-
grade step. For on September 27, 1650, Parliament
had abolished the old Recusancy Acts, and this was a
return to the bad old system of compulsory conformity.[2]
Hostile though Parliament was to the Catholics, it was
evident that the bill was far more stringent than the
exigencies of the moment demanded, and forty-three
members voted against its passing. Some, it is true, were
probably inspired by self-interest rather than any love of
toleration. ‘ There is one desperate clause in it,’ said a Dec. 3,
member : ‘ if my wife turn papist I shall suffer the confis- 1656
cation of two-thirds of my estate.’ Another replied that

---

[1] Scobell, *Acts and Ordinances*, ii. 443–9.
[2] Gardiner, *Commonwealth and Protectorate*, i. 399.

the provision in question was one of the best things in
the bill. For it was against the Scriptures to marry an
unbeliever, and the late King lost not two-thirds of his
estate but the whole of it through marrying a papist
woman.[1] The part of the bill which raised most opposition was the oath of abjuration. It might be right to
make Catholics abjure the Pope's supremacy, and his
power to depose sovereigns; but to inquire whether they
held certain doctrines and to oblige them to renounce
those doctrines was inconsistent with liberty of conscience.
The oath, it was urged, was worse than the *ex-officio* oath
by which the bishops had forced men to accuse themselves, and the procedure was like that of the Spanish
May Inquisition. Two members of the Protector's Council,
29, Strickland and Pickering, spoke strongly in this sense,
1657 but the most outspoken champion of the rights of
recusants was Lambert Godfrey, a lawyer who sat for
Kent. ' Admit them to be never so bad ; to be the
worst of men, to give the Devil his due ; this is no argument for you to do injustice. I think they are the worst
of men, and imitating their practices, is to imitate the
worst of men in the worst of their practices. I know no
difference between it and the Inquisition, only the one
racks and tortures the purse, the other the person.'
A soldier backed him by saying that it was against the
rights of Englishmen to make them accuse themselves.
' I grant,' answered Major-General Boteler, ' an oath
to accuse a man's self ought not to be put to an
Englishman, but I look upon the recusants as persons other than Englishmen. I look upon them as
enemies, and upon that account would not have
them have the liberties of the laws.'[2] Against the
belief that English Catholics were the secret allies
of the foreigner no theory of the rights of conscience

---

[1] Burton, *Diary*, i. 6–8.   [2] Ib. ii. 152, 153.

and no tradition of individual rights was strong enough

to prevail.

To the Protector this revival of the Catholic question
by Parliament was extremely inconvenient. The complaint of the non-execution of the penal laws was
practically a censure of his domestic policy; and any
aggravation of those laws might embarrass his foreign
policy. Parliament did not see this. One speaker had
suggested that foreign powers might retaliate on English
Protestants abroad,[1] but the danger had been lightly
regarded, and no one had pointed out that the proposed
measure might affect the relations between England and
France. Mazarin cherished a hope that the public
toleration of the English Catholics would follow his
alliance with the Protector. Bordeaux, whilst telling
the Cardinal that any formal declaration in their favour
was utterly impossible, had continued, until the beginning of December, 1656, to assure him that toleration
practically existed already. Catholic priests, said one
of his letters, could walk about London without fear ;
and lately, when some were arrested on suspicion of
being concerned in affairs of state, though they confessed their profession they were not handed over to the
executioner as the law demanded. Every Saint's day
hundreds of Catholics attended service at the ambassadors' chapels, and went away unmolested. English-
born priests who performed the service escaped unpun-
ished.[2] In December the French ambassador's note
changed. He reported to Mazarin the alarm which the
discussions in Parliament had roused amongst the
Catholics. The new measure in prospect would totally
ruin them, by depriving them of any power to vest

[1] Burton, *Diary*, ii. 149.

[2] Bordeaux to Mazarin, November $\frac{6}{16}$ and December $\frac{1}{11}$. *French Transcripts, R.O.*

CHAP.
III
1656

their property in the hands of trustees, and the execution of the old penal laws was also about to be ordered. Some of them, he said, meant to appeal to the King of France to protect them against the impending storm. Apparently the Cardinal replied by ordering Bordeaux to intercede with the Protector on behalf of the Catholics; for on December 25 the ambassador had an interview with Lockhart in which he introduced the question. Lockhart at first replied that the intervention of a foreign power would not be well received; but when Bordeaux reminded him of his own intervention on behalf of the Huguenots and the Vaudois his tone became more conciliatory. It was agreed that each might make representations on behalf of his co-religionists.[1] Next day the Protector himself wrote to the Cardinal in order to explain his position. ' I may not,' said he, '(shall I tell you I cannot ?) at this juncture of time and as the face of my affairs now stands, answer to your call for toleration. I say, I cannot, as to a public declaration of my sense in that point ; although I believe that under my government your Eminency, in behalf of Catholics, has less reason for complaint as to rigour upon men's consciences than under the Parliament. For I have of some, and those very many, had compassion, making a difference. Truly I have (and I may speak it with cheerfulness in the presence of God, who is a witness within me to the truth of what I affirm) made a difference ; and, as Jude speaks, "plucked many out of the fire," the raging fire of persecution which did tyrannise over their consciences, and encroached by an arbitrariness of power upon their estates. And herein it is my purpose, as soon as I can remove impediments, and some weights that press me down, to make a further progress, and

Dec.
26

[1] Bordeaux to Mazarin, $\frac{\text{December 25}}{\text{January 4}}$. *French Transcripts, R.O.*

discharge my promise to your Eminency in relation
to that.'[1]

For the moment Mazarin was content with the
Protector's promise that the Catholics should be
treated as leniently as possible ; indeed, he had no
other alternative. Six months later, on June 26,
1657, Cromwell gave his consent to the new Act, but
neither it nor the old laws against recusants appear
to have been seriously enforced. The Middlesex
Sessions Records show no sign of any increased activity
against the Catholics.[2] In December, 1657, eight priests
or supposed priests were arrested in Covent Garden.
Their crosses and jewels were confiscated, and
Cromwell made some of his gentlemen try on their
' copes and other popish vestments,' which caused
' abundance of mirth' in him and other spectators.
But the priests themselves were neither indicted
nor punished.[3] It is not possible to determine the
amount of revenue raised from the estates of the
recusants under this Act, but there is reason to believe
it was very small.[4]

Besides Catholics, another class of persons were
excluded from toleration, and during the course of the
session their case came into consideration. The Instrument of Government laid down the rule that the freedom
of worship it guaranteed was not to extend either to
those who abused that liberty ' to the civil injury of
others and the actual disturbance of the public peace,'

[1] Thurloe, v. 735 ; Carlyle's *Cromwell*, Letter ccxvi.

[2] *Middlesex Sessions Records*, iii. 255, 265, 273.

[3] *Clarke Papers*, iii. 129; *Mercurius Politicus*, December, 1657, pp. 152, 192;
Pepys to Montagu, December 8, 1657; *Carte MSS.*, lxxiii. 175; *Macmillan's
Magazine*, November, 1893, p. 35; Vaughan, ii. 299, 309.

[4] On the revenue derived from the recusants see *Calendar of the Committee
for Compounding*, i. p. xxi ; v. p. xxxii. A list of recusants under sequestration
drawn up in 1655 shows that they numbered 1582 persons (ib. i. 741). In the
revenue for 1658–9 there is an entry, ' By Receivers General arising chiefly by
Papists and Delinquents' estates, £54,087 5s. 9d.'

or to those who ' under the cover of Christ hold forth and practise licentiousness.' This provision, which represented the views of the officers who drew up the constitution, was far more liberal than any clause which the civilian supporters of the Protectorate would have drawn up. It allowed almost every variety of religious belief to be freely professed, provided the person professing it was moral and law-abiding in his conduct. Accordingly the Protector's first Parliament persistently endeavoured to restrict this freedom within certain theological limits. It held that whatever the conduct of a man might be, he ought not to be allowed to profess publicly certain doctrinal views. At first, therefore, that Parliament had proposed to require belief in a number of doctrinal truths as the condition of toleration. Afterwards, instead of fixing the amount of Christianity necessary to secure toleration, it determined to fix the amount of heresy which should entail punishment. Certain doctrinal heresies were to be specified as outside the pale of toleration, and what these heresies were Protector and Parliament were to settle by agreement. Bills were to be brought in to restrain blasphemy and profaneness, and to prevent the promulgation of doctrines contrary to the public profession of faith accepted by the nation.[1]

The sudden dissolution which took place prevented this constitutional amendment from becoming law; but the Protector's second Parliament was inspired by the same views as the first. It also found the liberty granted by the Instrument too large to be reconciled with its zeal against heretics. Yet though ' intolerable ' heresies had never been defined there were existing laws which could be put in force against those who

---

[1] Gardiner, *Commonwealth and Protectorate*, iii. 46, 61, 85.

publicly professed certain opinions. The Presbyterian blasphemy ordinance, passed in May, 1648, enumerated a score of doctrinal errors made punishable with death,[1] and though it was generally held to be abrogated by the Act of 1650, the point was by no means settled. The milder Act, passed in August, 1650, when the Independents were in power, specified certain 'atheistic, blasphemous and execrable opinions' for which the first punishment was to be six months' imprisonment and the second banishment from England.[2] It was directed against those who maintained that some human being was God or a manifestation of God, or that certain acts of immorality might be committed without sin by the spiritually perfect. There was one clause in it condemning 'whosoever shall deny the holiness and righteousness of God' which might be stretched to include the Anti-Trinitarians as well as the Ranters at whom the Act was aimed. It is possible that Biddle might have suffered under it, if he had not been banished without a trial.[3] Other offenders were from time to time proceeded against.

In December, 1655, some Kentish justices, at the instigation of Major-General Kelsey, committed Richard Coppin to prison. According to Kelsey he was guilty of ' preaching and maintaining several blasphemous tenets, saying Christ's human nature was defiled with sin, and that he offered sacrifice for his own sins as well as for the people's ; and that all men should be saved, denying hell or heaven to be other than what was within him, and many such damnable tenets.' The Major-General felt it necessary to defend his action to the Protector, 'knowing that many scandalous

[1] Scobell, *Acts and Ordinances*, i. 149.
[2] Ib. ii. 124 ; Gardiner, *Commonwealth and Protectorate*, i. 398.
[3] Ib. iii. 209.

CHAP.
III
1656

professors, that have fallen off from the worship and
services of God, and are ready to follow anything that
is evil, are ready to cry out for liberty of conscience,
and are not backward to say it's persecution worse
than in the bishops' time, and the like.' Kelsey proposed that Coppin should be banished like Biddle,
lest he should corrupt others; but he escaped with
some months' imprisonment, and the case probably
confirmed those who thought fresh legislation
necessary.[1]

To orthodox Puritans in general, the minor sects
were not so much a source of anxiety as the growth and
spread of Quakerism.   The Quakers attracted universal
unpopularity.   Puritan ministers in general hated them
because they disturbed their congregations, and scoffed
at the 'priests' and the 'steeple-houses.'   Puritan
justices of the peace were inflamed to fury by their contempt of court and defiance of authority.   The mob
was always ready to join in an assault upon a Quaker
missionary, and absolutely indifferent to the sufferings
of a Quaker prisoner.   James Parnell, a young Quaker
of eighteen years old, was arrested for disturbing a congregation at Coggeshall in July, 1655, fined £40, and
committed to Colchester Castle in default of payment.
There he died in May, 1656, from ill-treatment and
starvation.   It was said by the orthodox, though without truth, that he had wilfully starved himself to death,
and a ballad-maker exulted at the fate of the false
prophet who had promised his disciples to perform a
miracle :—

---

[1] Thurloe, iv. 486.   A life of Coppin is contained in the *Dictionary of National
Biography*, where it is said that he was committed to prison on December 24,
1655, and that before June 26, 1656, he had been set free by *habeas corpus* (xii. 192).
There is no account of his trial, but if the ordinance of 1648 had been held to be
still in force he would certainly have been condemned.   Under the Act of 1650
it is doubtful whether he could be touched.

As Christ had fasted forty days,
   And never at all did drink nor eat,
Nor in his body entered not
   So much as one small grain of wheat,
' So will I do,' James Parnell said,
   ' Because you all shall know and see
That I am a prophet of the Lord ;
   And those that will believe in me
Shall have eternal joys in Heaven
   Amongst the souls whom God hath blest ;
But those that will not me believe
   Shall never come where saints do rest.'

CHAP.
III
1656

On the thirteenth day of his fast Parnell died, and the ballad-maker, expressing a pious hope that all such hypocrites might be so served, invoked God with His powerful hand to protect the souls of men from such snares of the devil, and bade all Quakers to be warned by this example.[1]

Quaker was a name which at this time was very loosely used. The doctrine preached by Fox was not at first so definite, coherent, and sober as it afterwards became. The movement attracted to it a number of wild enthusiasts of every kind, and public opinion classed as followers of Fox sectaries who drew their inspiration from other sources. Fox continually

---

[1] On Parnell's case, see Francis Glisson's *True and lamentable Relation of the most desperate Death of James Parnel, Quaker*, and the answer to it, entitled, *The Lamb's Defence against Lies* (E. 879 (3), and E. 881 (1)). A life of Parnell is given in the *Dictionary of National Biography*, xliii. 347. The ballad in question, which is signed L. P., i.e. Lawrence Price, is to be found in the Bodleian Library.

' The Quakers Fear, or, Wonderfull strange and true News from the famous Town of Colchester in Essex, showing the manner how James Parnel, a Quaker by profession, took upon him to fast twelve days and twelve nights without any sustenance at all, and called the people that were his followers or Disciples, and said that all the people of England that were not of their Congregation were all damned Creatures. Of his blasphemous Life and scandalous Death in the Jayl at Colchester this present month of April 1656 you shal here have a full Relation. The tune is, "Summer time." Or " Bleeding Heart." ' —*Wood, folio Ballads*, 401, fol. 165.

disputed with the Ranters and controverted their teach-
ing; but Baxter regarded the Quakers as themselves an
offshoot of the Ranters. ' The Quakers,' he says, ' were
but the Ranters turned from horrid profaneness and
blasphemy to a life of extreme austerity on the other
side. Their doctrines were mostly the same with the
Ranters.' [1] Another writer described the Ranter as
' an unclean beast much of the make with our Quaker,
of the same puddle.' [2] Many held that the Quakers
were crypto-Catholics, and their preachers Papists in disguise.[3] For that reason some local authorities attempted
to impose upon them the oath of abjuration directed
against Catholic recusants.[4] But neither the suspicion
of Popery nor the confusion with the Ranters brought
so much odium upon the Quakers as the follies and
extravagances of one of their own leaders. James
Naylor was one of Fox's first converts. He had entered
the Parliamentary army when the war began, rose to
the rank of quarter-master in Lambert's regiment of
horse, and left the service in 1651. ' A very useful
person,' said Lambert ; ' we parted with him with
great regret. He was a man of very unblameable life
and conversation, a member of a very sweet society of
an Independent church.' [5] When Naylor was converted
he became first the helper of Fox, and afterwards his
rival. His fervid eloquence gained him an influence
which almost equalled that of Fox, and he became the
idol of female Quakers. But he lacked the sanity and
self-control which underlay the eccentricities of his
leader, and was carried away by the emotional

---

[1] *Reliquiæ Baxterianæ,* i. 77.

[2] E. Pagitt, *Heresiography,* ed. 1661, p. 259.

[3] ' Many Franciscan friars and other Papists have been proved to be disguised speakers in their assemblies,' says Baxter.

[4] E. 934 (7). *To the Protector and the Parliament of England.*

[5] Burton, *Diary,* i. 33.

enthusiasm which his preaching roused. His appearance
was singular and striking ; men saw in his face and features a resemblance to the traditional portraits of Christ, which he artificially heightened by the arrange- ment of his hair and beard.[1] His excited disciples addressed him in language which the Bible applied to Christ. He was ' the fairest of ten thousand,' ' the hope of Israel,' ' the Lamb of God.' ' Thy name,' wrote one, ' is no more to be called James, but Jesus.' They reported that he had raised a woman from the dead, and professed to see in him an emanation of the divinity, a new Messiah.[2]

During Naylor's imprisonment at Exeter, in the summer of 1656, these demonstrations multiplied. Fox, who heard that his friend James ' had run out into imaginations, and a company with him, which raised up a great darkness in the nation,' came to Exeter to remonstrate with him. But Naylor slighted Fox's remon- strances, and remained unconvinced by his arguments.[3] As soon as he was liberated he made a triumphant entry into Bristol, which was a parody of Christ's entry into Jerusalem. A man went before him bare-headed ; two women led his horse ; some threw their garments before him ; others sang hosannas and cried, ' Holy, Holy, Lord God of Israel.' The Bristol magistrates at once arrested Naylor, with seven of his followers, and sent them to London for trial. On October 31, 1656, the matter was brought before Parlia- ment, which appointed a committee of fifty-five members to examine him. The chairman of the committee was Thomas Bampfield, the Recorder of Exeter, a man who

---

[1] There is a portrait of Naylor in Pagitt's *Heresiography*, p. 244. See also *A True Narrative of the Examination, Trial, and Sufferings of James Naylor,* 1657, p. 6, E. 899 (6).

[2] *A True Narrative*, pp. 15–28.

[3] Fox, *Journal*, i. 327, ed. 1901.

so truly represented the feelings of his fellow-members that he became Speaker of the next Parliament. For many days Naylor and his disciples were examined; but at last, on December 5, Bampfield brought his report to the House.[1] The accused, it declared, assumed the gestures, words, honour, worship, and miracles of our blessed Saviour, and also His titles and incommunicable attributes. As soon as the report had been read, Major-General Skippon was on his feet. He was an infrequent and unskilful speaker, but no man was heard with more respect by Puritans of every shade. All remembered that he had dared to take up arms for the Parliament long before Essex became Lord General of its army or any peer drew his sword for the people's rights. They remembered, too, that when Essex deserted that army in Cornwall, the patient valour and devotion to duty of his Major-General shone brightest in disaster. In an age when soldiers were religious his faith was conspicuous as his courage, and it was not without right that he styled himself ' the Christian Centurion.' ' It has always been my opinion,' declared Skippon, ' that the growth of these things is more dangerous than intestine or foreign enemies. I have often been troubled in my thoughts to think of this toleration.' Then, referring to the Quakers, he said that their growth and increase was too notorious both in England and Ireland, and that their principles struck both at ministry and magistracy. ' Should we not be as jealous of God's honour as we are of our own ? Do not the very heathen assert the honour of their gods, and shall we suffer our Lord Jesus to be thus abused and trampled upon ? ' [2] Major-General Boteler followed Skippon—Boteler, the most odious of all Cromwell's Major-Generals—a typical Independent as Skippon was a typical Presbyterian. His

---

[1] *Commons' Journals*, vii. 448, 464.   [2] Burton, *Diary*, i. 24.

ears, he said, tingled and his heart trembled, to hear CHAP.
III
1656
the report.   Never had he heard such blasphemy.   ' It
is not intended to indulge such gross heresies and
blasphemies as these, under the notion of a toleration
of tender consciences.' [1]   The rest of the debate
mainly related to the question of procedure ; some were
for erecting a special court to try Naylor, some for
drawing up a bill of attainder against him.   It was
finally decided to call him to the bar and to bid him
answer to the charge.

Next day Naylor appeared before the House and Dec. 6
was questioned by the Speaker.   Substantially he admitted all the facts alleged against him except the charge
of immorality, though he attempted to show that the
expressions which seemed to imply his divinity had
been used and received in an innocent and spiritual
sense.   What he had done, a revelation from God had
ordered him to do, even to the manner of his entrance
into Bristol, which had merely an allegorical significance.   ' I was set up as a sign to summon this nation,
and to convince them of Christ's coming.   The ful-
ness of Christ's coming is not yet, but he is come
now.' [2]

After Naylor had withdrawn, a furious and rambling
discussion began which lasted for nine days.   Some
few members urged that his offence was not blasphemy.
Pickering argued that he did not give himself out to
be the Son of God, but to be a prophet, a type or sign to

---

[1] Burton, *Diary*, i. 25.

[2] *Commons' Journals*, vii. 465 ; Burton, *Diary*, i. 46–8.   At the close of
his examination by the committee, Naylor had thus summed up what he had
to say: ' I do abhor that any of that honour which is due to God, should be
given to me as I am a creature; but it pleased the Lord to set me up as a sign
of the coming of the righteous one ; and what hath been done in my passing
through the towns, I was commanded by the power of the Lord to suffer such
things to be done to the outward as a sign.   I abhor any honour as a creature.'
—*A True Narrative*, p. 28.   See the comments of Dr. Stoughton, *Church of the
Commonwealth*, ii. 364.

warn men of Christ's second coming. Naylor's followers
were more guilty than himself. ' I do not believe,' said
Lawrence, the President of the Council of State, ' that
James Naylor thinks himself to be the only Christ;
but that Christ is in him in the highest measure. This,
I confess, is sad. But if you go about to adjudge it
blasphemy, I am not satisfied. It is hard to define
what is blasphemy.' Another member of the Council,
Walter Strickland, thought Naylor a man under ' a
high delusion, as believing that more of Christ is in
him than in any other creature,' but yet not absolutely
a blasphemer. A fourth councillor, Colonel Sydenham,
pointed out that the Quakers in general affirmed that
Christ dwelt personally in every believer, an opinion
which was near akin to a most glorious truth, and that,
if Naylor were condemned as a blasphemer, it might
be made a precedent against the whole sect. But the
House was not in the mood to listen to any arguments
which mitigated Naylor's offence. ' Let us all stop our
ears and stone him,' said one zealous member, and it
was voted without a division that Naylor was guilty
of horrid blasphemy, a grand impostor and a great
seducer of the people.[1]

The question of the procedure against Naylor, and
the nature of the punishment to be inflicted upon him,
were less easily settled. The view that he was protected
by the Instrument of Government was suggested, but only
to be summarily dismissed.[2] ' These Quakers, Ranters,
Levellers, Socinians and all sorts,' said Skippon, ' bolster
themselves under clauses thirty-seven and thirty-eight
of the Instrument of Government, which at one breath
repeals all the acts and ordinances against them. I

[1] Burton, *Diary*, i. 56, 62, 65, 69, 75. The member who suggested stoning
was Thomas Clarges, Monck's brother-in-law.
[2] *Ib.* i. 59, 78.

heard the supreme magistrate say it was never intended
to indulge such things ; yet we see the issue of this
liberty of conscience. If this be liberty, God deliver
me from such liberty. It is to evil, not to good, that
this liberty extends.' ' As to the Instrument of Government,' observed Downing, ' I hope it shall never be
made use of to let this wretch escape. I am as much
for tender consciences as any man, but I deny that this
has any share in such liberty.' Major-General Goffe
was still more emphatic. ' I shall not,' he declared,
' entertain an irreverent thought of the Instrument of
Government. I shall spend my blood for it. Yet if
it hold out anything to protect such persons, I would
have it burnt in the fire.' [1] It was too clear that, even
if the letter of the constitution protected Naylor, the
House was in no mood to be bound by it. Like
the last Parliament, it held that in this respect the
Instrument allowed heretics a freedom which no
Christian commonwealth could safely permit them to
enjoy.

Some members, perceiving the constitutional question involved, wished to leave Naylor to the ordinary
courts. ' I wish we had not meddled with this business,
but sent him over to the Upper Bench,' said Whitelocke.
But by what law could the courts condemn him ? One
member said that, by the common law, blasphemy and
heresy were punishable with death. ' I know no law
nor statute,' said another, 'which has repealed that *de
haeretico comburendo*.' ' I hope,' chimed in a third,
' that the abuse of it, and turning it against the Lollards,
does not take away the law.' Thurloe, on the other
hand, said he should be sorry to see the old laws against
heretics put into execution now, adding : ' I know no
law in force this day against blasphemy, unless it be

---

[1] Burton, *Diary*, i. 50, 61, 110.

that of the old Parliament.' He referred to the Act of
1650; and Whitelocke backed him up by saying that it
annulled the severer ordinance against blasphemy passed
by the Long Parliament in 1648. If this was true,
Naylor could only be sentenced to six months' imprisonment (which was the penalty the Act of 1650 imposed
for a first offence), or at most, if the highest punishment
the act permitted were inflicted, to banishment from
England. The House was in no mood to let him escape
so lightly, and, since its zeal demanded the infliction
of some severer sentence, it was obliged to take the law
into its own hands.[1]

Two alternatives, it was agreed, lay before Parliament. It might proceed either by its legislative or its
judicial power. Supposing that it decided to proceed
in its legislative capacity, it might draw up a bill of
attainder against Naylor, as Boteler, Whitelocke,
Bacon, Shapcote, and many other members recommended. Or it might, as Thurloe proposed, ' make a
law *ex post facto*,' by passing a bill to heighten the
punishment inflicted on such offenders. The drawback
was that, if the House proceeded by a bill of any kind,
the consent of the Protector was necessary to make it
law. Charged as he was to protect liberty of conscience,
Cromwell might consider it his duty to use his right of
veto and to negative the bill. Captain Baynes at the
very beginning of the debate pointed out this difficulty.
If they went by way of bill the Lord Protector must have
a negative. ' We may bring him into a snare unless he
heard the matter. His opinion may stick and demur
as to the offence ; for the Instrument of Government
says, all shall be protected that profess faith in Jesus
Christ, which, I suppose, this man does.' [2] Accordingly,

---

[1] Burton, *Diary*, i. 111, 118, 130, 133, 141 ; Scobell, ii. 124, Act of August 9,
1650.   [2] Burton, *Diary*, i. 59.

without passing any express resolution for the purpose,
the House fell back upon its supposed judicial power.
It was generally assumed that it possessed a judicial
power, and the assumption was supported by precedents showing that the House had punished various
persons for defaming its members, and for other breaches
of privilege.   Floyd's case was cited as a precedent,
although in that instance the Commons had been obliged
to abandon their claim to be a court of judicature.   It
was argued, however, that the House of Lords had
undoubtedly possessed a judicial power, and that on
the extinction of the House of Lords this power had
devolved upon the House of Commons.   The present
Parliament, it was said, possessed the combined powers
of both Houses.   ' Whatsoever authority was in the
Houses of Lords and Commons, the same is united in
this Parliament.'   This was affirmed by no less a person than Lord Chief Justice Glyn, and the theory was
eagerly accepted.   Major-General Goffe went a step
further, and assured his fellow-members that the
ecclesiastical jurisdiction by which the bishops once
punished blasphemy had, since the abolition of the
bishops, devolved also upon the House.[1]

Weak as these arguments were, the House had no
hesitation in accepting them, and in proceeding to
pass sentence upon Naylor.   The only question which
remained to be decided was the nature of the punishment to be inflicted.   Many held that death was the
only adequate penalty for such blasphemy as Naylor's.
The judicial law of Moses was appealed to, and there
was an animated discussion whether it was still binding
upon Christians.   Lawyers and soldiers rivalled each
other in explaining texts from Leviticus and Deutero-
nomy with as much assurance as if they had been

[1] Burton, *Diary*, i. 30, 109, 157, 248.

passages from Coke's 'Institutes' or the 'Articles of War.'
The case of the Hebrew who was put to death for gathering sticks on the Sabbath day was cited, though a little
doubt was expressed whether it was applicable.   Zecha-
riah xiii. 3, which says that a man who speaks lies in
the name of the Lord shall be thrust through the body
by his father and mother, was held to be more to the
point.   Major-General Goffe triumphantly brought forward the instance of the Church of Thyatira, which is
severely condemned in Revelation ii. 20, for not
punishing a blasphemous female, and urged it as a
reason for inflicting the death penalty on Naylor.
Two other Major-Generals, Kelsey and Packer, answered
Goffe; and the poet Waller made an excellent speech
in favour of a more just and merciful sentence.   But
moderate men were heard with impatience.   Even the
recorder of the debate lost all pretence of impartiality
when he reported a plea for Naylor.   'He said a great
deal more to extenuate the crime, but I minded it not,'
is Burton's note on Waller's speech.   The orator Burton
most approved was Bampfield, who made 'a large
and handsome speech' in answer to what 'the merciful
men' had said.   It was 'such as they were scarcely
able to reply to,' for he proved 'that it was the mind
of God to punish this offence with death.'[1]

In spite of Bampfield and the bigots, 'the merciful
men' gained the victory, and on Tuesday, December 16,
when the debate ended, the proposal that a bill should
be brought in for the punishment of James Naylor by
death was defeated by ninety-six to eighty-two votes.[2]
The bigots had their revenge when the nature of the
minor punishment which was to be inflicted came to
be determined.   To be pilloried, to be whipped, to

---

[1] Burton, *Diary*, i. 91, 99, 100, 109, 121, 123, 151.
[2] *Commons' Journals*, vii. 468.

be branded, to have his lips slit, hard labour, and
transportation were successively suggested. 'You
ought,' said Downing, 'to do something with that
tongue that has bored through God. You ought to
bore his tongue through.' 'You had better take his
life,' replied President Lawrence; 'that tongue may
afterwards praise the Lord. I was ever against that
punishment.' Another member pointed out that
boring the tongue was an ordinary punishment for
swearing, and that he had known twenty cases in
which it had been inflicted, so Lawrence's objection
was set aside.[1] The sentence finally voted ran as
follows :—

'Resolved that James Naylor be set on the pillory,
with his head in the pillory, in the New Palace, Westminster, during the space of two hours on Thursday
next; and shall be whipped by the hangman through
the streets, from Westminster to the Old Exchange,
London; and there likewise to be set on the pillory,
with his head in the pillory, for the space of two hours,
between the hours of eleven and one on Saturday next;
in each of the said places wearing a paper with an in-
scription of his crimes; and that at the Old Exchange
his tongue shall be bored through with a hot iron; and
that he be there also stigmatised in the forehead with
the letter B. And that he be afterwards sent to Bristol,
and be conveyed into and through the said city, on a
horse bare-ridged, with his face backwards; and there
also be publicly whipped on the next market day after
he comes thither. And that from thence he be committed to prison in Bridewell, London, and there
restrained from the society of all people and kept to
hard labour, till he shall be released by Parliament;
and during that time shall be debarred from the use of

[1] Burton, *Diary*, i. 153-5.

pen, ink, and paper, and shall have no relief but what he earns by his daily labour.' [1]

On December 17 Naylor was brought to the bar of the House to receive his sentence. It had been resolved, by 107 to 85 votes, that he was not to be allowed to say anything in his defence before judgment was pronounced, so the proceedings were brief. The Speaker told him that the House had mingled mercy with justice, as it desired his reformation rather than his destruction, and then read the catalogue of penalties which were to be imposed upon him. ' God,' replied Naylor, ' has given me a body ; God will I hope give me a spirit to endure it. The Lord lay not these things to your charge.' [2]

Dec.
18
Next day the first part of the sentence was duly carried out. Naylor stood for two hours in the pillory in Palace Yard, and was then flogged through the streets from Westminster to the Old Exchange, and finally committed to Newgate.[3] On the same morning Parliament received petitions against the Quakers from the cities of Bristol, Chester, and Exeter, and from half a dozen counties. Member after member rose in his place to demand the enactment of some new law to prevent this spreading mischief, which, if unchecked, would lead to the overthrow of magistracy and ministry. Some two or three objected to the use of the general word Quakers. ' It is a word that signifies nothing,' said Colonel Sydenham. ' It is like the word Lollards or Puritans, under the notion whereof many godly persons are now under the altar, their blood being poured forth. It is of dangerous consequence to make a law under general terms, and leave it to after ages to

---

[1] *Commons' Journals*, vii. 468.
[2] Ib. vii. 459 ; Burton, *Diary*, i. 166.
[3] *Mercurius Politicus*, December 18–24.

interpret your meaning. Let it be plainly explained
what the offences shall be.' He was backed by Walter
Strickland. 'We know,' said Strickland, 'how laws
against Papists were turned against the honestest men.
We may all in after ages be called Quakers. It is a word
nobody understands. We all know how the edge of former laws against Papists has been turned upon the best
Protestants, the truest professors of religion, the honest
Puritan, as they called him, a good profession, but hard
to be understood, as this word Quaker will be in after
ages.' The House answered by referring the petitions
to the committee which had been appointed to examine
Naylor—a body not very likely to err in the direction
of tolerance.[1] It seemed as if a general campaign
against Quakerism was about to begin. The editor of
the official newspaper inserted, in the number which
contained the record of Naylor's punishment, a long
account of the trial of nine Quakers at Boston, and
the measures taken by the government of Massachusetts
to suppress 'that abominable brood.'[2]

Yet there were some Puritans left in England who
held that doctrinal errors should not be punished by
barbarous cruelty. Naylor had at least one defender.
For some days a Quaker named Robert Rich, called
'the mad merchant,' had haunted the doors of the
House with petitions and letters in his favour. He
asked to be allowed to prove to the House, out of the
Scriptures, that nothing which Naylor had said was
blasphemy or worthy death or bonds. On the day
when Naylor suffered the first part of his sentence Rich
was at the door of the House as usual, crying to the
members as they passed in, and upbraiding some who

---

[1] Burton, *Diary*, i. 168–73.
[2] *Mercurius Politicus*, December 18–24, p. 7466. The case of Mary Prince
and others is reported at length.

pretended to be friends to innocency and justice, and warning them. 'The Lord,' he cried, 'is coming to separate between the sheep and the goats, to gather up the wheat into garners, and to burn the chaff with fire that is not to be quenched.' No one sought to hinder him. 'These words past with such a power (mixed some time with singing) that none resisted or gainsaid.' From the door of Parliament he passed into Westminster Hall, singing very loud, and stood over against the Court of Chancery, where the Commissioners of the Great Seal were sitting, and cried to them 'that the land mourned because of oppression, and for want of justice and true judgment.' Then, with a great multitude following him, he went into Palace Yard, and marched, singing still, round the pillory. The mob which had gathered to witness Naylor's sufferings made way for him ; none harmed him ; even the soldiers who arrested him let him go, for his madness was his protection.[1]

Happily the cause of humanity and tolerance had saner champions too. Naylor was to undergo the second part of his punishment on Saturday, December 20 ; but on that morning four persons presented a petition, stating that he was too weak to undergo that part of his sentence at present, and begging for the respite of a week, 'that he may recover a little strength before he be called forth again.'[2] Some members subsequently grumbled that the whipping had been too lenient, and that it was but a 'mock punishment.' But the hangman, who was an exact arithmetician, computed that his patient had received precisely 310 stripes, and the woman who dressed Naylor's back testified that the conscientious official had done his business with thoroughness. Parliament, having no wish that its

[1] *A True Narrative*, pp. 38–42.
[2] Ib. pp. 49–52; Burton, *Diary*, i. 482 ; *Commons' Journals*, vii. 471.

xhibition of orthodoxy should be interrupted by the CHAP.
·remature death of the heretic, answered by postponing III
he second part of the sentence to December 27. It also 1656
ent five ministers to Newgate to try milder methods
f conversion.[1]

On December 23 another petition, signed by some
ighty-seven persons in and about London, was pre-
ented to the House. The deputation which brought
t was headed by Joshua Sprigge, once chaplain of the
New Model, and they prayed that the remainder of the
entence against Naylor might be entirely remitted,
leaving him to the Lord, and to such Gospel remedies
s he hath sanctioned.' The House, which had only
greed to receive the petition by one vote, promptly
·ejected their demand. ' We are God's executioners,
nd ought to be tender of his honour,' said George
Downing, and the phrase exactly expressed the feeling
f the majority.[2]

The petitioners, who had expected this, turned now
o the Lord Protector. They were concerned, they
aid, in the proceedings against Naylor, solely ' out of
enderness to the good cause of spiritual and civil
iberties.' They pointed out that the constitution gave
he Protector a joint interest in the legislative power,
nd that its thirty-seventh article guaranteed liberty of
onscience. They requested Cromwell therefore, according to all his former declarations and their past
experience of his care for liberty of conscience, to weigh
he consequences of the late proceedings of Parliament,
nd ' to stand up for the poor people of God.' [3]

This was an appeal to which Cromwell could not

---

[1] Burton, *Diary*, i. 247; *Commons' Journals*, vii. 471; *A True Narrative*,
. 53.
[2] Burton, *Diary*, i. 216-20; *Commons' Journals*, vii. 474; *A True Narrative*,
. 54.
[3] Ib. p. 55.

turn a deaf ear. He had no particular sympathy with the views of the Quakers, so far as he understood them, and he had the strongest objection to their habit of disturbing congregations at their worship and reviling the ministers of the Established Church. In the pro- clamation of February, 1655, announcing his intention of punishing such disorderly practices, the Quakers were especially named. On the other hand, he had as strong an objection to the excessive severity with which they were punished by country justices, and the barbarous cruelty with which they were treated in country gaols. The meeting of Parliament had been followed by an order for the release of a number of Quakers imprisoned in Devonshire, Dorsetshire, Suffolk, and Essex; and the Protector had under consideration the case of a number of others who had been illegally committed by the Sussex justices.[1] Cromwell, therefore, could not remain insensible either to the barbarity of the sentence upon Naylor or to the constitutional questions involved in the proceedings against him, though he held that the liberty of conscience provided by the Instrument was not meant to cover opinions like those of Biddle and Naylor. He resolved to intervene.

On December 26 a letter from the Protector, refer- ring to the judgment against Naylor, was read in Parliament. 'Although,' it said, ' we detest and abhor the giving or occasioning the least countenance to per- sons of such opinions or practices, or who are under the guilt of such crimes as are commonly imputed to the said person ; yet we, being interested in the present government on behalf of the people of these nations, and not knowing how far such proceeding (wholly without us) may extend in the consequence of it, we desire that the House will let us know the grounds and

[1] *Cal. State Papers Dom.*, 1656–7, pp. 122, 123, 133, 229.

reasons whereupon they have proceeded.'[1] This letter roused once more a question which the Parliament had carefully avoided. By rejecting the proposal to bring in a bill against Naylor the House had seemed to decline proceeding by its legislative power, and by inserting the word 'adjudged' in the sentence upon Naylor it had seemed to claim a judicial power.[2] But it had not during the course of the debates, by any direct vote, either defined the nature of its procedure or the origin of its jurisdiction. It was now bluntly asked by what authority it had acted.

Lambert explained the meaning of Cromwell's intervention clearly enough. 'It is not without good reason that his Highness would be satisfied in the grounds. He knows not by what way you have proceeded, whether upon the judicatory or legislative. He is under an oath to protect the people both in freedom of their consciences and persons and liberties. He is bound to inform himself in whatsoever he finds encroaching upon either.' The Lord Chief Justice urged that a committee should be appointed to consider precedents. He admitted that past Parliaments had exercised a judicial power in punishing offences, but asserted that it ought to be very charily exercised, and that, while the legislative power of Parliament was boundless, its judicial power was, and ought to be, limited. For Parliament observed none of the ordinary rules of courts of justice; it was 'a court of will and power.'

The Chief Justice went on to say that the Lord Protector was under an oath to protect the lives and liberties of the people. 'If we proceed in this manner, judicially, against any man as we please, we divest

---

[1] *Commons' Journals*, vii. 475; Carlyle's *Cromwell*, Letter ccxvii.
[2] *Commons' Journals*, vii. 469.

him of that power, and take the sole power of judging
men without law or against law. It is true such things
have been done by Parliament alone, but never without great regret.' He added that, though he did not
advise them to annul their sentence, they must beware
lest it was made a precedent. 'Provide against it in the
future, for it may be of very dangerous consequence to
Englishmen to be governed by a court of will.' Sir
Gilbert Pickering took the same line as Glyn. 'It is
very fit this jurisdiction should be debated. It seems
though the judicial power of Parliament cannot extend
to life, yet by this means by a vote of to-day you may
pull out a man's eyes; to-morrow slit his nose, or cut off
his hands, ears or tongue.' [1]

Other speakers abandoned the legal argument, alleging
that the sentence was contrary to natural justice. 'You
ought not,' said Major Audley, 'to have denied the person
to have spoken when he desired it at the bar. Were he
never so wicked you ought to give him the liberty of an
Englishman.' Sydenham backed him. 'We live as
Parliament men for a time, but we live as Englishmen
always. I would not have us so tender of the privilege
of Parliament as to forget the liberties of Englishmen.'
'We cannot tell,' said Lambert, 'what Parliaments
in other ages may produce. We ought to take care to
leave things certain, and not to expose the people's
liberties to an arbitrary power.' [2]

Some members of the majority endeavoured to
confuse the issue by misinterpreting the meaning of
the Protector's letter. 'I understand not,' said Downing, 'that the Protector does at all question or desire an

[1] Burton, *Diary*, i. 255, 256, 275. The debate was spread over two days,
December 26 and December 27, and was resumed on December 30. This
summary of the arguments does not observe the chronological order of the
speeches.
[2] Ib. i. 246, 274, 282.

account of our jurisdiction.' The letter, he asserted, _{CHAP.}
was drawn from the Protector by importunity. ' I am _{III}
confident it is not in his heart to give the least counten- ₁₆₅₆
ance to such persons. I know it is not in his heart to
have this punishment respited.' Whalley, whose kin-
ship to the Protector gave his words more weight,
asserted with great confidence that Cromwell was not
against the sentence. Colonel Markham went further,
declaring that the Protector abhorred Naylor's crime
and did not desire a reprieve. ' For my part,' he said,
' if he did not abhor it I would never serve him.' The
result of the debate was that the consideration of the
Protector's letter was adjourned, and that by nearly two
votes to one, that is by 113 to 59, the House decided
not to suspend the execution of Naylor's sentence.

On December 27 the second part of Naylor's punish- _{Dec.}
ment was carried out, by branding him in the forehead ₂₇
and boring his tongue. One of the members of the
Parliament who had condemned him to those penalties
went to see them duly inflicted. Naylor was bound
with a cord by both arms to the pillory. He ' put out
his tongue very willingly, but shrinked a little when the
iron came upon his forehead. He was pale when he
came out of the pillory, but high-coloured after the
tongue-boring. . . . Rich, the mad merchant, sat bare-
headed at Naylor's feet all the time. Sometimes he
sang, and cried, and stroked his hair and face, and
kissed his hand, and sucked the fire out of his forehead.
Naylor embraced his executioner, and behaved himself
very handsomely and patiently.' A great crowd of
people witnessed the spectacle, and their behaviour
was strangely sympathetic. ' Notwithstanding there
might be many thousands of people, yet they were
very quiet, few heard to revile him, or seen to throw

---

[1] Burton, *Diary*, i. 254, 260, 264 ; *Commons' Journals*, vii. 476.

anything at him ; and when he was aburning, all the people before him and behind him, and on both sides of him, stood bareheaded.' [1]

Though the House resumed the debate about the Protector's letter on December 30, and proposed to devote yet a third day to the subject, it never arrived at any conclusion. For the question the letter raised was both difficult and dangerous. One section of the House held that the authority of Parliament was based on the Instrument of Government and defined by its provisions. That was the view of the government. Another section of the House held that Parliament possessed by inherent right all the powers which any former Parliaments had possessed. The majority, in claiming the judicial powers of the defunct House of Lords, was claiming by inference the unlimited sovereignty which the Long Parliament had exercised. It was denying the validity of the limitations which the constitution imposed upon Parliament, and by inference the validity of the constitution itself. If the House persisted in maintaining this claim, the Protector as guardian of the constitution would be obliged to demand that Parliament should restrict its action to the sphere marked out for it in the Instrument of Government.

Moreover, even if the authority of the Instrument was admitted, a dispute about the meaning of its provisions was equally dangerous. There was no authority which could decide whether the Protector's interpretation or Parliament's was the right one. Mr. Godfrey put his finger on this defect in the constitution. ' Here,' said Mr. Godfrey to the House, ' is your power asserted on the one hand ; the supreme magistrate on the other desiring an account of your judgment. Where shall there be *tertius arbiter ?* It is a hard case. No judge

[1] December 27. Burton, *Diary*, i. 265, 266 ; *A True Narrative*, p. 42.

upon earth.'[1] As the House was not prepared to recede from its position, the discussion was adjourned, and the subject was quietly dropped. It returned no answer to the Protector's letter, and remained more than ever convinced that some amendment of the constitution was necessary, if heresies and blasphemies were to be efficiently repressed.

Though an open breach was thus avoided, the claims which Parliament had put forward produced their effect both upon the Protector and the army. No conviction was more deeply rooted in the minds of the soldiers and officers than the belief that it was necessary to limit the authority of Parliament in the interests of individual liberty. This belief had given birth to the Proposals of the Army, the Agreement of the People, and the Instrument of Government. It was now plain that the Instrument of Government had failed to attain this object, and that some amendment of the constitution would be necessary to effect it. The idea of instituting some third authority to arbitrate between the Protector and the representatives of the people, and to strengthen in case of need the hands of the former, began to penetrate the minds of military politicians. A couple of months later, when the Protector sought to calm the minds of the officers at the proposed revival of a House of Lords, it was to Naylor's case that he referred to prove the need of amending the constitution.[2] ' By the proceedings of this Parliament,' said he, ' you see they stand in need of a check or balancing power, for the case of James Naylor might happen to be your case. By their judicial power they fall upon life and member, and doth the Instrument enable me to control it ? ' And those most opposed to the House of Lords were equally

---

[1] Burton, *Diary*, i. 249.
[2] The speech to the hundred officers about Kingship. Burton, *Diary*, i. 383.

convinced that the dealings of Parliament with Naylor
threatened sober and peaceable Christians, unless some
remedy was devised.

The Protector could not pardon the culprit without
a quarrel with Parliament, even if he was inclined to
do so ; but he repeatedly endeavoured to lighten
his sufferings. On January 23, 1657, Naylor, after
having undergone the part of his punishment he
was doomed to suffer at Bristol, was brought back
to London and conveyed to Bridewell.[1] There he
was to lie ' without being visited and relieved by
any,' and with no food save what he could earn
by his labour.

On January 29, Parliament, at his wife's petition,
allowed her to visit him, and ordered that he should be
provided with the necessaries of life.[2] On February 20,
she petitioned the Protector, representing the obstacles
which the keepers of Bridewell put in the way of her
visits, the cruelty with which her husband was treated,
and the failure to supply him with food fit for a sick
man.[3] The Protector at once enforced the order.
Three months later, on May 26, 1657, Parliament, on
the motion of Sir Gilbert Pickering, who declared that
he was acting at the request of the Protector, appointed
a special attendant to take care of Naylor during his
confinement, and sent a minister to confer with him.[4]
Later still, in August, 1658, just a month before Cromwell's own death, he commanded his secretary, Malyn,
to inquire into Naylor's condition, for it was said that
he was very ill. Malyn could not get a word out of the

[1] Burton, *Diary*, i. 370; *Commons' Journals*, vii. 483; *Mercurius Politicus*,
January 15–22, 1657, p. 7541.
[2] *Commons' Journals*, vii. 483.
[3] Her petition is printed at length in Barclay's *Inner Life of the Religious
Societies of the Commonwealth*, p. 426.
[4] Burton, *Diary*, ii. 131.

prisoner, though he told him that he came from the
Lord Protector. He reported that Naylor had declined the offer of a doctor, saying that God was his
physician, and he needed no other. Malyn held him
to be a man ' under a resolved stubbornness through
height of pride,' and earnestly deprecated any thought
of his release. ' I hope,' he said, ' I should not go about
to dissuade your Highness from a work of mercy, which
is pleasing to God, which we have seasons and objects
enough for without doing that which may offend God
through want of zeal for His glory and honour against
such horrible impieties, which may minister an occasion
of offence or jealousy in those who are truly godly.' [1]
The servant's conception of true godliness differed
from that of his master. There were some of Cromwell's contemporaries who had a clearer conception of
the intellectual basis of toleration than the Protector,
and demanded for all men a larger freedom of specu-
lation about things divine than he was willing to
concede. But the liberality of Cromwell's practice
often redeemed the comparative narrowness of his
theory; with him toleration was rather a strong
feeling than a logical conception. In an ideal commonwealth, he once told Parliament, the words of
the Psalmist would be realised, and Mercy and Truth
would meet together. ' Here there is a great deal of
truth amongst professors and very little mercy. They
are ready to cut the throats of one another; but when
we are brought into the right way we shall be merciful
as well as orthodox, and we know who it is that saith
that if a man could speak with the tongues of men and
angels, and yet want that, he is but sounding brass and
tinkling cymbal.' [2] Cromwell was right in holding that

---

[1] Nickolls, *Letters and Papers of State addressed to Oliver Cromwell*, p. 144.
[2] Carlyle, *Cromwell*, Speech v.

CHAP.
III
1656

charity was the one thing needful if religious peace was to prevail between the various sects into which the English nation was divided ; but no government could do much to promote it.   The task of reconciling mercy and orthodoxy was not easy for a ruler who had to deal with a Puritan Parliament and a Puritan army.

CHAPTER IV

THE MILITIA BILL

BEFORE the excited debates on Naylor's case were over a new occasion for discord revealed itself, and that was the question of the maintenance of the new militia. The proceeds of the decimation tax imposed upon the Royalists were insufficient to provide the pay of the various county troops raised by the government.[1] The deficit was met by reducing the number of men contained in each troop from one hundred to eighty, and by other economies. By this method the cost of the militia had been reduced from £80,000 to £67,000 per annum. It was doubtful, however, whether it would be possible to continue to raise this sum, and consequently, whether the militia could be permanently maintained. For though it might be argued that the provisions of the Instrument allowed the government, during the intervals of Parliament, to raise an extraordinary tax to meet a temporary emergency, it was clear that, when Parliament met, the consent of that body was necessary to the prolongation of such a tax.[2] The Major-Generals and the military party in the Protector's Council resolved to apply to Parliament for the purpose.[3]

[1] Gardiner, *Commonwealth and Protectorate*, supplementary chapter, p. 2; popular edition, iv. 250.

[2] Article thirty of the Instrument; cf. Whitelocke's speech, Burton, *Diary*, i. 318.

[3] Cromwell does not appear to have suggested this application, and possibly disapproved of it. In his speech to the hundred officers, on February 28, 1657,

On Christmas Day, 1656, the House met as usual. A languid discussion took place about the hardships of the forest laws, occasioned by a bill for the preservation of the Forest of Dean. The House was very empty, and one member observing that this was caused by observance of the day, asked leave to bring in a bill to prevent it for the future. He was eagerly supported. ' I could get no rest all night for the preparation of this foolish day's solemnity,' cried one member. ' I doubt we are returning to Popery.' Others said that the bill's introduction was unseasonable when so much more important business was on hand. It was answered that it was never more necessary than now. People kept up their superstitious observances in defiance of Parliament. In many places Christmas Day was observed more strictly than the Lord's Day. One might walk all the way from Westminster to the Tower and not find a shop open, or a creature stirring. The bill was read the first time at once, and its second reading was fixed for the next morning.[1]

When this was over, Major-General Desborough stood up and asked leave to introduce what he deprecatingly termed a bill ' for continuance of a tax upon some people for the maintenance of the militia,' or, in other words, for making the decimation tax a permanent imposition on the Royalist party. It was necessary, he said, for the security of the public peace. Hitherto friends and enemies had borne an equal part in supporting the burden; but it could fall on no persons so fitly as those that occasioned the charge. ' Let us lay the saddle on

he said: 'You thought it was necessary to have Major-Generals and the first use to that motion (there was then the late general insurrection) was justifiable and you Major-Generals did your parts well. You might have gone on. When bid you go to the House with a bill and there receive a foil ? '—Burton, Diary, i. 384; see pp. 135-8, post.

[1] Ib. i. 228-30 ; Commons' Journals, vii. 475.

the right horse.' At once the face of the House was changed, and a hot debate sprang up. Desborough's motion recalled the House to the realities of the political situation. The question before it was no longer whether England should be made outwardly Puritan, but whether the rule of Puritanism should continue to exist. It was a question of self-preservation. The Cavaliers, argued the supporters of the motion, were only waiting for an opportunity to rise in arms. They were implacable and irreconcilable enemies. By letters and agents they maintained a constant correspondence with the exiled King, and kept Charles Stuart's interest still warm amongst them. The whole party had been implicated in the late rising ; all knew of it beforehand and all kept the secret. What would have been the fate of their unsuspecting opponents, if that design had succeeded ? ' Though I,' said Luke Robinson, one of the members for Yorkshire, ' was least believing or sensible of the plot, yet it was within three miles of me, and I am sure my throat had been cut in the first place.' [1]

Robinson seconded Desborough's motion, and five members of Cromwell's Council—Sydenham, Strickland, Pickering, Lambert, and Secretary Thurloe—followed with speeches in its favour. Major-Generals Whalley and Kelsey, with Colonel Hewson and other officers, united in supporting it.

The answer made to all this was that the proposal was against the Act of Indemnity.[2] Ex-Speaker Lenthall, now Master of the Rolls, enforced this view with all the weight of his authority and political experience. ' If any,' said he, ' since the Act of Oblivion have plotted or acted anything against the public peace, let them suffer severely ; but it is not for the honour of

---

[1] Burton, *Diary*, i. 232.
[2] Passed February 24, 1651–2. Scobell, ii. 179.

a Parliament to break the faith of a Parliament. Never was an Act of Oblivion violated by a Parliament in any age of the world.' Other eminent lawyers, such as Whitelocke and Bampfield, took the same line. In reply to them, some members declared that they had been against the Act of Oblivion from the first, but the chief argument was that there were two sides to the Act. It was not only a promise but a contract. In every bargain there must be some reciprocity, and the Cavaliers had not kept their share of it by living peaceably. ' I am as guilty of the Act of Oblivion as any man,' said Lambert. ' I have laboured to oblige that party and to win them as much as may be, but find it impossible till time wear out the memory.' He wound up by drawing a picture of a Cavalier household at the present moment, ' merry over their Christmas pies,' and drinking the health of the King and confusion to the Parliament.

Dec.
25
In the end, by eighty-eight to sixty-three votes, Desborough was given leave to bring in his bill.[1]

The bill was accordingly introduced and read for the first time on January 7, 1657. The debate which took place made it clear that the opposition which the bill roused was not solely confined to the lawyers. John Claypole, husband of the Protector's daughter Elizabeth, at once rose to move its rejection. The bill, he said, consisted of two parts ; the first was for continuing the tax of a tenth upon the Royalists, the second for indemnifying those who had taken part in the levying this tax. He approved of the proposed indemnity, but the first part of the bill was unjust.[2]

The mere fact of Claypole's intervention was significant, for he usually took no part in the debates of the

[1] Burton, *Diary,* i. 233, 240; *Commons' Journals,* vii. 475.
[2] Burton, *Diary,* i. 310.

House.   It was taken for granted that he had delivered
the sense if not the very words of Cromwell, and ' the
sycophants of the court' hastened to follow his lead.[1]
Broghil, who followed Claypole, was a politician of more
importance.   The members for Ireland looked to him
as their leader.   He represented the new Cromwellian
party, the men who looked to Cromwell to protect
England from the arbitrary rule of the sword, and
were desirous to make the Protectorate hereditary.
Broghil did not confine himself to the narrow question
of the breach of the Act of Indemnity, or content himself with showing that the tax was unjust.   He demon-
strated that it was politically inexpedient, because it
would perpetuate the division between the two sections
of the nations.   'How is it possible that we should
gain that party by punishment when we could not by
grace ?   Surely this will harden them.   I wish this do
not make them a corporation, and make men of estates
and no estates desperate.'[2]   Trevor echoed Broghil's
argument.[3]   'You provoke your enemies,' said he, 'by
taking away a tenth part from them, and leave them
the nine parts to be revenged with.   I like not this
middle way of policy, neither to oblige nor destroy.'
He added a new argument, which was in everybody's
minds, though no one had yet ventured to allege it,
saying frankly that he dreaded military rule.   'A new
militia raised with a tendency to divide the commonwealth into provinces ; a power too great to be bound
within any law ; in plain terms to cantonize [4] our nation,
and prostitute our laws and civil peace to a power that

---

[1] Ludlow, *Memoirs*, ii. 19, 20.

[2] Burton, *Diary*, i. 312.

[3] Ib. i. 315.   The report of Broghil's speech in the *Tanner MSS.* attributes
Trevor's and Whitelocke's arguments to Broghil.—*Tanner MS.*, lii. 186.

[4] ' He divided England into cantons over each of which he placed a Bashaw
under the title of Major-General,' says Ludlow, *Memoirs*, i. 405.   Cf. Heath's
Chronicle, p. 698, for a similar phrase.

was never set up in any nation without dangerous consequences.'

Desborough defended the bill with great violence. If
anything it was too lenient. A tenth was too light a
tax, and he would like to see a higher amount fixed.[1]
For it was useless to attempt to conciliate the Cavaliers.
'It was blows, not fair words, that settled and must
settle the peace of England.' The interest of all honest
men was concerned in the bill. 'I believe none will
be against it that are for the true old interest of the
nation.'[2] Lambert was more conciliatory in his
language, but he, too, declared that good words were
useless with the Cavaliers. 'The quarrel is now between
light and darkness; not who shall rule, but whether
we shall live or be preserved, or no.' He declared that
the maintenance of the militia as it was now established
was the only way to secure them against their common
enemies.[3]

It was evident, however, that the feeling of the
House was hostile to the bill. Amongst civilians fear
of a Cavalier rising was less strong than dread of military
rule; and the general aversion to the bill was strengthened
by the insolent and arbitrary expressions of some of
the Major-Generals. When Broghil spoke of indemnifying them for what they had done, Major-General
Lilburne interjected that he scorned to accept that
indemnity. 'We are much beholden to the gentleman that would give it us,' added Desborough. 'It is
our swords that must indemnify us.'[4]

These speeches showed that a long and bitter struggle
was inevitable before the question was decided. 'There

[1] In the bill as introduced, the precise amount of the tax was not specified;
there was a blank in it to be filled up afterwards.

[2] Burton, *Diary*, i. 315.

[3] Ib. i. 319.

[4] Ib. i. 313, 317; cf. Ludlow, *Memoirs*, ii. 19.

was a pretty full House,' says the diarist who recorded CHAP.
them, 'and a very mettled and serious debate for the $\underset{\smile}{IV}$
time, and will be, before all is done : for one might per- 1657
ceive by many men's countenances that they stood
full charged for speaking to the business.' [1]

For some weeks the decision was deferred. Next
morning, when the debate should have been resumed,
the illness of the Speaker prevented its continuance.
Parliament adjourned for that reason from the 8th to
the 12th of January, and then again from the 12th to
the 19th.[2] When that day came the revelation of a
new plot against the government once more diverted
the attention of the House from the Militia Bill. During
the autumn the great design of the Royalists and
Levellers for the invasion of England had steadily
developed. The King, as he told the Spanish government, had promised his supporters in England to go
over before Christmas, and to land at some place of
strength to be put into his hands, whilst one of his
brothers was to land at the same time in another part
of the country. By Christmas his little army amounted
to 2000 men, and he was pressing the Spaniards for the
money and men needed for his expedition. As they
delayed their answer to his memorials, the enterprise
was postponed till February.[3] Sexby was at the same
time pressing them for similar assistance. His plans
and demands were set forth in detail in a paper addressed
to Don Juan in December, 1656. It was necessary, he Dec.
said, to prevent Cromwell from doing further damage $\underset{1656}{14,}$
to the King of Spain by giving him a war to deal with
at home. Such a diversion he would undertake to
provide, if the Spanish government would supply him

---

[1] Burton, *Diary*, i. 320.
[2] Ib. i. 331, 337.
[3] *Cal. Clarendon Papers*, iii. 198, 204, 214.   The Spaniards estimated the
cost of the expedition at 400,000 florins.

CHAP.
IV.
1656

with 1000 foot and 500 horse. The foot should be Irish, but if he were furnished with arms and horses he would himself find efficient and experienced men. As for a landing-place, there were three fortified towns, all seaports, of whose governors he was as sure as a man could be. He was certain that the greater part of Cromwell's army would join this force after its landing, and that the most considerable places and persons in England would declare against Cromwell. But there was one thing essential to success which the ministers of Charles II must guarantee. No mention was to be made of King Charles ' before such time as Cromwell be destroyed ' ; till then those Royalists who took up arms in conjunction with the Levellers and with Sexby's expedition were ' to speak of nothing but the liberty of the country.' [1]

Sexby's project had little chance of success, though the Spanish authorities were inclined to favour it. The difficulty lay not in effecting the seizure of a port, or in landing 1500 men in England, but in uniting such discordant parties as the Levellers, Royalists, and the rest of the English malcontents, for any combined attack on the government. The ministers of Charles II, to whom Sexby's scheme was submitted by the Spanish government, regarded it with coldness and suspicion. They feared lest a premature attempt should afford Cromwell an easy victory, and damage the prospects of the enterprise which they themselves were planning. It would be best to delay Sexby's expedition till near the time when the King's was ready. They were willing that the Spaniards should supply troops to hold any post or fortress of which Sexby's partisans could obtain possession; but they protested against any proposals that the little Royalist army which King Charles

---

[1] *Clarendon State Papers*, iii. 315.

had painfully collected should be placed at Sexby's disposal for his expedition. All they would promise was, that orders should be sent to the King's friends in England to co-operate with Sexby's forces. The Royalists were ' to join with them in order to destroy the usurper, and without any public declaration or so much as mention of the King's interest.' On one point Hyde, who drew up the memorandum on Sexby's proposals, was emphatic. The King would make no serious political concessions to secure the support of the Levellers and the Republicans ; he would promise no great alterations in Church and State, such as ' lessening the power of the crown and devolving an absurd power to the people.' Nine-tenths of the people of England were really attached to the old constitution. On the other hand, the party which Sexby represented consisted of those bent upon the establishment of a republic, and though numerous enough they were absolutely disunited. They were ' persons of very different opinions and resolutions in all the essentials of that government, who hope to cozen one another till Cromwell be removed, and then each to advance his own particular designs.' [1]

An expedition to England, under the command of Sexby, did not suit the plan of the Royalist leaders ; but, while they sought to prevent the acceptance of his proposals by the Spanish government, they encouraged him in his design against Cromwell's life. Peter Talbot, who endeavoured in November, 1656, to arrange a secret interview between Sexby and the King, informed Charles at the same time that the prospects of the assassination plot were favourable. Sexby, he said, ' doth not yet despair of Cromwell's being cut off, and hath lately sent some strange engines

[1] *Clarendon State Papers*, iii. 315–7.

CHAP.
IV
1656

for that purpose.' Hyde answered on behalf of Charles that the King would receive him as graciously and secretly as could be wished, and said that something should be done soon, for Cromwell was daily becoming more formidable.[1] Hyde's agent, Titus, kept Sexby to the point when he seemed inclined to expend his energies on the larger enterprise. 'Sexby,' he wrote to Hyde, 'shows rather confidence that he shall be able to make a division in the army than to procure Cromwell to be killed, but I have always endeavoured to divert him from that opinion, and I think I have. The truth is, if they do not make Cromwell's death the beginning of their design, I shall much fear it will have but a sad conclusion.' [2]

Meanwhile in England Sindercombe and his comrades were doing their best to carry out Sexby's commission. After the abandonment of the attempt to kill the Protector at the opening of Parliament, they resolved to seize the opportunity which his journeys to Hampton Court afforded.[3] Cromwell usually went there on Saturdays to spend a day or two in fresher air than Whitehall. Sindercombe hired a house at Hammersmith from the Earl of Salisbury's coachman. It was admirably chosen, for it stood upon the roadside ' in a narrow, dirty place of passage where coaches use to go but softly.' Upon the garden wall was a little building described as 'a banqueting house,' which overlooked the road. ' Their intention was to shoot the Protector as he passed by, out of the little house, with screwed guns which

[1] *Cal. Clarendon Papers*, iii. 202, 206 ; *Clarendon State Papers*, iii. 311.

[2] *Clarendon MSS.* Titus to Hyde, January $\frac{9}{19}$, 1657.

[3] The account which follows is partly from the depositions of Toop and Cecil, printed in Thurloe, partly from the evidence at the trial of Sindercombe. —*Mercurius Politicus*, February 5–12, 1657, and *State Trials*, v. 842.

were prepared on purpose, which should break the coach in pieces, and kill him where he sat.' The guns, which were, no doubt, the 'strange engines' provided by Sexby, carried twelve bullets apiece, and a slug in addition : one of the conspirators described them as something like a harquebus. To make things sure, Toop, one of the Protector's bodyguard, was bribed by Sindercombe, with the promise of a captain's commission and £1500 in money, to supply information as to the Protector's movements. He was to let them know in what part of the coach the Protector sat, so that they could not miss him. Everything was carefully arranged. The house was 'very convenient for their purpose'; at the back of it were stables where they could keep their own horses, and there was an outlet to another road, so that they could escape without difficulty when they had 'done the fact.'

Unluckily for the conspirators the Protector gave up his usual visits to Hampton Court during the autumn, no doubt because the sitting of Parliament kept him in London; so they were obliged to change their plans. They determined, therefore, to catch him when he rode out to Turnham Green or Kensington, or as he was taking the air in Hyde Park. Toop promised 'to give notice of the life-guards going abroad, or of the saddling of the pad-nags.' Sindercombe, who was well furnished with money, bought the fleetest horses he could find for himself and his companion. For himself he purchased a bay that cost £80, and for Cecil a black horse at £75. For many days they lurked about waiting and watching for an opportunity, armed with swords and pistols only, and trained their horses as if to run a race. Cecil boasted that he could have ridden his black horse a hundred miles without drawing bit, and at such a speed that in ten miles he would have distanced most horses in England.   He wore a thin holland shirt and thin clothes in order to make himself the lighter.   Once, when Cecil was riding in Hyde Park, an opportunity offered itself.   Cromwell alighted from his coach, and, seeing Cecil, admired his horse, and asked him ' whose horse that was he rode on.'   At that very moment Sindercombe was waiting outside the Park ;   the hinges of one of the gates had been filed nearly through, and some of the palings cut, so as to secure an exit.   Cecil was ready to have done the deed, but the black horse had a cold that day, so he postponed the operation for the present.

After this the conspirators again changed their plan. The design for killing the Protector was to be put off till the spring, but in the meantime it was resolved to fire Whitehall.   This would at least give their friends abroad something for their money.   ' Their party would have been satisfied that they were not idle, but were at work to accomplish what they had designed.' If the Protector did not perish in the flames the destruction of Whitehall would make him easier to attack in future.   Sindercombe said that Whitehall ' was so strong a place and had so many turnings and windings therein, that it was the fittest hole for a tyrant to live in, and if that were burned there is never another place in England where he could hide and secure himself.' By means of Toop, Sindercombe and Cecil obtained access to the interior of Whitehall, and after some searching pitched upon the chapel as the best place to lay their train in.   Thither about six o'clock on Thursday, January 8, they conveyed ' a fire work in a hand basket,' made, it was said, by ' one that came over from beyond the seas on purpose to make it.'   The basket contained tar, pitch, tow, gunpowder and other combustibles, and had two slow-matches attached to it.

The conspirators lit the matches, calculating that by CHAP.
IV. twelve o'clock that night the combustibles would be fired, and that Whitehall would be in a blaze soon after. 1657

But by this time Toop had become either penitent or frightened; and some hours before the firework was deposited he informed the Protector of the plot.   Consequently, as soon as the incendiaries went away, an officer of the guard put out the matches, and next morning Cecil and Sindercombe were arrested.   Sindercombe, although he was unarmed at the moment, fought desperately, and could not be taken till he was wounded ; he remained stubborn and would say nothing.   Cecil told all he knew, confessed the fact that Sexby was the originator of the plot, and revealed its ulterior object. ' When the Protector was despatched,' he said, ' forces were to come over from Flanders in ships to be hired of the Dutch with the King of Spain's money.' [1]

Such was the story which, on January 19, 1657, Secretary Thurloe related to the House.[2] He read at length the confessions of Toop and Cecil; and as the members heard them they realised that the Protector had been dogged by assassins for the last four months, and that more than once his life had been at their mercy if these hirelings had been willing to risk their own.   They realised, too, that the Protector's assassination meant the overthrow of the government and perhaps ruin for themselves. ' I believe,' said one, ' none of us that sit here had been safe, if this design had prospered.' With one accord, therefore, they ordered a general public thanksgiving, and resolved to wait on the Protector in a body to congratulate him on his escape.[3]

---

[1] Thurloe, v. 776 ; on the arrest see Burton, *Diary*, i. 333 ; *Clarendon State Papers*, iii. 327.

[2] Burton, *Diary*, i. 354 ; *Commons' Journals*, vii. 481.   The informations of Toop and Cecil are printed in Thurloe, v. 774, 775.

[3] The thanksgiving, at first ordered for February 13, was finally fixed for February 20. *Cal. State Papers Dom.*, 1656-7, p. 258.

When these votes had been passed, a debate suddenly sprang up, in which each of the two parties in the House endeavoured to utilise the opportunity for its own political ends. Ever since Jephson had proposed that the Protector should be made King, the question of the revival of monarchy had filled the dispatches of foreign ambassadors and the minds of English politicians. During November, Giavarina and Bordeaux repeatedly informed the Venetian and the French governments that the subject of the succession was about to be raised in Parliament. In private letters the same expectation of some change in the constitution was freely expressed, and in the meetings of the officers the respective merits of hereditary and elective governments were acrimoniously discussed.[1] In December the excitement about Naylor's case pushed the question into the background just when people thought it was about to be decided; and when those debates ended, the introduction of the Militia Bill had roused a new and dangerous controversy. But now Thurloe's communication had opened up a wider subject than the mere question who was the instigator of Sindercombe's plot. The precariousness of the government, so long as it depended on Cromwell's life alone, was thrust into prominence, and the question of the succession naturally came into people's minds.

Old John Ashe, member for Somersetshire, and one of the leaders of the Presbyterian party, moved that the Speaker's address to the Protector should contain something more than congratulations on his escape. ' I would have,' said he, ' something else added, which in my opinion would tend very much to the preservation of himself and us, and to the quieting of all the designs of our enemies ; that his Highness would be pleased to take upon him the government according to the ancient

---

[1] See ' Cromwell and the Crown.' *English Historical Review*, July, 1902.

constitution, so that the hopes of our enemies in plots
would be at an end.'[1] The supporters of the Militia
Bill were at once up in arms. Ashe's expedient for the
Protector's preservation, said Desborough, would be but a
slender prop unless care were taken to secure his enemies.
' You have a bill before you,' chimed in Luke Robinson,
' I would have you go on with that as the best expedient
for your preservation.' To them the discovery of the
assassination plot seemed merely a fresh argument for
severe measures of repression against the Cavaliers.
Highland, an Independent of the most pronounced type,
denounced Ashe's motion as a crime. ' Are you now,'
said he, ' going to set up kingly government which for
these thousand years has persecuted the people of God ?
Do you expect a better consequence ? Do you expect
a thanksgiving day upon this ? This will set all the
honest people of this nation to weeping and mourning.
I desire the motion may die as abominable.' On the
other side, Edmund Waller, Downing, Bodurda, and
more, urged that an early day should be appointed for
the discussion of Ashe's motion. Some suggested the
next morning, but the House wisely decided to take
a longer time to think over so serious a subject, and to
resume the debate on the Militia Bill instead.[2]

Accordingly, from January 20 to January 22, the
Militia Bill occupied practically the whole time of the
House. A fortnight's suspense had rather heightened
than diminished the feeling against the measure. The
more time members had to think about it the less they
liked it. In the committees, which continued to meet
throughout the adjournment, or whenever a little group

[1] Burton, *Diary*, i. 362. The address was presented on Friday, January 23,
1657. The speech made by the Speaker is printed in *Mercurius Politicus*,
January 22–29, p. 7558. It contains no reference to any proposal for changing
the government.

[2] Burton, *Diary*, i. 363–6.

CHAP.
IV.
1657

Jan.
22

Jan.
21

of members met together, they grumbled against the bill. Who were these Major-Generals who demanded to be established as permanent authorities, and dared to dictate to the Commons of England ? ' Colonel Philip Jones, who has now £7000 per annum, was born but to £8 or £10 a year ; Sir John Barkstead was a thimble-maker ; Kelsey sold leather points ; Major-General Bridge was a common dragooner in Yorkshire ; and they reckoned up the mean extraction of many more Major-Generals.' [1]

Such being the temper of the opposition, the three days' debate was stormy and disorderly. Personal reflexions were not spared, and two quarrels required the intervention of the House. James Ashe, who was member for Bath, exchanged high words with Major-General Desborough.[2] Major-General Boteler, against whom a charge was pending in the law courts for oppressive conduct in Northamptonshire, made a hot speech for the bill. Harry Cromwell, the Protector's cousin, who sat for Huntingdonshire, answered him with equal heat. ' The gentleman that spoke last,' said Cromwell, ' thought it just that, because some of the Cavaliers had done amiss all deserved to be punished. By the same reasoning, because some of the Major-Generals have done amiss, which I offer to prove, all of them deserve to be punished.' At this Major-General Kelsey called him to order, and demanded the names of the persons who had done amiss. Harry jumped up again, and begged the leave of the House to name the persons to whom he alluded, promising to prove that they had done unwarrantable acts. Then followed a scene ; but old and prudent members intervened, allayed the heat, and restored order. ' This fire was put out by the grave water-carriers.' [3]

---

[1] Burton, *Diary*, i. 331.   [2] *Commons' Journals*, vii. 482, 483.
[3] *Commons' Journals*, vii. 481 ; Thurloe, vi. 20.

Again the decision on the second reading was
adjourned. ' What the issue will be, I know not,' wrote Secretary Thurloe. To impartial observers it seemed ' an even cast ' whether the power of the Major-Generals would be established or abolished.[1] The Protector's Council was divided on the subject. Not only the military men amongst its members, but civilians like Pickering and Thurloe, steadily voted in favour of the bill.[2] Thurloe made a long speech on its behalf. He recounted the misgovernment of Charles I, and went back to the breach between the Long Parliament and the King. On the one side had ranged themselves all those who loved their country, on the other men debauched by the King and his counsellors, who hated reformation and liberty. The quarrel was the same to-day. ' These are the men, sir, this is the old de-linquent, that we have to do with in this bill.' The Act of Oblivion referred to the past offences of the Cavaliers, not to those they might commit in the future. ' It was not like the Pope's pardons that are of all sins committed and to be committed.' New offences, therefore, might justly be followed by new penalties. It was notorious that the Cavalier party, as a whole, still retained its old principles, and still continued to hatch plots against the State. But the bill was directed only against the guilty: ' The question will not be of every individual man, but of such only as have not nor can give any testimony of their having changed their interest and principles, but on the contrary have given a just ground of suspicion that they do retain them.' [3]

Thurloe's argument hardly touched the real issue. As he confessed in a private letter to Henry Cromwell,

---

[1] Thurloe, vi. 8 ; *Clarke Papers*, iii. 87.

[2] Bordeaux to Mazarin, $\dfrac{\text{January 28}}{\text{February 8}}$. *French Transcripts, R.O.*

[3] Thurloe, v. 787 ; cf. vi. 8.

the fear of permanently establishing the Major-Generals was the motive which really influenced the opposition. Politicians who looked beyond the moment saw that it was not a question whether a petty sum was to be extracted from the pockets of the Cavaliers, many of whom richly deserved such punishment, but whether the government of the Protector was to be based on military force or the consent of the nation. 'That which makes me fear the passing of the bill,' wrote Vincent Gookin, 'is that thereby his Highness's government will be more founded in force, and more removed from that national foundation which the people in Parliament are desirous to give him ; supposing thereby he will become more theirs than he now is, and will in time find the safety and peace of the nation to be as well maintained by the laws of the land as by the sword.' Lambert and the officers were in favour of the bill, because they wished to maintain the power of the sword ; and their motive was obvious. 'If any others have pretensions to succeed the Protector [1] by their interest in the army, the more of force upholds his Highness living, the greater when he is dead will be the hopes and advantages for such a one to effect his aim.' [2]

The Protector himself seemed to stand neutral between the two contending parties. 'I cannot tell how it is relished at Whitehall,' wrote Thomas Burton. 'Various reports upon it.' [3] Yet though Cromwell would not openly declare against the supporters of the bill, he let it be seen that he did not consider its opponents his enemies. After Harry Cromwell's quarrel with Boteler in the debate of January 21, some of the military party threatened him and said 'that his Highness did and would take it ill.' On this Harry went to Whitehall, repeated what he had said to the Protector, and stuck

[1] In the original, ' him.'   [2] Thurloe, vi. 20.   [3] *Clarke Papers*, iii. 88.

to it manfully; he took his papers with him to show that he had evidence for his assertions. Cromwell answered him with raillery, and, taking a rich scarlet coat from his back and a pair of gloves from his hands, gave them to his cousin. It was the very cloak the Protector had worn on the day when he opened Parliament. Harry strutted about the House in it a few days later, ' to the delight of some and the trouble of others.' [1]

On January 28 the debate on the bill recommenced. ' It was a serious debate, not without sharpness and reflections,' says a newsletter, but nothing is known of its details. The upshot of it was that on January 29 the bill was rejected by 124 to 88 votes.[2] The military party took their defeat very ill. ' Some gentlemen,' wrote Feb. 3 Thurloe to Henry Cromwell, ' do think themselves much trampled upon by this vote, and the truth is it hath wrought such heat in the House that I fear little will be done in the future.' [3] Half a dozen of the Major-Generals went to the Protector, and complained ' how much thereby the House reflected on him, and discouraged the godly; and that their aim was to pass nothing which might tend to his accommodation, and that they would raise no money.' Cromwell answered this gloomy prediction by saying that he hoped better things of Parliament, and the event proved that he was right.[4] Thankfulness for the overthrow of the Major-Generals overcame the objection of the House to fresh taxes. The majority were anxious to prove to Cromwell that the loyalty and liberality of civilians would be the best support of his government.

Accordingly, the very next day, January 30, Parliament resolved that it would raise money to carry on

---

[1] Thurloe, vi. 21. [2] *Commons' Journals*, vii. 483.
[3] Thurloe, vi. 38. [4] Ib. vi. 37.

CHAP.
IV
1657

Feb. 3

the Spanish War, and voted a special grant of £400,000 for that purpose.[1] This was moved by the very persons who had so strongly opposed the Militia Bill, while those who had supported it ' were exceedingly cold in the debate for raising money and seemed to repine that Parliament did so well.' Gookin drew the conclusion that the military party would be glad to abolish parliamentary government altogether. ' It is judged by some,' said he, ' that the interest of the godly cannot be preserved but by the dissolution of this if not of all parliaments; and their endeavours in it have been plainly discovered to the party most concerned to know them, which will I believe suddenly occasion a reducing of the government to kingship, to which his Highness is not averse.' [2]

The arguments in favour of restoring the monarchy acquired fresh weight in the minds of all those who loved constitutional government. The motive for this reaction in favour of kingship was clear. As a shrewd observer remarked,' they are so highly incensed against the arbitrary actings of the Major-Generals that they are greedy of any powers that will be ruled and limited by law.' [3] Whatever unpopularity the Protector's intervention in Naylor's case had earned him amongst the Presbyterians was now forgotten in the tide of feeling against military domination. The known hostility of the officers to the principle of hereditary succession or the revival of monarchy only strengthened the popular feeling in favour of both. Lambert had been heard to say that the question between the maintenance of the republic and the re-establishment of monarchy meant a choice between progress and reaction ; it was not merely a question whether Richard or John was

---

[1] *Commons' Journals*, vii. 483.   [2] Thurloe, vi. 37, 38.
[3] *Clarke Papers*, iii. 91.

to succeed the Protector.[1]   To people outside the army the great objection to the retention of the elective Protectorate was that, if it were retained, John Lambert would be the next Protector.   They preferred the hereditary principle in some form or other, even if it involved the succession of a young man about whom they knew nothing, rather than accept one whom they knew too well.   Hence the dispatches of Bordeaux, during the weeks which followed the defeat of the Decimation Bill, show that the subject of kingship was again filling the public mind.   'People talk,' said one of his letters, ' of nothing but the crowning of the Protector, and public fame declares that the proposal is to be made to Parliament within the next three days.' [2] It was not only in political circles that this was talked about, but in the street and the market-place.   'Many citizens of London,' says a newsletter dated February 7, 1657, ' have laid several wagers of late that we shall have suddenly an alteration of the present government, but what their meaning is we cannot yet discern.' [3]

---

[1] Bordeaux to Mazarin, February $\frac{5}{15}$.   *French Transcripts, R.O.*   See *English Historical Review*, 1903, p. 53.

[2] Bordeaux to Mazarin, February $\frac{16}{26}$, 1657.   *French Transcripts, R.O.*

[3] *Clarke Papers*, iii. 88.

CHAPTER V

THE OFFER OF THE CROWN

WHILE the nation at large was divided between fear and hope, those who supported a change in the constitution of the Protectorate were secretly maturing their plans. In private they had determined upon adopting a new policy. Instead of attempting simply to alter the thirty-second article of the Instrument of Government so as to make the succession to the chief magistracy hereditary instead of elective (which was the proposal originally put forward), they had resolved to submit to Parliament a revised constitution conferring upon the Protector the office and title of King. We know very little of the origin of this Remonstrance, as it was at first entitled. It was the work of a small group of men who desired the revival of monarchy and were not anxious to claim the authorship of the scheme after they had failed to carry it out. One of the chief of this group was Lord Broghil; and associated with him were Glyn and several of the lawyers who subsequently took part in the conferences in which the representatives of the Parliament pressed Cromwell to accept the crown.[1]

---

[1] Broghil and Glyn, according to the testimony of Ludlow and Whitelocke, seconded Pack's motion that the paper he introduced might be read (*Memorials*, iv. 289; Ludlow, *Memoirs*, ii. 22). Captain Baynes, speaking of the introduction of the Petition and Advice in a debate during February, 1659, says it was brought in ' by a gentleman that found it by the way as he came from Lord ——' (Burton, *Diary*, iv. 216). I have no doubt that this refers to Broghil. The support given by the Irish members throughout to the Petition, and the fact that Jephson, an Irish member, was the first to propose the alteration of the succession, also suggest Lord Broghil as the inspiring influence.

When the draft of the new constitution had been CHAP.
drawn up [1] there was considerable difficulty in selecting ⌄ V ⌄
a person to introduce it. Broghil himself was a good 1657
speaker, but as an ex-Royalist who had fought against
the Parliament throughout the first civil war he was
disqualified from the foremost part. His advocacy
would have been too suspected. Whitelocke was asked,
but he was too cautious to take the lead, though willing
to follow. ' Not liking several things in it, I declined,'
says he. Other lawyers seem to have been equally
prudent, and at last a bold citizen of London was
pitched upon to bring forward the scheme. Sir Christopher Pack, knighted by the Protector on September
20, 1655, was one of the members for the City. He had
made a fortune in the woollen trade, had been Lord
Mayor in 1654-5, was a member of the Committee of
Trade, master of the Merchant Adventurers Company,
and one of the Commissioners of Customs.[2] Upon all
financial and commercial questions his opinion had
great weight, and no man had more influence with the
moneyed classes. Besides this, he was a ready speaker.
In the conferences at Whitehall about the admission of
the Jews he was thought by one of the audience ' to
give the strongest reasons against their coming in of
any man.' In a debate at the Committee of Trade he
had lately distinguished himself by the pertinacity with

---

[1] It was probably drawn up at the end of January or the beginning of
February, after the discovery of Sindercombe's plot, which is referred to in the
preamble.

Bordeaux, writing to Mazarin on February 19, 1657, says that the act
making Cromwell King had been seen in the hands of his son Richard. ' Le
parlement n'a point parlé de la royauté, bien que l'acte ayt esté vu tout dressé
entre les mains du fils aisné de M. le Protecteur.' $\frac{\text{February 19}}{\text{March 1}}$, 1657. *French
Transcripts, R.O.* Colonel Packer and Whitelocke both saw the Remonstrance
before it was introduced.—Burton, *Diary*, iii. 161. Whitelocke, *Memorials*, iv.
289.

[2] See his life by Mr. Welch in the *Dictionary of National Biography*, xliii. 28.

CHAP. which he defended the monopoly of the Merchant
V Adventurers Company against the free-traders. Sir
1657 Christopher Pack, we are told, ' turned in the debate
like a horse and answered every man.' He spoke at
least thirty times, and ' was very angry he could not be
heard *ad infinitum*,' so that ' the committee was forced
at last to come to a compact with him, that he should
speak no more after that time.' [1] An intrepid orator of
this kind was just what was required; for it was certain
that the introduction of the Remonstrance would be
the signal for a scene, and that an attempt would be
made to refuse its proposer a hearing. Self-confident,
and eager to distinguish himself, Pack had no hesitation in accepting the task offered him.

On Monday, February 23, after the House had
passed a bill for establishing a godly minster at Totnes,
and rejected one in favour of poor prisoners, Pack
suddenly stood up and presented a paper to the House.
He declared ' it was somewhat come to his hand tending
to the settlement of the nation, and of liberty and
property ; and prayed that it might be received and
read.' [2] How it came to his hands he did not clearly
explain, nor did he give the name of its authors.[3] He
confined himself to asserting that the proposals it contained were for the public good, and urging the House
to take them into consideration.

A storm immediately sprang up. Pack was charged
with ' great presumption in bringing a business of that

---

[1] Burton, *Diary*, i. 308.

[2] *Commons' Journals*, vii. 496.

[3] According to Colonel Packer, speaking February 9, 1659 : ' He said he
had found by Providence a paper, I know not where.' ' It was brought in,' said
Captain Baynes, ' by a gentleman that found it by the way as he came from the
Lord —— ' (Burton, *Diary*, iii. 160, 217). Both these members were present
at the debate, and they were speaking before others who were also present.
As to the rest of Pack's remarks, we have only the vaguest accounts, such as
that of Nieupoort, the Dutch ambassador.—Thurloe, vi. 84.

nature into the House in such an unparliamentary CHAP.
way.'¹ Captain Baynes moved that he should be V
called to the bar, and many other members backed the 1657
demand. Pack made things worse by privately con-
fessing, to a member who sat next him, that he had never
read the paper through; and the member, rising in his
place, promptly repeated the damning statement to the
House.² It became clear that the mover was merely the
tool of others—'like a puppet jerked with a wire,' it was
afterwards said.³ Colonel Sydenham moved, accordingly,
that a committee should be appointed to find out the
contrivers of this Remonstrance. Both these motions
fell to the ground; for the minority were more violent
than numerous, and the majority, guessing that the
Remonstrance contained the long-expected proposition
for the settlement of the succession, were anxious that
it should be considered. Broghil, Whitelocke, Glyn, and
others supported Pack's motion, Wolseley and some
of the Council took the same line; and at three in the
afternoon, by 144 to 54 votes, the House decided that
it should be read.⁴

The preamble revealed the secret at once. It
thanked God for His mercy in delivering England from
the tyranny and bondage which the late King had
designed to impose upon it, and the Protector as God's
instrument for preserving the peace and securing the
liberties of England. Then it abruptly demanded,
in the interest of the nation, the settlement of the
succession. 'We consider,' it said, addressing the

¹ Ludlow, *Memoirs*, ii. 22.
² Anthony Morgan to Henry Cromwell, February 24, 1656 (*Lansdowne MS.*,
821, f. 294). This is the best account of the debate. Thurloe says nothing of
what happened in the debate in either of his letters, confining himself to summarising the contents of the Remonstrance.—Thurloe, vi. 75; *Clarke Papers*,
iii. 91.   ³ Heath, *Chronicle*, p. 712.
⁴ The tellers for the majority were Wolseley and Col. Fitzjames, for the
minority Sydenham and Robinson.

Protector, ' the continual danger your life is in, from the bloody practices both of the malignant and discontented party,[1] it being a received principle amongst them, that no order being settled in your life time for the succession to the government, nothing is wanting to bring us into blood and confusion, and them to their desired ends, but the destruction of your person ; and in case things should thus remain at your death, we are not able to express what calamities would in all human probability ensue thereupon, which we trust your Highness, as well as we, do hold yourself obliged to provide against, and not to leave a people whose common peace and interest you are entrusted with in such a condition as may hazard both.' The first clause made the purpose of the appeal still clearer. It asked Cromwell to assume the ' name, style, title and dignity of King ' with all the rights annexed to it, and (in order to prevent the confusion which might follow his death) to appoint the person who should succeed him in the government of these nations.[2]

At this revelation the wrath of the opponents of monarchy rose to fury, and for three hours they discussed the question whether the subject should be resumed next morning, not so much with any hope of preventing the discussion as in order to display their unalterable hostility to the proposal. Lambert led the opposition. The re-establishment of kingship, he said, was contrary to the oaths and protestations they had all taken, and to the principles for which the army had fought, and so much blood had been shed.[3] The significance

[1] Gardiner, *Constitutional Documents*, p. 448. For the amendments subsequently made in the preamble, see *Commons' Journals*, vii. 512.

[2] Compare the original form of the first clause (*Clarke Papers*, iii. 94) with the amended form (Gardiner, p. 449).

[3] Giavarina. $\frac{\text{February } 27}{\text{March } 9}$. *Venetian Transcripts, R.O.*

of his appeal to the soldiers was obvious. 'He will
put the army in a ferment, if he can,' wrote Thurloe
to Henry Cromwell.[1] It was also noted that 'pretences
of religion' played a large part in his speech, as if he
would appeal to the Independents against the Presbyterians; and as he had a reputation for caring very
little about religion, it was regarded merely as a party
move. Next to Lambert, Colonel Sydenham was most
vehement in his opposition. Major-General Desborough
spoke against it, but, as became the Protector's brother-
in-law, with more moderation; and Fleetwood, who was
also moderate in his language, apparently urged that
it was inopportune to divide men about the nature of
the constitution at the moment when Charles Stuart
was preparing to land in England.[2] The debate ended
without a vote, but it showed how opinion stood in the
House. For kingship were all the 'gentlemen of the
long robe,' most of the civilian members of the Council,
all the representatives of Ireland except three officers,
and a strong party of country gentlemen headed by
Sir Richard Onslow, one of the members for Surrey.
Against it were the Major-Generals and most of the
officers who had seats in the House. The members for
Yorkshire, where Lambert's influence was great, all
sided with the opposition, with the solitary exception
of Charles Howard. One of these Yorkshiremen,
Luke Robinson, went so far as to propose that Pack's
paper should be burnt by the common hangman.[3]

Tuesday was spent in disputing as to the manner in
which the Remonstrance should be discussed. It was
decided to read it in parts, beginning with the first article
after the preamble. On Wednesday the minority, faithful

[1] Thurloe, vi. 74.
[2] Fleetwood to Henry Cromwell, February 24, 1657: *Lansdowne MS.*,
821, f. 274. Jephson to the same : ib. f. 290.
[3] See 'Cromwell and the Crown': *English Historical Review*, 1903, pp. 55, 56.

CHAP.
V
1657
to their obstructive tactics, demanded that the subject should be referred to a Grand Committee which, as members would be able to speak more than once, offered greater facilities for obstruction; but this was rejected by 118 to 63 votes. By this time both sides were getting weary, and when it was suggested that a day should be set apart ' to seek the Lord upon this occasion,' all agreed in appointing Friday the 27th for that purpose, and in resolving not to sit on Thursday, in order that members might have time to prepare themselves for the religious duties of the next day.[1]

Rigid Puritans though they were, both parties seem to have spent a large part of their two days in mundane politics. Even the divines caught the infection; and Patrick Gillespy and Philip Nye, who preached fast-day sermons on the Friday morning, openly referred to the burning question of kingship in their discourses. Both were against it, but Nye spoke moderately, while Gillespy was very bitter.[2] In the evening came a pre-concerted military demonstration on the subject. The officers of the regiments quartered in London were accustomed to meet every Thursday, at Whitehall, either for business or prayer. On the 26th they had met as usual, and naturally fell to discuss the question of kingship. Hearing that the Major-Generals were holding a similar meeting at Desborough's lodgings, they sent a deputation ' to acquaint them with the fears and jealousies that lay upon them in relation to the Protector's alteration of his title, and to desire the knowledge of the truth of things.' The Major-Generals replied by inviting the officers to join them; and the gathering was then addressed by Lambert, who explained the substance of the Remonstrance, pointed out the desirability of joint action, and invited them to

Feb.
27

---

[1] *Commons' Journals*, vii. 496.   [2] *Clarke Papers*, iii. 92.

moderation and patience in this weighty business.[1] The
effect of this was soon seen. Next day when the
observances of the fast were over, a hundred officers,
including the Major-Generals, waited upon the Protector, and by the mouth of their spokesman, Colonel
Mills, explained their dissatisfaction with the provisions
of the Remonstrance, and their hope that he would
refuse the title of King. Cromwell answered them
very vigorously and plainly.[2]

He said that he knew nothing of the Remonstrance
before it was introduced, and had not seen it till yesterday, when he was shown it by Colonel Mills. He loved
the title of King as little as they did, but he might
have been King long since if he had delighted to wear
a feather in his hat. Time was when they themselves
were not so averse to kingship, ' when they boggled
not at the word King.' They had offered to make him
King after the Long Parliament was dissolved; and the
title was again offered him in the first draft of the
Instrument of Government, as some present could
witness. Each time he had refused to accept the offer.

Then the Protector reviewed the revolutions of the
last few years, pointing out that the policy he had
adopted had been the policy of the army, not his own,
and that it had resulted in repeated failure. ' They
had made him their drudge upon all occasions.' At
their instigation, for it was against his own judgment,
he had dissolved the Long Parliament; and to satisfy
them he had called the Little Parliament, ' a hundred

---

[1] *Clarke Papers*, iii. 92.

[2] There are two fairly full accounts of this speech which agree in substance
though not in phraseology.   One is a letter from Anthony Morgan to Henry
Cromwell, dated March 3, in *Lansdowne MS.*, 821, f. 314 ; this is printed in
English Historical Review, 1903, p. 60.   The other is a long unsigned letter to be
found in *Add. MS.*, 6125, f. 61.   It is printed in Burton, *Diary*, i. 382.   A
summary of the speech by Mabbott is given in *Clarke Papers*, iii. 93, and a
brief account of it by Thurloe in *State Papers*, vi. 93.

and forty honest men named by themselves, not by him.' What happened then ? These hundred and forty honest men could not govern ; they attacked a settled ministry ; they flew out at liberty and property, insomuch that both were like to have been destroyed. They held that if one man had twelve cows, another that had none ought to share with his neighbour. Who could have said anything was his own, if they had gone on ? After the Little Parliament was ended, seven of the officers drew up the Instrument of Government and brought it to him to accept. 'There was not much counsel or consideration had in the making of it, and accordingly it proved an imperfect thing, which will neither protect our religious or civil rights.' The Parliament of 1654 followed, and as soon as its members met they began to attack the Instrument, and he was obliged to dissolve them. In his opinion the Instrument stood in need of mending, but the officers would not suffer Parliament to mend it ; 'was not the case hard with me to be put to swear to that which was so hard to be kept ? ' Then the officers undertook to mend the Instrument themselves; but he could not allow that, for as they knew, he was sworn not to suffer it to be altered but by Parliament. If he had permitted them to alter the constitution at their pleasure, his own authority would have had no basis but their will. 'You might have given me a kick and turned me going.'

Then came the meeting of this present Parliament. It was called against his judgment, but the officers would have it. 'I could have no quietness till it was done.' 'You were confident by your own strength and interest to get men chosen to your hearts' desire. How you have failed therein, and how much the country hath been disobliged, is well known.' As the elections did

not turn out to their liking, the officers had excluded
the members they objected to. 'When they were
chosen you garbled them, kept out and put in whom you
pleased, by the Instrument.' The responsibility fell
upon him as Protector. 'I am sworn to make good all
you do, right or wrong, and because a hundred and
twenty are excluded, I must think them malignants
and scandalous, whether they are so or not.'

Now, after the officers had remodelled the House
to suit themselves, they came and complained to him
of the conduct of the members they had admitted and
allowed to sit. It was a little too much. Cromwell
was naturally choleric, and at this point in his speech
he quite lost his temper and defied the officers. 'I
never courted you,' he said, 'nor never will. If the
members do good things, I must and I will stand by
them. They are honest men and they have done good
things. I know not what you can blame them for,
unless because they love me too well.'

'It is time,' he added, 'to come to a settlement, and
to lay aside arbitrary proceedings so unacceptable to
the nation.' The officers might dislike a House of Lords,
but it was necessary to have some assembly of the kind
as a check or balancing power. 'I tell you that, unless
you have some such thing as a balance, we cannot be
safe. Either you will encroach upon our civil liberties
by excluding such as are elected to serve in Parliament—
next time for aught I know, you may exclude four
hundred—or they will encroach upon our religious
liberty. By the proceedings of this Parliament, you
see they stand in need of a check or balancing power,
for the case of James Naylor might happen to be your
case. By the same law and reason they punished
Naylor, they might punish an Independent or
Anabaptist. By their judicial power they fall upon

life and member, and doth the Instrument enable me
to control it ?   This Instrument of Government,' he
concluded, ' will not do your work.'

The Protector then wished the officers good-night,
saying that he would be glad to discuss the matter
further with them, if they would choose six or seven of
their number to confer with him.   The officers had not
expected to be received in this way, and they went
away with their tails between their legs.   Cromwell was
in the position of a minister addressing a meeting of
recalcitrant supporters, or a member of Parliament
tackling an influential deputation from aggrieved con-
stituents ;   the officers were the representatives of the
Cromwellian party, the army was the constituency
Cromwell represented.   To hear the constitutional
history of the last few years treated with such uncon-
ventional freedom, and to be told so many home truths
was a salutary shock to their political self-sufficiency.

It had the best possible effect.   ' Next day,' says a
letter, ' they were very much quieter and very willing
and desirous to be satisfied.'   ' Their heat,' says another,
' was abated.'   ' Since that time,' adds a third, ' the
officers are quieted, and many are fallen from the
rest.' [1]   Report said that three of the Major-Generals
were converted, and were now prepared to accept the
revival of a House of Lords and the settlement of the
succession.[2]   On March 5, when the little committee
waited upon the Protector, a sort of reconciliation took
place.   On behalf of the officers the committee assured
him ' of their satisfaction in his Highness, and of their
resolution to acquiesce in what he should think to be
for the good of these nations.'   The Protector answered
by declaring ' his constant regard to his army, and to

---

[1] Burton, *Diary,* i. 384.   *English Historical Review,* 1903, p. 61.
[2] Burton, *Diary,* i. 385.

the ancient cause of the honest people under his govern- ment, and gave such christian assurance thereof that amounted to a large satisfaction both to them and to the council.' [1]

In consequence of this lull in the opposition, the consideration of the Remonstrance in Parliament went on rapidly. During the interval caused by the two days' fast, Thursday 26th, and Friday 27th February, the supporters of the measure had not been idle. In their deliberations they devised a compromise, which had the result of diminishing hostility and facilitating progress. When the House reassembled on Saturday, February 28, it was resolved that no vote passed on any part of the scheme during the debates should be held binding unless the whole was assented to. On the Monday this was followed by a still more important resolution postponing the paragraph of the first article of the Remonstrance, in which Cromwell was asked to take the title and dignity of King, until all the rest of the scheme should have been considered. Both these resolutions were passed unanimously.[2] The author of this compromise seems to have been Sir Richard Onslow, who is described in a contemporary letter as 'the head of the country party,' that is the unofficial members who supported the bill. He was a man of large estates, had fought for the Parliament throughout the war, and though excluded by Pride's Purge in 1648, had accepted both the republic and the protectorate, so that his position made him an excellent mediator.[3] It

---

[1] *Clarke Papers*, iii. 94, 96 ; Thurloe, vi. 107.

[2] *Commons' Journals*, vii. 497.

[3] A life of Onslow is in the *Dictionary of National Biography*, xlii. 22. His part in this compromise is mentioned by Giavarina in a letter dated March $\frac{6}{16}$. *Venetian Transcripts, R.O.* Arthur Onslow's account of his family, printed in the *Fourteenth Report, Hist. MSS. Commission*, part ix, p. 478, says simply that Sir Richard ' was very earnest for making Cromwell King.'

was also known that the postponement of the kingship clause had been approved by the Protector; and
this rendered the supporters of the Remonstrance ready
to agree to it. On one point, however, the majority of
the House were firm. The question of the succession
must be settled without any further delay. The opposition pressed to postpone the whole of the first article of
the Remonstrance, that is, not only the first paragraph
of it, which requested Cromwell to take the title of
King, but also the second paragraph which requested
him to appoint during his lifetime the person who
should succeed him. They insisted upon a division on
this question, and were soundly beaten by 120 to 63
votes. The result was seen next day, on Tuesday,
March 3, when the House unanimously passed the
resolution asking Cromwell to be pleased to appoint
and declare, during his lifetime, the person who should,
immediately after his death, succeed him in the
government of these nations.[1] The opposition was too
dejected by Monday's defeat to demand a division. Its
leaders seem to have given up the struggle. Colonel
Sydenham for a time absented himself from the House.
Lambert remained, but neither on the Saturday nor the
Monday did he take any part in the debate. He seemed
to be sullenly submitting to the inevitable, and to have
resigned himself to be, as a foreign observer put it, the
subject instead of the 'demi-colleague' of the Protector.[2] The supporters of the Remonstrance were
jubilant. 'We are of opinion,' wrote one, 'that our
work is more than half done, and the rather because the
opposite party either lay down the cudgels or leave the
field, and many (and those not of the least consequence)

---

[1] *Commons' Journals*, vii. 498; *Clarke Papers*, iii. 94.
[2] Jephson to H. Cromwell, March 3, 1657. *Lansdowne MS.*, 821, f. 312;
cf. Thurloe, vi. 101.

come over to us.'[1] 'We go soberly but slowly on,' said another letter. On Thursday, March 5, the House discussed article two of the Remonstrance, which declared that future Parliaments should consist of two Houses.[2] People had expected that this proposed revival of a House of Lords would rouse great opposition. 'That we fear will most stick with us is the balance or House of Lords, as some call it,' wrote Colonel Bridge. Thurloe told Henry Cromwell that this would prove ' a very hard and doubtful question.' To the surprise of both, it passed unanimously and without a division. The fact is, that when the opposition considered this second House, they found there was a good deal to be said in its favour. Cromwell regarded it as a device to keep the balance of the constitution by preventing one power from encroaching on another. Thurloe looked upon it as a sort of citadel in which the party of progress could hold out when the party of reaction got possession of the town. 'It would preserve,' he said, 'the good interest against the uncertainty of the Commons' House.' ' The other House is to be called by writ, in the nature of the Lords' House; but is not to consist of the old Lords, but of such as have never been against the Parliament, but are to be men fearing God and of good conversation, and such as his Highness shall be fully satisfied in, both as to their interest, affection, and integrity to the good cause. And we judge here that this House thus constituted will be a great security and bulwark to the honest interest, and to the good people that have been engaged therein ; and will not be so uncertain as the House of Commons, which depends upon the election of the people. Those that sit in the other House are to be for life, and as any die, his place is to

---

[1] Col. Bridge to Henry Cromwell, March 3, 1657. *Lansdowne MS.*, 821.
[2] *Commons' Journals*, vii. 498 ; *Clarke Papers*, iii. 95.

be filled up with the consent of the House itself, and not
otherwise ; so that, if that House be but made good
at first, it is likely to continue so for ever, as far as man
can provide.'[1]

Thurloe's commentary helps to explain why this
creation of a second House was accepted by the opposition. The soldiers who led the minority in the House
were not entirely blind. They had felt the ill results of
giving unlimited power to a House of Commons alone,
during the period from 1649 to 1653, when a Parliament
of one House governed England with sovereign power.
For that reason they had devised the constitutional
scheme embodied in the Instrument of Government,
with all the restrictions on the authority of future
Parliaments which it contained. They were beginning
to see now that it was impossible to maintain these
paper restrictions, without a direct appeal to force, unless there was some power in the constitution able to
enforce them. The Protector's veto was not enough,
and they began to appreciate the validity of the Protector's argument that a second House of Parliament
was required to balance the House elected by the
people. Moreover, they knew very well that the supporters of the Protectorate were a minority in the
country, and that if the people could freely express its
will in Parliament it would recall the exiled King. On
reflexion, therefore, they were not sorry to see a
sort of senate established as a check to the popularly
elected lower House, thinking that it would serve
to maintain the principles for which they had fought
against the reactionary tendencies of the nation in
general. They were so much convinced of this that,
in 1659, the necessity of ' a select senate ' became

[1] *English Historical Review*, 1903, pp. 56, 59; Thurloe, vi. 93; *Clarke
Papers*, iii. 93.

one of the chief planks in the political platform of
the army.

After this knotty point had been settled, Parliament took in hand articles three, four, five and six, which
dealt with the powers of the two Houses and the
qualifications of their members. It was easy to draw
up a number of provisions excluding from election unfit
persons, such as Royalists, Catholics, and delinquents of
various kinds ; the question was how these provisions
were to be enforced. Parliament was determined not
to allow the Protector's Council to decide in future upon
the fitness of its members : it had suffered too much
from that interference already. The third article of
the Remonstrance demanded ' that those persons who
are legally chosen by a free election of the people
to serve in Parliament may not be excluded from
sitting in Parliament, but by judgment and consent of
that House, whereof they are members.' But, as it was
necessary to have some body empowered to see that
members possessed the legal qualifications enumerated,
it was declared, by the fourth article, that forty-one
commissioners should be appointed by Act of Parliament ' to try whether the members to be elected for
the House of Commons in future Parliaments be capable
to sit,' and if they were not qualified to suspend them
from sitting till the House itself decided their cases.
Each successive Parliament was in like manner to pass
an act appointing ' triers ' of this kind for the following one. Henry Cromwell and other friends of the
Protector approved this plan, because ' the distaste of
rejecting such whom the country hath chosen will less
reflect on his Highness.' [1]

The seventh article took a little more time. On
March 13 the House voted that there should be a

---

[1] See Henry Cromwell's comments : Thurloe, vi. 94.

constant revenue for the support of the government
and the defence of the nation. The amount fixed
was £1,300,000 per annum; of which it was calculated that £600,000 was to go to the maintenance
of the fleet, £400,000 for the army, and £300,000 for
the civil government and household expenses of the
Protector. It was supposed that the customs and
excise would supply £900,000 out of this sum, and the
Exchequer £200,000. By an express provision, no part
of it was to be raised by a land tax.

This was a great improvement on the Instrument of
Government, which had declared (art. xxvii) that a
constant yearly revenue should be raised, but had not
specified the amount. Moreover, the determination of
ways and means for raising the revenue, which the
Instrument left to the Protector and his Council, was
now given entirely to Parliament.[1] 'In point of
money they have dealt very well,' said Thurloe. The
eighth article settled the composition of the Council,
which was now enlarged from fifteen to twenty-one
members. By a special proviso, which was added, the
appointment of the commander-in-chief, and of all field
officers on land or generals at sea, was to require the
consent of the Council. But this proviso was only to
come into force in the case of Cromwell's successors, and
his power to appoint remained unlimited.[2] 'As for
that reservation as to the choice of the chief officers of
the militia,' wrote Henry Cromwell, 'I look upon it as
an high respect to his Highness, inasmuch as they
would entrust him during his own life with that power,
which I myself also do not think fit to be entrusted to
any of his successors.'[3]

---

[1] *Commons' Journals*, vii. 502 ; *Clarke Papers*, iii. 97 ; Thurloe, vi. 123.
[2] *Commons' Journals*, vii. 505.
[3] Thurloe, vi. 94.

Next came the question of religion and toleration, which caused far more trouble. The debate upon it began in the afternoon of March 17. 'By the beginning,' said Thurloe, 'I perceive it will·last very long.'[1] It lasted till March 23, and the original tenth article was greatly amended and made into two. The Instrument of Government had vaguely stated that 'the Christian religion as contained in the Scriptures' was 'to be held forth and recommended as the public profession of these nations.'[2] The new constitution went much further. It attempted to establish a national church with a definite dogmatic creed. For years this had been the constant aim of Puritan divines. The Westminster Assembly had drawn up a detailed Confession of Faith, but this had never received the confirmation of Parliament, though it had been adopted by the Church of Scotland. In 1652 John Owen and a number of Independent divines had attempted a definition of the fundamental principles of Christianity, but without achieving any practical result.[3] Another trial had been made in Cromwell's first Parliament, when a committee of the House, aided by a committee of divines, had drawn up twenty Articles of Faith with their Scriptural proofs; but the abrupt dissolution of that Parliament had prevented the further progress of the scheme.[4] The idea of drawing up a creed was now revived; and on the proposal of Sir Richard Onslow, a proviso was inserted declaring that a 'Confession of Faith,' to be agreed on by Protector and Parliament 'according to the rule and warrant of the Scriptures,' was to be 'asserted, held forth, and recommended to the

[1] Thurloe, vi. 123.
[2] Article xxxv.
[3] Gardiner, *Commonwealth and Protectorate*, ii. 31 ; Shaw, *The English Church during the Civil Wars and under the Commonwealth*, i. 366 ; ii. 81–4.
[4] Shaw, i. 366 ; ii. 94.

people of these nations.' No divine who did not accept this confession was to be ' capable of receiving the public maintenance appointed for the ministry.' [1] This pointed to the establishment of a national church, based on a union between moderate Independents and moderate Presbyterians; and it was warmly approved of by Cromwell, his son Henry, and many supporters of the government.[2]

The provisions for toleration outside the national church were much less liberal than those of the Instrument. Catholics and Episcopalians were excluded in both, but whereas by the Instrument it was only necessary that Dissenters should ' profess faith in God by Jesus Christ,' to obtain protection in the profession of their faith and the exercise of their religion, in the new constitution it was necessary to believe in the Trinity. Unitarians were excluded, as they subsequently were in the Toleration Act of 1689. And not only was a stringent clause inserted against those who reviled the ministers of the national church or disturbed them in the worship of God, which was evidently aimed at the Quakers; but there was a proviso that, where the laws against such offenders were defective, new laws should be enacted. Finally, whilst in the Instrument only such as ' under the profession of Christ hold forth and practise licentiousness ' were to be denied liberty of worship, blasphemy and profaneness were now added to licentiousness, and what these two words might be interpreted to include it was impossible to say. It was clear, however, that henceforth neither Biddle, nor Naylor, nor any minor heretics of the same class, would be able to plead that the constitution gave them liberty to utter their religious opinions.

---

[1] *Commons' Journals*, vii. 506.
[2] Thurloe, vi. 183.

It is not surprising, therefore, that men like Downing, who had shown his persecuting zeal in Naylor's
case, approved these changes. ' This day,' he wrote on
March 19, ' the House passed the clause for Liberty of
Conscience, and indeed much more to satisfaction
generally than as in the Instrument of Government.'[1]
On the other hand, the sectaries outside the House
bitterly complained that the resolution ' to bring in a
public profession of faith, and to tie up the public
maintenance to conformity thereto ' threatened a re-
novation of ecclesiastical tyranny. They asked
' whether the several professions amongst us, that by
the national faith shall be concluded unorthodox, may
not from these beginnings, and other foundations
already laid, expect to receive the like entertainment
at the hands of this generation, as the godly and faithful
followers of Christ have at the hands of the worldly
powers and national church in times past ? ' [2]

At last, on Tuesday, March 24, the time came to
discuss the postponed clause of the first article, asking
the Protector to assume the title of King. Encouraged
by the calm of the last three weeks and the apparent
acquiescence of the officers, the supporters of kingship
thought that the clause would be carried with very
little trouble or delay. ' I was somewhat confident in
the morning,' wrote Colonel Bridge, ' that we should
have laid the top stone of that great and noble structure
we have been so long in framing before this time. But
we have not been able to bring it to an issue.' [3]
Instead of acquiescence there came a pitched battle
about the title, which consumed both morning and afternoon. Nine orators spoke on each side—Lisle, Broghil,

[1] *Clarke Papers*, iii. 98 ; *Cal. State Papers Dom.*, 1656–7, p. 315.
[2] ' A Narrative of the late Parliament.' *Harleian Miscellany*, iii. 466, 467.
[3] *English Historical Review*, 1903, p. 64 ; *Lansdowne MSS.*

and Whitelocke in favour of the proposal, Desborough
violently hostile, Whalley and Goffe opposed to it, but
moderate, and almost, it seemed, indifferent.[1] On the
25th, when the debate was resumed, the House was
fuller than usual; those who had absented themselves
returned to make a last fight against the hated title.
Lambert and Fleetwood both spoke. The latter delivered himself of a long invective against monarchy,
and was so moved by it that he burst into tears. He
had the gift of tears, and sincerely believed, as he told
Henry Cromwell, that the passing of the vote would be
'a sad grief to the hearts of all good people.'[2] Nevertheless some observers thought that these great officers
were not as much opposed to kingship as they professed
to be, and affected an exaggerated repugnance to it in
order to preserve their influence over the inferior
officers. Their speeches gained no votes; and by
123 to 62 it was resolved to ask the Protector to
assume the title and office of King.

The three days which followed the great fight were
spent in improving the wording of the Remonstrance,
and in adding half a dozen explanatory articles to complete the work.[3] The name of the document was
finally altered from Address and Remonstrance into
Petition and Advice, it being thought that this change
would the more engage the Protector to conform to the
desires of Parliament. The most important alteration,
however, was the addition of an eighteenth article by
which, in case the Protector was not pleased to give
his consent to all the matters and things in the Petition,
then nothing in the same was to be deemed of force.[4]
Cromwell must either accept the whole constitution

---

[1] Reynolds to Henry Cromwell, March 24, 1657; *Lansdowne MSS.*
[2] *English Historical Review*, 1903, p. 64.
[3] Articles numbered 9, 14, 15, 16, 17, 18 in the Petition and Advice.
[4] *Commons' Journals*, vii. 511-3.

or nothing. It was thought by Bordeaux that this CHAP.
V
1657 was added in order to give Cromwell a decent pretext for accepting the title in spite of his old hostility to it, by enabling him to say that he was obliged to acquiesce in all that Parliament wished.[1]

Having made these changes, Parliament on March 27 asked the Protector to fix time and place for an audience; and he named Tuesday, March 31, at eleven o'clock in the Banqueting House at Whitehall. At the appointed time the Speaker and members assembled in the Banqueting House. The Protector, attended by some of his Council and by many officers, met them there, and it was noticed that Lambert was not one of them. On such occasions it was usually the function of Lambert to bear the sword of state; but now he purposely absented himself at Wimbledon, and Montagu bore it instead.[2] The Speaker made a long and flowery oration, urging Cromwell to take the title of King and representing that the name and office of King were better known and more suitable to the laws and constitution of these nations than that of Protector, which was never known but in a prince's minority. He then proceeded to explain the provisions of the Petition and Advice. ' The Parliament,' he concluded, ' hath so good an apprehension of this frame of government, in all the articles of it, that it is their humble desire that you may be pleased to accept of them all. They are bound up in one link or chain, or like a building well knit and cemented; if one stone be taken out it loosens the whole. The rejection of one may make all the rest unsuitable and unpracticable.'[3]

The Protector replied that the matter was of such

[1] *English Historical Review*, 1903, p. 65; see Thurloe, vi. 183, for Henry Cromwell's comments.

[2] *Clarke Papers*, iii. 99; *Commons' Journals*, vii. 516.

[3] Burton, *Diary*, i. 411.

weight that he must have time for deliberation. To resolve suddenly in an affair of such moment, and without seeking the direction of God, would be wrong. ' Some short time to consult God and my own heart,' said he, was absolutely needful, and promised that he would consider the problem with an unbiassed mind. ' Neither the humour of any weak or unwise people or the desires of others that may have lusting after things that are not good' should influence his answer.[1]

For the moment, therefore, the decision was postponed. The general belief was that Cromwell would accept. After the vote of the House on March 25 many of the officers seemed inclined to accept the accomplished fact and abandon their opposition. Half a dozen of them went to the Protector, on the night of March 30, and told him that ' although, whilst it was in debate they opposed it, yet now observing a series of Providence in it they were satisfied, and that it was his duty to accept it.'[2] Amongst these officers was Colonel Thomas Cooper, who wrote to Henry Cromwell to announce his conversion. ' Having,' said he, ' according to what light and understanding I have received from the Lord, discharged my conscience, I can and do freely acquiesce in the will of God ; and though this matter, so long as it was in debate, was against my mind, yet being now concluded by the major part, I can and shall, through the assistance of God, I hope, approve myself with as much faithfulness to it, as if I had been never so much for the thing in the first promoting of it ; and this I do not upon a politic but Christian account, well knowing that if a hair of a man's head fall not to the ground without the Lord's

---

[1] Carlyle, *Cromwell*, Speech vii ; *English Historical Review*, 1903, p. 66 ; *Clarke Papers*, iii. 99 ; Thurloe, vi. 156 ; *Mercurius Politicus*, p. 7702 ; Vaughan, ii. 139.

[2] *English Historical Review*, 1903, p. 66.

providence, much less do so great things as the govern- CHAP.
V
1657
ments of the world suffer alteration without special
providence.'[1]

Others shared Cooper's view. It is probable that
Whalley, Boteler, and Goffe were amongst the deputation mentioned. A letter written on March 31 says
that they, and divers others, grow more good-natured.[2]
Most of the officers of the Irish army who were in
London were in favour of kingship, and at the beginning
of March contemplated a public demonstration on behalf of it, which they abandoned because they found
'the heat of the others abated.'[3] As for those in
Scotland, it was asserted about the middle of March
that they were well disposed to the change. ' For the
officers here,' wrote Monck, ' by so much as I can perceive as yet by their tempers, they will be very well
satisfied with what his Highness and the Parliament
shall think fit for the settlement and peace of the three
nations and the good people in them.'[4]

On the other hand, even after the vote of March 25,
some of the greatest officers remained fixed and firm in
their opposition. 'Lambert, Sydenham and Desborough,'
said a letter dated March 31, ' still stand out upon the
sullen posture. Fleetwood does not mutiny but
lament.' Hewson is 'as obstinate as could be imagined.'[5]
According to rumours circulated amongst the Royalists,
with whom the wish was father to the thought, these
irreconcilables even contemplated an appeal to arms.[6]
There was no truth in these rumours. The officers of
the army were too divided for such action on the

---

[1] Col. Thos. Cooper to Henry Cromwell, March 31, 1657. Thurloe, vi. 157.
[2] *English Historical Review*, 1903, p. 67.
[3] Ib. p. 61.
[4] *Clarke Papers*, iii. 98 ; Thurloe, vi. 106.
[5] *English Historical Review*, 1903, p. 67.
[6] *Clarendon State Papers*, iii. 336.

part of the dissidents, nor was the Protector the kind of ruler to yield to mutineers what he refused to petitioners. Moreover, at this moment the dissentient officers were by no means assured that Cromwell would accept the crown. So long as they thought he would yield to arguments and the moral pressure they could bring to bear upon him, they were not likely to think of more dangerous methods of persuasion. They thought that moral pressure might suffice, because they knew that they were not alone in their opposition. Outside Parliament, so far as it is possible to judge, public opinion gave them considerable support in their resistance. The bulk of the nation remained curious but interested spectators of the struggle in the House. They did not exactly regard it with indifference, but they did not share the passions which it roused. The Royalists scoffed openly at the whole of the proceedings. Some, it is true, hoped that Cromwell would accept the crown, because they believed it would cause a reaction favourable to the rightful King, or possibly a division in the army of which they might reap the advantage. Their views could scarcely find expression in a press which was rigidly under the control of the government; but now and then a pamphlet stole out and showed what they felt. On January 27, for instance, a pamphlet was published, entitled ' The Difference between an Usurper and a Lawful Prince explained in their several characters for the satisfaction of all men.' After describing various kinds of usurpers, it gave ' the character of an usurper that hath no title at all,' which was evidently meant for Cromwell. On March 1, when the excitement was at its height, the indefatigable William Prynne published his ' King Richard the Third revived,' with a title-page suggesting the obvious parallel. It

contained, said the title: ‘The memorable petition
and declaration contrived by himself and his instruments while Protector, in the name of the three Estates of England, to importune and persuade him to accept of the kingship and the crown of England by their joint election (as if he were unwilling to accept, though he most ambitiously aspired after them, by the bloody murther of King Henry VI, Edward V, and sundry others).’ Prynne did not name Cromwell; it was enough to mention the traditional tyrant of English history. He contented himself with reprinting the original petition, and adding a quotation from Ecclesiastes: ‘That which hath been is now, and that which is to be, hath already been; and God requireth that which is driven away.’

As a rule people were too cautious to say what they thought, unless they were in very safe company. Occasionally there occur, in the Middlesex Sessions Records, indictments of persons for using seditious language about Cromwell, drinking confusion to the Lord Protector, and so on; but they are not very numerous, nor are they particularly frequent at this crisis.[1] Ballads were under as rigid a censorship as the press; and no contemporary productions of that kind have reached us excepting two songs published after the Restoration by Alexander Brome.[2] Now, considering the scores of political ballads printed in periods such as 1647 and 1659, it is evident either that this crisis of 1657 caused little excitement amongst the London populace, or that the police was uncommonly efficient. Probably the two things worked together.

There was excitement, but it seems to have been

---

[1] *Middlesex Records*, iii. 247, 250, 252, 259, 264, 266, 268, 270.
[2] *The Rump*, p. 335 (Cromwell's Coronation); p. 326 (upon Cromwell's refusing the kingly power).

CHAP. confined to the class whose feelings found expressions
V in psalms and sermons rather than songs and pamphlets.
1657 The moderate Puritans were generally favourable to the
change ; the extreme sectaries bitterly hostile, especially the Anabaptists.   One of the earliest protests which
reached the Protector came from twelve congregations
(of which one was in Warwickshire, two in Oxford-
shire, three in Worcestershire, six in Gloucestershire),
urging him utterly to reject the title.   It was written
apparently about February, 1657 :

'We cannot be ignorant of a present design, noised
about the whole nation, to raise your Highness to a
greater title and style of regal power, under pretence of
greater honour to your Highness ; which having been
weighed in our spirits before the Lord, we cannot but
give forth our own and other saints' apprehensions, as
to this concernment.

'We do already discern that the assuming such a
title and power will generally rejoice the hearts of the
profane party ; and will also open their mouths to
blaspheme God, and all profession of religion, and
reproach the saints with self-seeking and hypocrisy,
and that they fought not for the exalting of Jesus
Christ, as they pretended, but themselves; especially
your Highness having so solemnly and publicly
professed against it.' [1]

Next came 'The Serious Attestation of Many
Thousand religious and well-disposed People living in
London and the parts adjoining,' protesting against
the 'endeavour to introduce the old demolished
fabric of government in its essential parts.' [2]   Then
followed a still more plain-spoken address to the

---

[1] Nickolls, *Original Letters and Papers of State addressed to O. Cromwell,*
1743, p. 140.
[2] British Museum, 669, f. 20 (52).   Dated March 26, 1657.

Protector from nineteen Anabaptist ministers in
London (April 13) :

'We cannot but spread before your Highness our
deep resentment of, and heart bleedings for, the fearful
apostasy which is endeavoured by some to be fastened
upon you, upon plausible pretences, by such who for
the most part had neither heart nor hand to engage
with you, and the good people of the nation, in the day
of straits and extremities, by persuading you to re-
edify that old structure of government, which God by
you and them, had signally borne testimony against and
destroyed, and assume that office which was once
declared and engaged against by the Parliament,
March 17, 1648, . . . as unnecessary, burdensome,
and destructive to the safety and liberty of the
people. Sir, we have in the capacities wherein we
stand, with freedom and faithfulness to the good
old cause, borne our testimonies against this retro-
gradation, and should with much peace and satisfaction to our consciences, acquiesce therein, but that
we are persuaded the honour of God, the interest of
His people, the safety of yourself and family, and the
peace and tranquillity of the nations, lie so eminently
at the stake. . . .' [1]

It was evident that the opinion of about half
the party which had made Cromwell Protector was
hostile to the proposed change. The opposition did
not come merely from a cabal amongst the officers ;
it came also from the rank and file of militant Puritanism.
On the other hand the supporters of the change outside
Parliamentary and official circles seemed to be few. No
petitions came pouring in to encourage and support the
action of the Parliamentary majority. The press was
open to the supporters of kingship if they chose to

---

[1] Nickolls, *Original Letters*, p. 142.

use it, but they scarcely attempted to discuss the question. There was a pamphlet entitled 'Antitheta or Political Reasonings,' which stated the arguments for and against Monarchy and an Elective Succession in the manner of one of those modern political handbooks which set forth the pros and cons upon questions of the day for the instruction of young politicians. But the only advocate of the change in print was a champion calculated rather to discredit than to recommend the cause he adopted. Marchamont Needham, the editor of the official newspaper *Mercurius Politicus*, was a journalist of great ability and versatility, who possessed a gift of humour rare amongst the pamphleteers of the time. His pen had been at the service of all parties in succession. A Republican opponent characterised him as ' an old malignant pamphleteer ' who had formerly written *Mercurius Britannicus* for the Parliament against the King, then *Mercurius Pragmaticus* for the King against the Parliament, and afterwards *Mercurius Politicus* for the Protector against both King and Parliament. His most notable political writings had been expositions of Republican principles, ' The Case of the Commonwealth of England Stated ' (1650), ' A True State of the Case of the Commonwealth ' (1654), and ' The Excellency of a Free State ' (1656). The latter was a collection of leading articles, originally published in *Mercurius Politicus* to prove the advantages of republican over monarchical government. All three are serious works, written in a remarkably clear and vigorous style, and well suited to convince those who were half convinced by events. In the controversial pamphlets, of which he wrote many, he adopted a lighter method of treatment, which his friends termed witty and satirical and his adversaries scurrilous.

A Royalist describes him as 'transcendently gifted in opprobrious and treasonable droll'; a Republican denounces him as a 'lying, railing Rabshakeh'; he himself called his method drolling, and defended its employment in political writing by the example of Sir Thomas More. More, he said, was 'an eminent statesman' who 'had the right knack of living in the world, his motto was "joco-serio," betwixt jest and earnest,' which might be translated 'drolling.' Sir Thomas was true to this motto for a long time; but at length, 'falling from his principle by being once in his days in earnest,' he stood up for the Pope's supremacy and 'brought himself to the block by it,' leaving his memory as a sad example to those who ventured to be in earnest amongst the great politicians of this captious world.[1] As Needham was a complete sceptic in politics it was easy for him to assume this attitude, and as he was cynically shameless, he had no difficulty in advocating the change from a republic to a monarchy as emphatically as he had defended the establishment of the republic. Everyone around him was changing his principles, and, as he hinted to Cromwell, still more startling changes were in prospect. One day, at Whitehall, the Protector asked Needham what the news was; in reply he told Cromwell that *vox populi* said Mr. Nye should be Archbishop of Canterbury, and Dr. Owen Archbishop of York. It was a good jest, for if the Protector was to become King in spite of his former professions against kingship there was no reason why his chaplains should be more consistent. His newswriter could not afford to be.[2]

Accordingly, on March 12, 1657, Needham commenced a series of articles in *Mercurius Politicus* intended to prepare the minds of the public for the

---

[1] *Mercurius Politicus*, March 5-12, 1657.
[2] *Cal. State Papers Dom.*, 1656-7, p. 318.

CHAP.
V
1657

restoration of monarchy. Imitating Harrington, he cast his articles into the form of letters from an imaginary state, the city and commonwealth of Utopia. For seven years past this renowned state had been ' sorely afflicted with an infectious itch of scribbling political discourses. The world there had run mad in ' disputes about government, that is to say about notions, forms, and shadows.' All the people of the country were ' arrant statesmen,' born so, not bred. The Greeks were a dull people ; they had but seven wise men ; Utopia had 7000 who understood all except themselves. Hence confusion reigned in the commonwealth, and all kinds of disorders. To cure this, ' that most excellent prince,' the Lord Basilides, assembled the senate ' to consult about the ways and means of reducing the commonwealth to a happy establishment.' One after another, in their resolutions, the senate pointed out the errors which the Utopians had committed in their seven years' madness. They had been mistaken in their notions of liberty and government. All their reasoning about government had been based upon a wrong foundation. ' They fetch their arguments from principles of natural right and freedom, whereas the truth is government is an art or artifice found out by man's wisdom, and occasioned by necessity.' To constitute a government man was ' necessitated, in order to the more secure enjoying of his freedom, to resign up his natural private right for the public convenience of himself, and the community where he lives.' Granting that government was merely established for the general convenience, it followed that there was ' no everlasting principle in government,' and no particular form eternally right for all times and places.

' For the rules and reasons of government cannot be

always the same, it depending upon future contingents,
and therefore must be alterable according to the variety
of emergent circumstances and accidents ; so that no
certain form can be prescribed at all times, seeing that
which may be most commendable at one time, may be
most condemnable at another, and that is ever best
which befits the present state and temper of affairs, and
is most conducible to the end of government ; and so
a free state may be no less, and many times much more,
in that which men call monarchy, than in any other
form. 'Tis not the name of a free state or commonwealth which makes it so indeed, but that is a free state
in every form, where men are put into the way of a free
enjoyment and security of their rights and properties.
. . . Men are as free every jot under a right principality
as under a popular form.'

Seeing this, the Utopians began to understand that
they had been extremely mistaken in their supposition
touching the ground of their quarrel with the foreign
race of kings which had once ruled Utopia.   It was not
against the name and office of King that they had taken
up arms, but against the ' enormities and irregularities '
of their kings.   When they found it impossible to
secure the interest of liberty and religion any other way,
they had been obliged to change the old form of government and introduce a new one, substituting what was
called a free state for a monarchy ; and since then one
form of government had succeeded another as each
proved ineffectual for its purpose.   Therefore the
Senate of Utopia now resolved, ' That every one of those
forms ought to be looked upon in their times but as
ultima tabula post naufragium, that is to say, the last
plank, as it were, after shipwreck, laid hold on out of
necessity to save a commonwealth from sinking, and
so no longer to be made use of than till they could get

ashore upon some sure and lasting settlement.' The people of Utopia, as well as the senate, now understood this. They began to see ' That all forms of government are but temporary expedients, to be taken upon trial, as necessity and right reason of state enjoins, in order to the public safety ; and that as 'tis a madness to contend for any form, when the reason of it is gone, so 'tis neither dishonour nor scandal, by following right reason, to shift through every form, and after all other experiments made in vain, where the ends of government cannot otherwise be conserved, to revert upon the old bottom and foundation.' [1]

This was good sense from whatever mouth it came, and though it was disguised in the dress of a political allegory. It agreed very closely with the view of the question taken by Cromwell himself. An enemy had once described him as declaring ' that it was lawful to pass through any forms of government for the accomplishing his ends,' and in a sense it was true.[2] He had once termed himself a man who was not ' wedded and glued to forms of government.' During the debates of the army in 1647 he had championed the cause of monarchy against those who asserted that a republic was the only legitimate government. All forms, he had argued, were lawful. Had not the Jews been governed successively by patriarchs, judges, and kings ? The important thing was that the particular form adopted should be acceptable to the people who lived under it. ' In the government of nations that which is to be looked after is the affections of the people.' Moreover, all forms of government were but temporal things, trifling in comparison with those

---

[1] *Mercurius Politicus*, March 26–April 2, 1657.

[2] ' Major Huntington's Reasons for laying down his Commission,' Maseres, *Select Tracts*, i. 406.

eternal ends for which men and societies of men existed. CHAP.
V
In St. Paul's phrase, they were 'dross and dung in
comparison with Christ.'[1]   Thinking thus, Cromwell had 1657
been slow to be converted to republicanism; and when
he had been converted, it was because no other government seemed possible at that particular moment.   Even
after the republic had been established he had not disguised his abstract preference for monarchy, and had
avowed his belief ' somewhat with monarchical power
in it would be most effectual for the settlement of the
nation.'[2]

Time had now brought the majority of Cromwell's
supporters to Cromwell's point of view.   They had
come to think that, of all forms of government, monarchy was that most suitable to the condition of
England and most acceptable to the English people; and
they believed that it was the only form that promised a
permanent settlement of the nation.   Was the Protector to refuse what Parliament demanded, and to
reject what he himself thought best for England, just
because another section of his supporters thought
another form of government the only legitimate one ?
Some of these dissentients were moved by factiousness
and by personal ambition rather than higher motives;
or, at least, higher and lower motives were so inter-
mixed that it was difficult to discriminate between them.
Henry Cromwell, writing to Thurloe, expressed the Mar. 4
hope that his father would not be deterred by such
opposition.[3]

' As for the matter and merit of the proposals themselves, I say in general, that I do not like them the
worse, because some of the great ones could no better

---

[1] *Clarke Papers*, i. pp. lxxi–lxxii. 277, 369, 370. The last phrase is a
reminiscence of Philippians iii. 8.

[2] Whitelocke, *Memorials*, iii. 374.

[3] Thurloe, vi. 93.

digest them ; for since they cannot allow of what a parliament of their own modelling hath done, I look upon them as persons very unapt to be quiet, nor able to endure (as I may call it) any settlement whatsoever ; and therefore I think that the depraved appetites of such sick minds ought the less to be valued ; besides, I look upon some of them as vainly arrogating to themselves too great a share in the right of his Highness's government, and to have too high an opinion of their own merit in subverting the old.   I have been credibly informed, that they have been talking of an heptarchy, and of cantonising the country, with such other conceits as are not consistent with settlement ; and therefore I am so far from a tender sense of their dissatisfaction, that I rather esteem it a providential opportunity to pull out those thorns, which are like to be troublesome in the sides of his Highness.'

Nevertheless it is certain that in most cases the aversion which the officers of the army manifested to monarchy was a simple and sincere feeling, unmixed with any thought of self-interest.   It was almost part of their religion.   Had not God, through Samuel, rebuked the Israelites when they demanded a king ? and would He not also rebuke the backsliding English if, in their madness, they made the same request ?   The obscure comrades who had toiled and fought with Cromwell, in the days when the very being of the cause was in danger, had a claim to be heard as well as those to whom its triumph had brought power and honour.   One of these, Captain William Bradford—a man who, like so many Puritan soldiers, afterwards became a Quaker— addressed an appeal to Cromwell which can hardly have left him unmoved.

Mar. 4   ' I perceive,' wrote Bradford, ' that there are a number in Parliament that have voted kingship for you.

I likewise perceive that there is a number there (though the less) that voted against it, and that the greatest part of the officers of the army now near you, are against it. I beg and beseech your Highness, nay again and again, with tears and prayers I beseech you, to consider what you are doing, after so many declarations and engagements, willingly taken by your direction, by most of the people now subject to you, and after an Instrument signed and sworn to by yourself. Consider, my Lord, I beseech you, and weigh between those two parties voting and dissatisfied. Those that are for a crown, I fear you have little experience of them; the other, most of them, have attended your greatest hazards. . . . My Lord, though the major part in Parliament hath voted this upon you, yet those that loved you, hoped you would have disowned it; but I hear the contrary, which [occasions] sad language given to the officers of your army, truly honouring you. Good my Lord, let not your own wisdom, nor the counsel of a few, persuade you beyond the practice of truth; the hazard will be more than their remedy can help; there will be more safety to yourself and nation, for you to disown the vote, than manage it with harshness. I am of that number, my Lord, that still loves you, and greatly desires to do so, I having gone along with you from Edgehill to Dunbar. The experiences that you have had of the power of God at these two places, and betwixt them, methinks, should often make you shrink, and be at a stand in this thwarting, threatened change. Good my Lord, remember you are but a man, and must die, and come to judgment; men of high degree are vanity, men of low degree are a lie. My Lord, those in power having parts and near unto you, I fear have much injured you, in not dealing freely with your Lordship, but rather feeding that in you, grasping after greatness, and aiming at their own self-interest; and so those now free with your Lordship in never so much love, may run the greater hazard. My Lord, neither my life, estate, nor relations were ever anything to me in comparison of the public, nor yet is; yet I would not be prodigal of them or your Highness's favour. My freedom proceeds from a large proportion of love and no bye-ends.' [1]

This was the consideration which made Cromwell hesitate—not fear of the loud pulpits denouncing the wrath of God against him, nor parrot-cries of 'apostate,' but the sense that many who had loved and followed him were beginning to sorrow over him as a lost leader and as one who had brought shame upon their creed and cause.[2]

His case was hard. There was the necessity of agreeing with Parliament if he wished to found anything that would endure, and it might be long before he found another Parliament in so complying a mood, and so eager to give the nation a settled government.[3] There was much in the proposed constitution which was good in itself, and seemed better calculated to secure the ends he desired than anything which the soldiers or statesmen of the age had yet devised.

April 3 'I must needs bear testimony for you,' he told the committee of the Parliament when he met them again, 'that you have been zealous of the two greatest concernments that God has in the world. One is that of religion and the preservation of the professors thereof, to give them all due and just liberty, and to assert the truths of God. The other is that of the civil liberty and interest of the nations, which although

---

[1] Nickolls, *Original Letters*, p. 141.

[2] John Forster's *Life of Cromwell*, published in 1839, is a modern embodiment of this feeling.

[3] Cf. Thurloe, vi. 243.

it be, and indeed ought to be, subordinate to that of the people of God, yet it is the next best that God hath given men in the world, and better than any words, if well cared for, to fence the people of God in their interest.'[1] But all these good things were clogged with the addition of that title which seemed a trifle of a feather-weight to him, but meant so much to some of his friends. Left to himself, Cromwell's natural inclination would have been to accept the constitutional scheme Parliament had drawn up, but to refuse the title. There was a rumour that he would do so, but it was generally discredited.[2] For the choice was not open to him. By the deliberate decision of Parliament he must accept all or nothing. If he refused anything ' the whole excellent structure,' as Henry Cromwell called it, fell to the ground. It would be a pity, wrote Henry, that ' all these fair advantages' which the scheme promised should be lost ' out of fondness for a matter of less moment,' because Parliament insisted on including the title of King, or the army on excluding it. He blamed Parliament for making the two things inseparable.[3]

---

[1] Carlyle's *Cromwell*, Speech viii. Thurloe uses very similar words. Some here, says he, ' think that the liberties of the nation and those of the people of God are met and do embrace each other in this paper, and that it doth carry with it a better foundation of government than hitherto hath been propounded.' *State Papers*, vi. 156.

[2] So Titus reported to Hyde, April 10, 1657. *Clarendon State Papers*, iii. 336.

[3] ' As I believe,' said he, ' . . . that it is but peevishness in some to oppose the title desired by the Remonstrance ; soe I cannot well satisfie my self, that those are alltogether blameless, whoe for not being humoured in a title and a verry word, should suddenly withhold what would make themselves and others happie. I would not have the sober and judicious partie soe much justifie the weakness of the other, as to contend over earnestly for a name ; for allthough it be but the same, which those other would of themselves have formerly given (whilst it might be taken for their owne gift), yet it being abroad in the world a gaudy feather in the hatt of authoritie, I feare least our friends should lye under the like temptation of desireing to sticke it in, and affect purchaseing to themselves that reputation at the rate of those choice concernments, which indeed are too precious and noble to be made use of upon such an account.' —Thurloe, vi. 183.

CHAP.
V

1657
April 3

Weighty though all these considerations were, the Protector was not long in deciding. On the third day after Parliament had presented the Petition and Advice to him, he sent for the committee which had been appointed to receive his answer and told them he could not accept it. 'I should be very brutish,' he said, ' should I not acknowledge the exceeding high honour and respect you have had for me in this paper. . . . Ever since I heard the Parliament were upon this business . . . I must say I have been able to attain no further than this, that seeing the way is hedged up as it is to me, that I cannot accept the things offered unless I accept all, I have not been able to find it my duty to God and to you, to undertake this charge under that title.' [1]

Without expressly saying so, he hinted that this negative answer was caused by conscientious objections to the title. ' Nothing,' he said, ' must make a man's conscience his servant, and really it is my conscience that guides me to this answer.' As he had warmly praised the constitutional scheme it could only be the title to which he objected; and his expressed regret that he had been necessitated to accept all or nothing clearly revealed his wishes. In deference to Parliament he accepted the restriction laid upon him, and told the committee that, if the House had resolved so to limit him, it would not be fit for him to seek to alter that resolution by any arguments addressed to themselves.

[1] Carlyle, Speech viii, April 3, 1657.

CHAPTER VI

THE HUMBLE PETITION AND ADVICE

CROMWELL'S answer was announced to Parliament on Saturday, April 4. As his acceptance had been confidently expected, the disappointment which his negative caused was correspondingly great. 'You cannot imagine,' wrote Jephson to Henry Cromwell, ' how great a damp fell upon the spirits of those who had been most active in promoting the business.'[1] In their dejection some absented themselves from the House : Lord Broghil, Chief Justice Glyn, Sir Charles Wolseley, and other members of the committee which had heard the Protector's refusal, were away when Whitelocke formally reported it. The Major-Generals and their followers openly exulted. All opponents of kingship mustered in full force, and Colonel Sydenham, who had been six weeks absent from the debates, once more appeared in the House. But, though this was ' no small discouragement ' to the supporters of the Petition and Advice, they stood their ground stoutly, and moved that Parliament should adhere to its former vote and renew its offer. The debate was short and sharp. Montagu led the adherents, Hewson and Desborough the opposition ; but before two o'clock in the afternoon the House had resolved

[1] Jephson to Henry Cromwell (*Lansdowne MSS.*, 822, f. 27). For longer extracts from this correspondence and further details on the subject of this chapter, see ' Cromwell and the Crown,' part ii, *English Historical Review*, 1903, p. 52.

CHAP.
VI
1657

that it would make a fresh application to the Protector.[1] This was carried by seventy-eight to sixty-five votes, and was a substantial victory, for the opposition had thought to win the day by a surprise. Their main argument was that it was unreasonable, since his Highness had declared that it was against his conscience to accept the title, for Parliament to put pressure upon him. But when the Protector's answer was examined it was easily shown that, whatever inference might be drawn from his words, he had made no such definite statement. This satisfied the majority, for they wished to believe it, and ' put no small life into the business.' [2]

On Monday, April 6, the debate was resumed. The absentees, perceiving the danger which their retirement had caused, came to the reinforcement of their friends. It was resolved to draw up a statement of the reasons why Parliament felt bound to adhere to the Petition and Advice, and to present this with the vote to the Protector. A committee was at once appointed for the purpose. The opposition was so out-numbered that they did not venture to divide on the question of appointing the committee, but some violent things were said against the proposal. ' Mr. Speaker,' Colonel Hewson was reported to have declared, ' this Parliament in which we are is worse than the Devil; for he offered the kingdoms of the world to Christ but once, and we must offer it twice ; and for it give reasons to destroy not only ourselves but all the three nations with us.' [3]

Next day, April 7, the committee reported the reasons to be alleged for renewing the application to the Protector, and the following address was agreed upon :—

---

[1] *Commons' Journals*, vii. 520.
[2] Col. Bridges to Henry Cromwell, April 7. *Lansdowne MSS.*, 822, f. 29.
[3] Sexby to Talbot, April 26, 1657. *Clarendon State Papers*, iii. 338.

'That the Parliament having formerly presented their humble Petition and Advice to your Highness, whereunto they have not as yet received satisfaction; and the matters contained in that Petition and Advice being agreed upon by the Great Council and Representative of the three nations; and which in their judgments are most conducing to the good of the people thereof both in their spiritual and civil concernments; they have therefore thought fit to adhere to this advice, and to put your Highness in mind of the great obligation which rests upon you, in respect of this advice; and again to desire you to give your assent thereto.'[1]

On April 8 the committee waited on Cromwell with this address. His reply was ambiguous: he made, wrote Samuel Morland, 'a speech so dark, that none knows whether he will accept it or not; but some think he will accept it.'[2] No man, declared Cromwell, could put a greater value than he did on the opinions and desires of Parliament; and he was equally sensible of the importance of the matters to which they referred. But they called their paper an 'Advice,' and they must give him leave to measure their advice and his infirmity together. Great authority was a great burden; he knew it as a fact, and not merely as a philosophical generality. He was convinced in his conscience that nothing less than assistance from above would enable a man to discharge it; and a man must be sure he was doing right before he undertook it. He had hesitated as to this thing, and hesitated still. What he asked for was liberty to vent his own doubts and fears and scruples. There were many other things in the document, besides the name and title, which deserved

---

[1] *Commons' Journals*, vii. 521.
[2] *English Historical Review*, 1903, p. 69. Vaughan, *Protectorate of Cromwell*, ii. 144; Hooke to Winthrop, *Mass. Hist. Coll.*, III. i. 181.

discussion. He was ready to give his reasons if they would put him in a position to do so, and he asked them to state their reasons a little more particularly than the resolutions of the House did.[1]

In answer to this speech, Parliament, on April 9, appointed a committee of some ninety-nine members, to receive the Protector's doubts and scruples relative to the particulars of the Petition and Advice, and to offer him reasons for his satisfaction and in support of the resolutions of the House. Those particulars in which they were unable to satisfy the Protector they were to report to Parliament.[2]

Accordingly a series of conferences took place between the Protector and the representatives of the committee. They began on the morning of Saturday, April 11, and were continued on April 13, 20, and 21. Bulstrode Whitelocke, Chief Justice Glyn, Nathaniel Fiennes (Commissioner of the Great Seal), John Lisle (his brother Commissioner), Lenthall (once Speaker of the Long Parliament, and now Master of the Rolls), Sir Charles Wolseley, and Lord Broghil were the spokesmen of the committee. All their arguments turned on the question of the title. Whitelocke, as their chairman, opened the discussion.[3] He said that the title of Protector being a new title, ' it was thought that the title which was known by the law of England for many ages, and many hundreds of years together received, the Law fitted to it, and it to the Law, might be of more certainty, clearer establishment, and more conformable to the laws of the nation.'

Lenthall followed. The name of ' King ' was not a bare title, but something more. ' The whole body of the Law is carried upon this wheel': it designated an

<hr />

[1] Carlyle, Speech ix.　　　　[2] Commons' Journals, vii. 521.
[3] Old Parliamentary History, xxi. 72.

office, not a title. Moreover, a name meant much. CHAP.
Witness the action of Parliament in refusing to change VI
the name of King James from King of England to 1657
King of Great Britain, because of the hazard to their
rights and liberties which it might entail. Witness
also the action of the Parliament of 1653, when they
refused to alter the name of the Parliament and call
it The Representative of the People.[1]

Glyn took a different line. The power of a King, he
argued, was limited by the laws, that of a Protector
was not; therefore, as he was sworn to govern according
to the laws, Cromwell must become King instead of Protector. This point he illustrated by an imaginary
dialogue:—

'Supposing your Highness should do any act, and
one should come and say: "My Lord Protector, why,
when you are sworn to govern by the Law, do you, as
Lord Protector, do thus and thus ? "

' " Do I ? why, how am I bound to act ? "

' " The King could not have done so."

' " Aye, but I am not King ; I am not bound
to do as the King ; I am Lord Protector. Show
me that the Law doth require me to do it as
Protector." '[2]

Fiennes argued that Parliament wished to give
Cromwell the authority of King, and that therefore it
was necessary for him to take the name too. Parliament did not think it agreeable to their wisdom to
inspect all the laws and all the cases, and make the
name of Protector suit them, or else leave it lawless and
boundless. Either they must fit all the laws to the

---

[1] *Old Parliamentary History*, xxi. 75.
[2] Ib. xxi. 79 ; *Somers Tracts*, vi. 359. The debates between Cromwell and
the committee were published in 1660, in a pamphlet called *Monarchy Asserted*,
which is attributed to Nathaniel Fiennes. It is reprinted in *Somers Tracts*, ed.
Scott, vi. 346. The Parliamentary History emends a little too freely here.

name—and that was impossible—or leave the name
unbounded—and that was intolerable.[1]

Wolseley enlarged upon the necessity of obeying
the voice of the nation. 'The Parliament,' he said,
'finds the minds of the people of these nations much
set upon this office and title. God hath by his Providence put a general desire of it into the nation; and
Parliament think that in things not unlawful they
ought to hearken and to be much inclined by the desires
of them that sent them. . . . Your Highness hath been
pleased to call yourself, when you speak to the Parliament, a servant; you are so indeed to the people, and
'tis your greatest honour so to be. I hope then, Sir,
you will give the people leave to name their own
servant.'[2]

Broghil, who spoke last, produced a new argument
—one which had great weight with every man who had
anything to lose, and consequently appealed to a wider
circle than any argument about the importance of
names. If Cromwell bore the title of King, all those
that obeyed and served him would be secured by a
law made long before any of the political differences of
to-day had a being. By the Act of Henry VII a
full provision was made for the safety of those who
served a *de facto* King; and if the Protector became
King, this law, hitherto pleaded on behalf of the Royalists,
would henceforth be on the side of those who had
fought for the Parliament and now supported Cromwell's government.[3]

The Protector spoke a few words, admitting the
weight of the arguments adduced, and asking time
to consider them. He promised to give his answer to
those arguments at their next meeting, which was to

[1] *Old Parliamentary History*, xxi. 84.   [2] Ib. xxi. 81.
[3] Ib. xxi. 88. Referring to 2 Hen. VII, cap. i.

take place on Monday, April 13. When the day came
he confined himself in his speech entirely to the
question of the title.[1] He began by summarising the arguments of the committee. Kingship, they had said,
was not a title but an office, so interwoven with the
fundamental laws of this nation that they could not
well be exercised and executed without it. To this he
replied that King was a name of office implying the
supreme authority and nothing more. The importance
was in the thing signified, not in the name. The
authority that christened the supreme authority by
that name could have given it any other name. That
authority was the will of the nation. Kingship ' had
its original somewhere, and it was in consent of the
whole, there was the origin of it.' Parliament represented that whole. ' Let us think what we will, what
the Parliament settles is that which will run through
the law, and will lead the thread of government
through the land,' as well as the title of King.

Experience as well as reason proved this. Under
another title than that of King the supreme authority
had twice received universal obedience—first in the days
of the Long Parliament, who called themselves *Custodes
Libertatis Angliae*, and secondly since he himself had held
that authority with the title of Lord Protector. The
judges had acted under these two supreme authorities
and the laws had been enforced. ' These two experiences
manifestly show that it is not a title, though never
so interwoven with our laws, that makes the law
to have its free passage and to do its office without
interruption.'

To himself the name he was called by was of
no importance. He had undertaken his present
place ' not so much out of hope of doing any good as

[1] Carlyle's *Cromwell*, Speech xi.

out of a desire to prevent mischief and evil. . . . We
were running headlong into confusion and disorder, and
would necessarily have run into blood, and I was [there-
fore] passive to those that desired me to undertake
this place.' For the preservation of the public peace
he was ready to serve in any post. 'I have often
thought that I could not tell what my business was,
nor what I was in the place I stood in, save comparing
myself to a good constable set to keep the peace of
the parish. . . . I do judge for myself that there is no
necessity for this name of King ; for the other names
may do as well.'

Then followed a plain statement that the cause why
he could not take the name of King was ' somewhat of
conscience.' The reason was this. When he was first
a captain of horse, he came to the conclusion that no
soldiers but conscientious and godly men would ever
be able to encounter the gentlemen who fought for the
King. And so he raised ' such men as had the fear of
God before them, and made some conscience of what
they did, and from that day forward they were never
beaten.' This should teach them to own men who were
religious and godly, that is to consider them and respect
them. There were many such men in the nation ; and
while they kept their integrity, men of a worldly or
carnal spirit would never beat them down. God would
not bless the undertaking of anything which would
justly and with cause grieve them. ' If I know as I
do that very generally good men do not swallow the
title . . . it is my duty to beg of you that there may
be no hard things put upon me ; things I mean, hard to
them, which they cannot swallow. . . . ' ' I would not
have you lose them. I would not that you should lose
any servant or friend who may help in this work : or
that they should be offended by that that signifies

no more to me than I told you. That is, I do not think
the thing necessary.'

To sum up the speech of April 13, what the Protector said was that he did not think they had proved that the title was necessary, and, since it would offend many tried friends of the government, he could not accept it. Yet, though the speech was carefully clear, it did not discourage the adherents of kingship. One hearer, noting certain admissions made by the Protector, argued: 'I conceive the conclusion is so natural from these confessions that I cannot believe his Highness would grant so much if he intended to refuse the title.' 'It seems to me,' wrote another, ' that since he allows an indifferency in the thing, his great reason will not permit him to balance the resolves of Parliament, made upon so great a debate and consideration, with the humour of persons without, that can give little of reason besides this, that godly men are dissatisfied.'[1]

On the other hand, the opposition were greatly pleased with this speech, especially with the reasons Cromwell gave for his dissatisfaction about the title. It seemed to Fleetwood, in his jargon, ' a full and signal witness-bearing to the interest of the people of God.' He thought that it would facilitate the compromise between the supporters and the opponents of the Petition, which was being discussed in private about this time.[2] Moderate men amongst the officers saw that some concession must be made on their part. It was now admitted on all hands that the Instrument of Government was not a good working constitution. Cromwell had plainly shown that in his speech to the

---

[1] *English Historical Review*, 1903, pp. 70, 71. Bridges to Henry Cromwell, April 13; Gookin, April 14, *Lansdowne MSS.* 822, ff, 37, 43.
[2] *Lansdowne MS.*, 822, f. 41.

hundred officers; and some of the soldiers who helped
in the making of it confessed as much. ' The Instrument,' wrote Colonel Whalley, ' is now become
very odious.' [1] It was, therefore, from the officers that
the proposal of a compromise came; and it took the
form of a suggestion that Cromwell, while refusing the
crown, should accept the rest of the new constitution.
' Fleetwood,' wrote Colonel Jephson to Henry Cromwell, on April 6, ' did this day profess himself to me
to be a great enemy to arbitrary government, and
manifested his unwillingness to a total breach, and persuaded rather to quit the title and accept of the rest.' [2]
About the middle of April a meeting was arranged
between some of the leaders of the two parties to discuss
this proposal, ' to see,' said Fleetwood, ' how near we
can come to a right understanding one of another in
this business, wherein if the Lord please to own us
that we can come to a right close, it may be of great
mercy to this distracted, divided condition we are in.' [3]
An agreement was not easy. ' We are at present in
suspense,' wrote Sir John Reynolds, ' that which is
offered by some as an expedient not being pleasing to
the House, viz. that the present settlement be
established without the title of King, which the sense of
Parliament doth much oppose and dislike.' [4] Thurloe
did not think it would be possible to persuade Parliament
to accept any compromise. On April 21 he told Henry
Cromwell that nothing but kingship would satisfy that
body. ' For aught I see, the Parliament will not be
persuaded that there can be settlement any other way.
The title is not the question, but it 's the office, which is
known to the laws and this people. They know their
duty to a king, and his to them. Whatever else there is

---

[1] *Lansdowne MS.*, 822, f. 49.   [2] Ib. 822, f. 27.   April 6.
[3] Ib. 822, f. 41.   April 14.   [4] Ib. 822, f. 47.   April 14.

will be wholly new, and be nothing else but a probationer, and upon the next occasion will be changed again. Besides, they say, the name Protector came in by the sword out of Parliament, and will never be the ground of any settlement; nor will there be a free Parliament so long as that continues; and as it savours of the sword now so it will at last bring all things to be military. These and other considerations make men who are for settlement steady in their resolutions as to this government now in hand; not that they lust after a king, or are peevish upon any account of opposition; but they would lay foundations of liberty and freedom, which they judge this the next way to.'[1]

Accordingly Cromwell's very explicit statement of his conscientious objection to the title produced no effect upon the House. They continued to press him to accept it; and the conferences went on, though they were interrupted for several days by Cromwell's illness. Both on April 14 and 15 the committee which attended at Whitehall to confer with him had to go away without seeing him. 'Lord Fiennes and Colonel Jones came and told us,' says a member of the committee, 'his Highness had got a cold and was indisposed, so could not, without prejudice to his health, wait upon us at that time. . . . We were forced to return both times as wise as we went; which did strongly build up the faith of the contrariants.'[2]

On Thursday, 16th, a meeting at last took place. Cromwell was still seriously unwell. 'He came out of his chamber half unready, in his gown, with a black scarf round his neck,' and apologised for making them lose their labour.[3] Then seven of the Parliamentary

[1] Thurloe, vi. 219.
[2] Burton, Diary, ii. 3, 4.
[3] Fifth Report, Historical MSS. Comm., p. 163.   MSS. of the Duke of Sutherland, Stephen Charlton to Sir R. Leveson.

leaders, ' the grandees,' as they are termed, answered the Protector's objection to the title, and repeated all the old arguments in its favour.[1] Whitelocke added a new precedent. Henry VIII had originally been styled Lord of Ireland, but, on account of ' the inconveniences which did arise there by reason of that title,' Parliament enacted that he should assume the title of King. This was in the thirty-third year of his reign.[2] Fiennes pointed out that though, as Cromwell said, two other names and titles, those of *Custodes Libertatis Angliae* and Protector, had been accepted as designating the supreme authority, these experiments were not convincing. As to the first, ' the experience of it was but of short continuance ' ; as to the second, ' it hath and doth still stand, but in a shaking and uncertain condition'; as to both, ' they attained the end but imperfectly, and through a great deal of force.' [3]

Nearly every one of the seven speakers referred to Cromwell's argument that the title would dissatisfy many pious men, and answered it in some way or other. It was felt to be one of the crucial points in the discussion. Fiennes pointed out that many old friends of the cause were dissatisfied when kingship was abolished, and yet the men in power were not deterred thereby from doing what was then judged to be for the good of the nation. There was the same dissatisfaction when Cromwell took upon him the government under the title of Protector; ' and yet it was not held any just obstacle to what was then thought for the good of the nation.' Therefore the opposition of many good men to the present change should not be allowed to weigh too heavily in the balance. ' There is a certain latitude

[1] Burton, *Diary*, ii. 5 ; *Old Parliamentary History*, xxi. 90–121.
[2] Ib. xxi. 120.
[3] Ib. xxi. 106.

whereby respect may be had to friends ; but when the public good of the whole nation is in question, other considerations than that ought not to take place.' If the dissentients were really pious and sober men, said one speaker after another, they would in the end peaceably submit, and accept the name which the nation thought best.[1]

Cromwell's answer was deferred till Monday, April 20. It was short and not very clear ; he argued that the legislative sanction of Parliament was not what made a government firm, but rather the acceptance of it by those concerned to yield obedience to it. That acceptance was the grand question. Then, after reiterating that he had no title to the government of the nation but had undertaken it to prevent general confusion, and would willingly resign his power if the wisdom of Parliament could find out a way to settle the interests of this nation upon the right foundations, he wound up by expressing a desire to dismiss the question of kingship for the moment, and to consider divers particulars in the Petition, as to which he had something to say. He handed them therewith a ' paper of exceptions ' containing some objections and criticisms.[2]

Cromwell was evidently ill; for he spoke in a very halting manner and expressed himself with unusual difficulty. The committee returned as unsatisfied as before. ' Nothing but a dark speech, more promiscuous than before,' wrote one of them.[3]

On Tuesday, April 21, at the fourth conference with the committee, the Protector resumed the subject of the detailed proposals contained in the Instrument,

---

[1] *Old Parliamentary History*, xxi. 97, 102, 107, 116 ; see also pp. 97, 101, 108, 113 on the ' blasted ' title.

[2] Carlyle, Speech xii.

[3] Burton, *Diary*, ii. 7.

CHAP.
VI
1657

April
21

prefacing it by a long discourse on the importance of obtaining a settlement and his own endeavours in the past to attain that end.[1] Once more he told the story of the dissolution of the Long Parliament, and the reasons which had enforced the army to put an end to its sitting. Then he related the history of the calling of the Little Parliament—'a story of my own weakness and folly,' he termed it—and explained why the sober majority of that body had finally abdicated the power into his hands. Thus the nation had been delivered from two evils. One was the domination of the Long Parliament, which had swallowed up all the other lawful powers in the nation, and claimed to be a legislative and a judiciary in one. This, he said, 'would have swallowed up all civil interest, and put us under the most horrid arbitrariness that ever was exercised in the world.' The other was the domination of the Little Parliament, which, claiming a spiritual right to dominion, 'had swallowed up all our religious interest, all our ministry, and all the things we were beholden to God for.'

For this reason he was 'in love with this paper,' and above all with the idea of a settlement which would secure both the religious and civil interests of the nation. If the existing form of government sufficiently secured those things, let them stick to that, and remain as they were; if it did not, let them have something better. He thought that the constitutional scheme contained in the Petition and Advice did secure those things better than the constitution embodied in the Instrument of Government. 'I think,' said he, 'you have provided for the liberty of the people of God and of the nation ; and I say he sings sweetly that sings a song of reconciliation betwixt these two interests, and

[1] Carlyle's *Cromwell*, Speech xiii.

it is a pitiful fancy to think they are inconsistent.' Nevertheless, in some respects, the scheme contained in the Petition might be improved. The things he had to offer were not very weighty, but they would tend to the completion of the business, so he would submit them to the deputation.

His criticisms were many in number. First, he thought that the qualifications of members of Parliament, as stated in article four, were too lax, and calculated to let in enemies of the cause. He objected to the disqualification of public preachers from sitting in the House; as phrased it would exclude many who were not really and actually ministers. There was also another point in the fourth article which was unsatisfactory—that providing for the appointment of forty-one commissioners to determine whether members were properly qualified; it would be better to content themselves with imposing a heavy fine on those who took their seats without the legal qualification.

In the third article, which concerned the House of Lords, he thought it desirable to make it clear how future vacancies in that body were to be filled. As to the seventh article, which dealt with the revenue, he had a much more serious criticism to make. Parliament had promised a fixed yearly revenue of £1,300,000 for the support of the government, and temporary supplies in addition when they should be needed. On the other hand, it had not provided how this money should be raised. He desired Parliament to make both forms of supply certain, to decide how the fixed revenue of £1,300,000 should be raised, and to determine the amount of these temporary supplies, and how long they were to be continued. In concluding his remarks on finance, he pointed out that much more money than they had voted was necessary. The

present charge of the forces by sea and land and of
the civil government came to £2,426,989. The whole
present revenue of the three nations amounted to
£1,900,000, so that there was a deficit of £542,689 in
the existing budget, and the revenue they promised
was £600,000 less than that already at his disposal.[1]
Twice, he recommended this question of finance to
their attention. It was the 'chief and main thing'
in his speech, according to Thurloe.

There were but two other criticisms of importance
in the 'paper of exceptions,' which Cromwell finally
handed to the committee. He wished to remind them
once more of the necessity of Law Reform and Reformation of Manners. He urged them to confirm more
explicitly the Acts and Ordinances made since the
late troubles, and especially those made since the
Protectorate began. The security of property and
religion, and the titles of private men to their estates
all depended upon it. In Ireland the whole fabric of
society rested upon what had been done during those
four years. 'We have settled,' said Cromwell, 'almost
the whole affairs of Ireland, the rights and interest of
the soldiers there, and of the planters and adventurers.'
In England, on the other hand, the great constructive
work of the Protector's government had been the re-
organisation of the Church. 'We have settled very
much of the business of the ministry,' said Cromwell,
adding: 'I dare bear my testimony to it, there hath not
been such a service to England since the Christian religion
was professed in England.' That settlement, however,
depended upon the validity of the ordinance instituting
the Triers, and certain supplementary ordinances, which
the Protector now urged Parliament to confirm.

[1] As Carlyle points out, Cromwell states the deficit thus, but '£526,989 is
what arithmetic gives.' See Carlyle's *Cromwell*, ed. Lomas, iii. 122, 469.

If they would take these matters into consideration, and let him hear what they thought about them, he would be ready to give a final answer. ' I do not say it as a condition to anything, but I shall be very ready, freely and honestly, and plainly, to discharge myself of what . . . may reasonably be expected from me, as God shall set me free to answer you.'

' Another long speech, almost as dark as before,' groaned Mr. Burton; but most people thought it promised well.[1] ' His carriage in this debate,' wrote Thurloe to Henry Cromwell, ' was such that it gave great hopes to some that he would at last comply with the Parliament.'[2] The general view was that these circumstantial objections to parts of the Petition signified approval of the rest, and that the Protector would hardly have taken the trouble to go into such details if he had not meant to accept in the end. ' In the conclusion of his Highness's discourse,' wrote Jephson, ' we made ourselves believe we had great reason to perceive that, if satisfaction were given in the particulars—the things in the Petition being so desirable and reasonable, and settlement a thing of so absolute necessity—he would hardly know how to deny it with all its appurtenances.'[3]

Under this impression Parliament set to work to discuss the Protector's amendments. Many of the things, as Thurloe remarked, were ' not of the essence of the paper,' and were such as Parliament would find no difficulty in complying with.[4] Others were more important. ' It is reported,' says a newsletter, ' that these proposals have given the House so much work to do that it will take them a month's time at least, if they

---

[1] Burton, *Diary*, ii. 7.
[2] Thurloe, vi. 220.
[3] Jephson to Henry Cromwell, April 21, 1657. *Lansdowne MS.*, 822, f. 51.
[4] Thurloe, vi. 220.

continue sitting.' Some thought they would decline to
sit so long. 'It is certain,' continues the letter, 'that
the major part of them are much discontented, and
would fain be gone into the country.' [1]

On April 23 the House set to work, and steadily
went through all the Protector's objections from first
to last. In a week they had completed their task,
and that in a very satisfactory manner. Over and
above the £1,300,000 fixed by the Petition as the
permanent revenue of the government, they voted
£600,000 a year for the next three years as a temporary
supply, thus raising the total to £1,900,000. And to
this they added the gross sum of £400,000, for this year
only, to defray the cost of the Spanish War.[2]

They then considered the question of confirming past
legislation, and went through all the legislative work
done since 1653. They resolved that all the Acts and
Ordinances passed by the Long Parliament from 1642
to April, 1653, were valid in themselves and needed no
confirmation, adding, however, a proviso that nothing
in them was to be held binding which was contrary to
the Petition and Advice.[3] As to enactments since that
date, they confirmed the Acts of the Little Parliament
and the Ordinances issued by the Protector in the first
nine months of his government, without any material
omission. The Civil Marriage Act of the Little Parliament was continued, however, for the period of six
months only ; and the Ordinance of the Protector concerning the Triers was amended by requiring that future
commissioners appointed for the purpose should be
approved by Parliament, while the operation of that for
the ejection of scandalous ministers and schoolmasters

---

[1] *Fifth Report, Hist. MSS. Comm.*, pp. 16, 163.
[2] *Commons' Journals*, vii. 523.
[3] Ib. vii. 529.

was limited to three years.[1] Practically the House
had accepted all the amendments and suggestions of Cromwell; and on Friday, May 1, when the committee laid the resolves of the House before him, they were justified in expecting a favourable answer.[2]

The Protector promised the committee a speedy and a positive answer, and said that he would let them know when he would meet the House for the purpose. Yet some days passed and no message came. While the people outside Parliament, and most men in Parliament too, believed that he would accept the Petition, those near his person were in a complete state of uncertainty as to what he would do. Thurloe was utterly in the dark. ' His Highness,' he wrote on April 21, ' hath very great difficulties in his own mind, although he hath had the clearest call that ever man had. . . . And surely whatever resolutions his Highness takes will be his own, there being nothing from without that should be any constraint upon him either to take it or refuse it. The greatest is, which indeed hath weight in it, the advice of a Parliament.'

On April 29, eight days later, the Secretary was equally dubious. ' Whether his Highness, when all this is

---

[1] *Commons' Journals*, vii. 524, 526. The ordinance for the visitation of the universities was also limited to six months (ib. 526).

[2] ' The parlament are in good hopes still ; otherwise they would scarce have done many thinges, which for a settlement sake they have consented to. There is not one thing in his H. paper of exceptions, but they have complyed with him in ; and one of the exceptions is a matter of vast consequence ; viz. the confirminge of the lawes made by the little convention (as it is called here) and the ordinances of H.H. and councell, wherein the parlament hath taken this course : They have perused all the several acts and ordinances, and all of them, which concerne either safetie or reformation, they have confirmed ; a thinge, which tends exceedingly to the settlement of mens mindes ; and, in the oppinion of most men, too much to have been expected from a parlament. But beinge weary of rollinge from one thinge to another, and haveinge an entire confidence in his H., they were willing to come to any thinge that is reasonable, and may be judged secure for the good cause soe longe fought for ; which is the rule, that this settlement hath beene planned by.'—Thurloe, vi. 261.

done, will accept of kingship, I am not able to say.   He
keeps himself reserved from everybody that I know of.
For my part, I profess I can take no measure of his mind
therein : if I did, your lordship should have an account
of it.   Every wise man without doors wonders at the
delay.   If this Parliament settle us not, there is no
hopes to have any settlement by a Parliament ; none
will ever be brought to spend so much time about it, or
to do half that this hath done ; but on the contrary, if
this miscarry, will be obliged to steer quite another
course.   The issue is in the hands of the Lord to whose
pleasure we must submit, yea wherein we ought to
rejoice.   I know his Highness is under great difficulties
from friends, which makes his way the more darksome.
I trust the Lord will be a light to him.' [1]

A week later, on May 5, Thurloe was still in the same
doubt and ignorance.   ' On Thursday he intends to give
his final answer to the Parliament; what this answer
will be God and his own heart only knows.' [2]

In the same way the ambassador in France knew
nothing as to Cromwell's intentions with reference
to kingship.   ' If his Highness can be moved to accept
April of it,' said Lockhart, ' the services he hath done the
21   nation abundantly deserve it ; but if he, who hath so
much merited it, do judge it fit to continue his refusal,
the contempt of a crown, which cannot but proceed from
an extraordinary virtue, will render him in the esteem of
all whose opinion is to be valued more honourable than
any that wear it.' [3]

The Protector's nearest relatives were as ignorant
as his confidential servants.   Richard Cromwell, in his
letters to his brother Henry, could tell him nothing.
When the debates on the Petition and Advice began,

---

[1] Thurloe, vi. 219, 243.   [2] Ib. vi. 261.
[3] *Clarendon State Papers*, iii. 338.

Richard, who represented the University of Cambridge, retired to the country. During the discussion, words were uttered which it would have been unpleasant for the Protector's son to hear ; and he congratulated his brother Henry on being ' out of the spattering dirt which is thrown about here.' What little he did know he was afraid to write. ' Things that might be whispered ought not to be committed to paper.' [1]

Another connexion of the family, Sir Francis Russell, who was both an old friend of the Protector's and father-in-law to Henry Cromwell, expressed first one opinion and then the opposite. On April 11, writing under the influence of the impression produced by Cromwell's first refusal, Russell was convinced that he would persist in declining. He described it as a great defeat to the wise and ambitious part of this world. ' Your father,' he added, ' is at present in a notable powerful spirit, tramples this world and the outward majesty of it under his feet ; he tells me, and I do believe so much, that he is in great peace and quiet this work being over.' [2]

A minister who came from Massachusetts, William Hooke, who saw Cromwell during this period of suspense, came to much the same conclusion. ' I suppose,' said he, ' his spirit inclineth to refusal, as the case is circumstanced.' He thought the Protector ' willing enough to betake himself to a private life, if it might be.' ' He is a godly man,' added Hooke, ' much in prayer and good discourses, delighting in good men and good ministers, self-denying and ready to promote any good work for Christ.' [3]

Whitelocke, writing after the Restoration, recorded

---

[1] Richard to Henry Cromwell, March 7, 1657 ; *Lansdowne MS.*, 821, f. 324.
[2] *Lansdowne MS.*, 822, f. 35.
[3] William Hooke to John Winthrop, April 13, 1657. *Mass. Hist. Coll.*, III. i. 181.

CHAP.
VI
1657

his recollection of the Protector's demeanour during these weeks. He would often shut himself up two or three hours together with Broghil, Wolseley, Thurloe, Pierrepoint, and other confidants. ' None were admitted to come to him ; he would sometimes be very cheerful with us, and laying aside his greatness he would sometimes be very familiar with us, and by way of diversion would make verses with us, and everyone must try his fancy ; he commonly called for tobacco pipes and a candle, and would now and then take tobacco himself ; and then he would fall again to his serious and great business, and advise with us in those affairs.' [1]

Towards the end of this period of suspense Cromwell's friends began to believe that he would change his mind and accept the crown. Circumstances seemed more favourable. ' Your father,' Russell wrote to his son-in-law, on April 27, ' begins to come out of the clouds, and it appears to us that he will take the kingly power upon him. That great noise which was made about the business not long since is almost over, and I cannot think there will be the least combustion about it. This day I have had some discourse with your father about this great business ; he is very cheerful, and his troubled thoughts seem to be over.' Russell was delighted at the prospect. He predicted that in his next letter to Henry he would have to address him by the title of Duke of York. Colonel Pride, he said, had told him that he was in favour of kingship because he hoped it would be Henry's turn next.[2]

Other observers, too, agreed with Russell in believing that there would not be the least combustion if Cromwell took the crown, and in thinking that the vehement opposition of the officers had blazed out and died away. Thurloe thought so. Writing on April 21 he said : ' My

[1] Whitelocke, *Memorials*, iv. 289.   [2] *Lansdowne MS.*, 822, f. 57.

Lord Deputy and General Desborough oppose themselves with all earnestness against the title but think
the other things in the Petition and Advice are very
honest. The other gentleman (i.e. Lambert) stands at
a distance, hath given over his opposition and lets
things take their own course. Many of the soldiers are
not only content but are very well satisfied with this
change. Some indeed grumble, but that's the most,
for aught I can perceive.' [1]

On April 24 Colonel Whalley openly declared his
conversion, telling Parliament : ' I believe we all agree
to come to settlement, and to all the things contained
in the Instrument except that of the title, and for my
part, rather than I would forego the other good things
contained in it, I could well swallow that of the title.' [2]

A week later it seemed as if even Lambert would be
reconciled to the change. ' The difference formerly
mentioned,' wrote Thurloe on April 29, ' begins to be
made up again ; great professions of fidelity have been
made very lately.' [3] The utmost the opponents of
kingship did was to threaten to resign. ' My Lord
Deputy and General Desborough seem to be very much
fixed against his being King, and speak of nothing
but giving over their commands and all employment,
if he doth accept that title; others also speak the same
language so that our difficulties are many.' [4]

Suddenly a change came : the old spirit of opposition flamed up from its ashes. On Wednesday, May 6,
after a week's deliberation, the Protector sent a
message to the committee, desiring the House to meet
him in the Painted Chamber at eleven o'clock the next
morning.[5] The committee received the news with gladness, for they were confident of an affirmative answer at

[1] Thurloe, vi. 219.   [2] Burton, *Diary*, ii. 43.   [3] Ib. vi. 243.
[4] Thurloe, vi. 261.   [5] *Commons' Journals*, vii. 531.

CHAP.
VI
1657

May 6

May 7

last.   Privately Cromwell told several of the members that he would accept the Petition with the title in it ; so that it seemed as if doubt and suspense were over.[1]   In the meantime something happened that made him hesitate again.   As the Protector was walking up and down the great walk of St. James's Park he met his brother-in-law, Colonel Desborough, and told him of his resolution.   Desborough had already prophesied to Cromwell that, if he accepted the crown, he would infallibly draw ruin upon himself and his friends.   He now declared that the cause and Cromwell's family were lost.   For his own part, he added, he was resolved never to act against him, yet after that time he would not act for him.[2]   Either from Desborough, or from Fleetwood and Lambert themselves, the Protector learnt that those great officers would adopt the same line.   'The three great men,' wrote Thurloe to Henry Cromwell, 'professing their great unfreeness to act, said that immediately after his acceptance they must withdraw from all public employment; and so they believed would several other officers of quality that had been engaged all along in this war.'[3]

Cromwell determined to gain at least a few hours for deliberation.   On Thursday morning he countermanded the meeting with the House, and asked that a committee should be sent to confer with him at five o'clock the same afternoon.   When the members of the committee came to Whitehall they found that the Protector had given up expecting them, under the impression that his message had not reached the House in time.   He was somewhere in the garden inspecting a

---

[1] Thurloe, vi. 281.
[2] Ludlow, *Memoirs*, ii. 24 ; cf. Burnet, *Own Time*, i. 125.   The latter apparently copies Ludlow.
[3] Thurloe, vi. 281.

new horse which had just arrived from Barbary, and CHAP.
they waited two hours.   At last he came into the room, VI
apologised for keeping them waiting, and dismissed them 1657
once again.   They went away grumbling, as may easily
be imagined.[1]

Meanwhile the opponents of kingship were not idle. May 6
After his talk with the Protector on Wednesday, Desborough went home and took counsel with his friend
Colonel Pride.   Pride had been knighted by the Protector a few months earlier, and was now Sir Thomas ;[2]
but the idea that Cromwell should take the title of King
was horrible to him. ' He shall not,' declared Pride.
' Why, how wilt thou hinder it ? ' retorted Desborough.
' Get me a petition drawn and I will prevent it,' promised
Pride.   As both of them were better hands with the
sword than the pen, they went to Dr. John Owen, one
of the Protector's chaplains and Vice-Chancellor of the
University of Oxford, whom they persuaded to draw
up a petition according to their desires.[3]   When it
was drawn, John Mason, Pride's lieutenant-colonel,
took it in charge, and ' went up and down from
man to man,' till he got twenty-six or twenty-seven
signatures.[4]

On Friday morning the House met, as usual, about May 8
nine o'clock.   The first piece of news they received was
a report from Whitelocke that the Protector would see
them that very morning in the Banqueting House
at Whitehall.   The second was a message that a deputation of officers were waiting at the door with a
petition they wished to present to the House.   Mason
was there with three or four comrades to represent the

---

[1] Ludlow, *Memoirs*, ii. 24 ; *Commons' Journals*, vii. 529, 531 ; *Clarke Papers*, iii. 107.

[2] See *Harleian Misc.*, iii. 456, 481.

[3] Ludlow, ii. 25.

[4] Thurloe, vi. 281.

rest of the signatories, who numbered the majority of the field officers then in town.[1]   They were early because they feared to be prohibited from petitioning by their superiors, or forestalled by Cromwell's acceptance. The three great malcontents had taken no part in the movement. Fleetwood thought the intention of the petitioners 'honest,' but the petition unseasonable. ' When I knew of that they were about,' says he, ' I went and acquainted his Highness with it, who desired it might be suppressed.'   Fleetwood came a quarter of an hour too late to find the petitioners; when he reached their meeting-place they had already set out for the House, and he followed them thither.[2]   On their arrival at the House, Mason sent in a message to Desborough requesting him to present the petition.   But Desborough had made up his mind to remain passive ; and all he did was to acquaint the House with the fact that certain officers of the army were at the door.[3] The House resolved to call them in, and Mason, standing at the bar, presented the petition.[4]   It prayed that Parliament would forbear to press the Protector to any further answer concerning their Petition and Advice, he having already given them his reasons why he could not accept it.[5]   While the House was considering whether the petition should be read, Fleetwood arrived upon the scene.   He told them that the petition ought

[1] Mason, says Morgan, ' came in with three or four more in the name of some twenty more' (*Lansdowne MS.*, 822, f. 71). 'Some twenty-six or twenty-seven officers came with a petition,' says Thurloe (vi. 281). It was signed, says Ludlow, by two colonels, seven lieutenant-colonels, eight majors, and sixteen captains (*Memoirs*, ii. 27).

[2] See Fleetwood's letter to Henry Cromwell.   Morgan and Ludlow (ii. 27) give account of the way in which the Protector received the news.

[3] Ludlow, *Memoirs*, ii. 27.

[4] *Commons' Journals*, vii. 531.

[5] *Clarke Papers*, iii. 108.   Thurloe says simply that it was ' to desire them not to press H. H. any further about kingship.'   Ludlow gives a longer account (ii. 27).

not to be debated, much less answered at this time, for CHAP.
the contents of it were to desire them not to press the VI
Protector to be King, whereas their present business 1657
May 8
was to receive his answer to what had been already
offered.[1] As Lieutenant-General, Fleetwood was the
highest officer in the army next to the Protector; and
his argument that the debate should be put off was
conclusive. Accordingly the petition was laid aside,
and all the members repaired at once to the Banqueting
House at Whitehall, where James had revelled and
Charles had suffered. The Protector's speech was
brief and very apologetic. He expressed his sorrow
for the expense of time and trouble he had caused the
House. The constitution they offered him was a good
one, which would settle the civil rights of the nation on
a good foundation, and provided well for the security of
honest men ' in that great natural and religious liberty,
liberty of conscience.' But, unhappily, he had not
been convinced by their arguments as to the necessity
of the title of King. ' I am persuaded therefore,'
he concluded, ' to return this answer to you, that I
cannot undertake the government with the title of
King.' [2]

It was a stunning blow to the supporters of kingship
and to the friends of the Protector. All the world,
wrote Bordeaux to Mazarin, ' believed him on the eve of
becoming King.' [3] The party which had promoted the
Petition and Advice hardly knew what to do; and for
some days did nothing. To give time for thought the
report of Cromwell's answer was deferred from day

---

[1] Fleetwood to H. Cromwell, May 12, 1657 (*Lansdowne MS.*, 822, f. 67).
Ludlow confirms this.

[2] Carlyle's *Cromwell*, Speech xiv, May 8.

[3] May $\frac{10}{20}$, 1657, *French Transcripts, R.O.* See *English Historical Review*,
1903, p. 75.

to day.   On Saturday the House discussed cases of
privilege and trivial private bills; on Monday it debated a bill for the probate of wills. 'His Highness's
refusal,' wrote Colonel Jephson on Monday, 'hath so
amazed his real servants as I know not what to write or
say concerning it. I am sure 'tis not a discourse fit for
a letter. What resolution will be taken upon the
report of it to Parliament is not yet known; for it hath
been deferred from day to day until to-morrow. The
counsel I find most inclined to is to raise money for the
summer's service and to adjourn the Parliament for
some months. God direct us to something which may
preserve these nations from total ruin.' [1]

At last, on Tuesday, May 12, the Speaker reported
the Protector's answer to the House; but feeling ran too
high amongst the members for them to confine the
discussion to that. They fell upon the question of the
army petition, to which they attributed the Protector's
refusal. It was affirmed to be a breach of privilege, and
Bodurda, member for Anglesey, moved that the House
should vindicate their privilege in respect to the petition.
John Goodwin seconded him. It greatly concerned
the House, he said, to take notice of those evil counsellors without its doors, who advised the Protector not
to hearken to the advice of his Parliament. In the
beginning that was the cause of the quarrel between
Parliament and the late King. The debate ended as
suddenly as it rose. As the Speaker was too ill to continue sitting, the discussion of the Protector's answer
was adjourned till the next morning; and the House
went into committee on the new taxes. Both parties
were getting exasperated. In one of the division
lobbies an altercation took place between two members.
Pride angrily denounced Goodwin's speech, and said

[1] *Lansdowne MS.*, 822, f. 69.

he ought to be called to the bar for it. But Pride was
not popular in the House. Sporting country gentlemen disliked him for putting down cock-fighting in
London, and suppressing the bear pit and the bears.
When Harry Owen retorted : ' 'Twere better to call you
to the bar for killing the bears,' the crowd in the lobby
warmly applauded.[1]

On Wednesday, May 13, as arranged, the debate on
Cromwell's answer began, and lasted for three whole
days. All sorts of proposals were discussed; but ' in
that time they were so far from coming to a result that
they could never agree upon the stating of the question.'[2]

The most determined of the supporters of kingship
still resolved to continue to press its acceptance. The
consideration of the question was to be deferred for a
time, till his Highness should be better informed. In
the meanwhile the House were to raise money and pass
what good bills they could, and then, with the Protector's
consent, to adjourn for the summer. They talked of
giving the Protector three months in which to make up
his mind, while the members returned home to look
after their private affairs.[3]

A second plan was to expunge the clause relating to
the title, and to offer the new constitution once more
to Cromwell with the present title of Protector.
Monck, far away in Scotland, urged this course. ' I
received your letter,' he wrote to Thurloe on May 19,
' by which I understand his Highness has denied the
acceptance of the government under the title of king ;
but I hope he will be ready to accept of it by the title of
protector ; and that God will direct the hearts of those
in the parliament to offer it to him upon those terms.

[1] Morgan to H. Cromwell, *Lansdowne MS.*, 822, f. 71.
[2] *Clarke Papers*, iii. 100 ; *Commons' Journals*, vii. 533, 534.
[3] *Clarke Papers*, iii. 99 ; *English Historical Review*, 1903, p. 77.

CHAP.
VI
1657

For truly I think all honest men desire, that his Highness and the parliament may come to some settlement
in this business; for otherwise, unless the chief
magistrate and the parliament agree, we shall never be
able to carry on our work safely or cheerfully, and so
my prayers shall be to Almighty God to direct them to
that end.'[1]

This was the course the officers had now come to
advocate.   They pretended now, said Thurloe, that they
were very well pleased with all the rest, and that this
was the only alteration they desired.   Bordeaux, who
had predicted the adoption of such a compromise when
Cromwell first gave his answer, was convinced that
solution would be finally adopted.[2]

But the opposition to this proposal in the House was
still very strong.   'I find the country gentlemen are
very averse from this,' wrote Thurloe; 'and so long as
they keep together it will scarce be effected; but they
being under great discouragement and discontent,
it is very probable many of them will be gone; and
then this, or whatever else shall be thought fit, may be
done.'[3]

Weary of the fruitless debates the House adjourned
itself from Friday, May 15, to Tuesday, May 19, hoping
that the agreement which public debates had failed to
produce might be reached through private deliberations.
The expedient succeeded in making the issue clearer.
When the House met again on the 19th a motion was
made that 'Lord Protector' should be the title to be
inserted into the Humble Petition and Advice; 'and
that it be referred to a committee to consider how that
title may be bounded, limited and circumstantiated.'

[1] Thurloe, vi. 292.
[2] Letters of Bordeaux dated May 10 and 14.   *French Transcripts, R.O.*
[3] Thurloe, vi. 282.

This was passed by seventy-seven to forty-five
votes.[1]

In this division two things are noticeable. First,
the diminution in the number of the House. Members
were beginning to go away in disgust. On May 12,
when the Protector's answer was reported, 142
members were present and voting; on the 15th there
were 127 voters, and now their number had fallen to
122. The second point to note is that the position of
parties was reversed. The country gentlemen, as
Thurloe had predicted, were, so far as we can judge
from the names of the tellers, against the motion. Lord
Broghil and Sir William Roberts, two of the leaders of
the ' court party,' as the supporters of kingship were
called, led the opposition. On the other hand, the
majority of seventy-seven which carried the motion
was headed by two determined opponents of kingship,
Strickland and Fleetwood.[2]

The committee which was to define the Protector's
authority met in the Speaker's Chamber on Tuesday,
May 19, and brought in its report on May 22.[3] Two
sections at once revealed themselves within it. One
section, presumably the men who had supported kingship, wished to give the Protector in so many words
exactly the power which a king might exercise. The
other, consisting mainly of the military party, wished
to restrict the Protector's authority by exactly defining
its limitations, and not to refer in any way to the kingly
power. They wished, in short, to create a new office
instead of rebaptising an old one.[4]

However, as it was evident that the task of laying

---

[1] *Commons' Journals*, vii. 535.
[2] Ib. vii. 535.
[3] Ib. vii. 537.
[4] Thurloe, vi. 291, 311 ; *Clarke Papers*, iii. 109.

down a set of detailed rules for the exercise of the Protector's power would be difficult, if not endless, the
committee finally agreed upon a compromise. The
Protector, it reported on May 22, was to exercise the
office of chief magistrate of these nations, 'and to
govern according to this Petition and Advice in all
things therein contained; and in all other things,
according to the laws of these nations and not
otherwise.'

The debate was not long; for the House, which was
now reduced to 103 members, wished to get the business
over. By fifty-three to fifty votes it was resolved
to insert the resolution of the committee into the
Petition and Advice, in place of the original clause
containing the title of King which had been voted on
March 25.[1]

On May 25, therefore, three days after the report of
the committee had been adopted, the Petition and
Advice was once more offered to Cromwell. This time
he accepted it without demur, only expressing his sense
of the responsibility imposed upon him. He came, he
said, 'not as to a triumph, but to undertake one of the
greatest tasks that ever was laid upon the back of a
human creature.' 'I can say in the presence of God,
that nothing would have induced me to have undertaken this insupportable burden to flesh and blood,
had it not been that I have seen in this Parliament
all along, a care of doing those things that might
truly and really answer the ends that we have engaged
for.'[2]

The long struggle had ended at last; and, though it
had not ended in complete triumph, very substantial
success had been attained. Instead of a constitution

---

[1] *Commons' Journals*, vii. 511, 537; cf. *Harl. Miscell.*, iii. 464.
[2] Carlyle's *Cromwell*, Appendix No. 30. Speech should be ' xv.'

drawn up by a few officers and imposed upon the
nation by the army, England had at last a constitution drawn up by the representatives of the nation in Parliament, even though it was a packed and mutilated Parliament. The settlement Cromwell longed for seemed one step nearer.

All that had been gained was admirably summed up by Henry Cromwell in a letter to Thurloe :—

'Seeing Providence hath disposed matters thus, let us be contented, and thankful to God, that there is this step made towards the freedom of these nations, although all that may be wished cannot be arrived at at one time. I confess, I like gradual proceedings best, and this the better, because it seems such ; for I take the late Instrument and way of government to have been a real relief against the wild courses of the Little Parliament ; and am glad no alteration in that Instrument was effected, till time and experience have taught us both its faults and remedies. Wherefore I am contented, that the finishing of our settlement be also deferred, till a competent trial hath been made of the present way ; and although we should at last return to that very form which was of old, yet I do not think these several tossings and tumblings have been in vain, for by them men will be the better convinced of the danger of levity, and take heed how they are too wanton and bold hereafter with long settled constitutions ; besides, these things come to pass, that the works of God might be made manifest.' [1]

On the other hand, the new Protectorate was obviously just as much a stop-gap as the old. It was but a half-way house to monarchy, and the nation could not tarry there. Already there were rumours that the proposal to revive kingship would be taken up again in

---

[1] Thurloe, vi. 330.

CHAP.
VI
1657

this or the next Parliament. The feeling in favour of the old form of government was so strong that it might safely be predicted one of two things would happen: either monarchy would be revived in favour of Cromwell and his family, or the nation would recall the exiled House of Stuart. The Petition and Advice is, from one point of view, the first step towards the Restoration of Charles II.

With the acceptance of the Petition and Advice the interest of the session ends, although it dragged on until June 26. On that day the House presented, and Cromwell accepted, a supplement to the Petition and Advice, containing a number of amendments and additions which had, for the most part, been suggested by himself. At the same time he gave his assent to a number of bills, some being measures of finance, others embodying some of the social reforms which he had pressed the House to undertake.[1]

On the same June 26, Cromwell was solemnly installed as Protector, and with far greater state and formality than when he first took that office upon him. Clothed in purple and ermine, invested with a sword of State and a sceptre of massy gold, he lacked nothing but a crown on his head, and the symbolic unction on his brow and breast, to make the ceremony seem a coronation.[2]

---

[1] *Commons' Journals,* vii. 577.
[2] *Mercurius Politicus,* June 25–July 2, 1657 ; *Cromwelliana,* p. 165.

CHAPTER VII

'KILLING NO MURDER'

THESE prolonged discussions on kingship raised the hopes of the various parties who were plotting the overthrow of the government. First one, then another, tried to take advantage of them. The expectation of a breach between the Protector and the army induced the Royalists to hold back, and the Fifth-Monarchy men to appeal to arms. The one party resolved to await the favourable opportunity for action which seemed to be coming; the other party believed that the moment had already come. The intended invasion from Flanders was once more deferred. In February, 1657, the Sealed Knot urged delay, on the ground that the attempt to convert the Protectorate into a monarchy would lead, in all probability, to a revolt amongst the soldiers. In the mercantile jargon which they used in their correspondence, Charles was recommended not to embark for England with his foreign troops till he found ' a quick and stirring market.' [1]

Delay seemed the more advisable to the King's

[1] ' The horse and foot here seem extremely displeased that Cromwell useth such unwearied diligence in engrossing the monarchy, and Lambert endeavours to heighten the discontent, whereon, in all probability, will follow some violent rising; and therefore John Russell, Sir Richard Willis and their company advise the King not to embark into England with those foreign forces till he finds a quick and stirring market. I know many others desire impatiently their despatch; but if my humble opinion can signify anything, I would join it to the former, and beg a longer expectation of so likely an accident.'—Broderick to Hyde, February 6, 1657. *Clarendon State Papers*, iii. 326.

councillors in Flanders, because the Spaniards had failed to fulfil their promises. The expedition was to have taken place in December; but neither money, men, nor ships had been forthcoming when the moment came. In a memorandum addressed to the Spanish ministers, the King declared that he did not blame them for this failure, which he attributed wholly to the accidents which had fallen out in their own affairs. But it was very unlucky, for at that time the temper of England was very well prepared for his reception, and all things in readiness there. Finding it impossible to embark at the time prefixed, he had sent messengers to tell his friends that he would be with them by the end of March. 'In this disposition, things stand there at present,' continued the memorandum, 'very considerable places undertaking to declare as soon as the King shall be in a readiness to embark, and his Majesty having as moral an assurance as affairs of that nature are capable of, to have more than one port at his devotion; and he supposes there will be little question of that assurance, when it is such as he will adventure himself and his brother upon it.' March had come, but once more the Spaniards proved unable to fulfil their promises. The King complained that the supplies placed at his disposal for the expedition were less than he expected, and had led his friends in England to expect. He was not provided with the 2000 cavalry stipulated in the treaty with Spain, and to land his foot without any horse to protect them would be dangerous. Under these circumstances his Majesty inclined 'to suspend any enterprise of his own in England till the next winter.' Yet there were reasons which might necessitate an earlier attempt. The King might not be able to warn some of his friends in England in time; or they might be too far engaged to

draw back. He must be in a position to succour
them if they should take up arms. In the second
place, it was probable, from the state of English
politics, 'that such divisions and altercations
may suddenly fall out in England' that the King
would be obliged to transport himself thither. In
order that he might be ready whenever action
was necessary, Charles demanded that the money
promised by the Spaniards should be immediately
placed at his disposal, and that adequate provision
should be made for the five regiments he had raised.
If no such accidents fell out in England his troops
would remain in Flanders, and would be applied to the
service of the King of Spain in that country.[1]

The Spanish government readily acquiesced in the
postponement of the expedition, promised that every
preparation should be made for an attempt in the
following November, and undertook to provide
money to equip the King's regiments for the field.[2]
Nothing could have suited the authorities in Flanders
better than this delay. Instead of being obliged to
furnish the King with 4000 or 6000 men at the moment
when the campaign was about to begin, they obtained
a reinforcement by no means to be despised. The
Royalist regiments now numbered between 2000 and
3000 men ; and it was probable that their ranks would
be further swollen by volunteers from England and
Scotland, and by deserters from the Irish regiments in
the service of France.[3]

---

[1] *Clarendon State Papers*, iii. 330. There are two copies of this memorandum
amongst Clarendon's papers ; one is dated March 5, the other April 27. It
seems to have been drawn up in March, but not sent till April, as Don Juan's
answer is dated May 12, and refers to the memorandum as dated April 27.
—*Cal. Clarendon Papers*, iii. 253, 279, 287.

[2] *Cal. Clarendon Papers*, iii. 287.

[3] Ib. iii. 283. Johan Somer, a spy, informed Thurloe on May 5 that the
King had mustered 4000 men a month. In the campaign 2000 of them fought

The King's change of plan relieved the English government from a source of embarrassment, if not of positive danger. Granting that the Protector was strong enough to crush any force which Charles and the Spaniards could throw into England, such a landing in March or April, 1657, when the excitement about kingship was at its height, might have led to serious consequences. It is not likely that there would have been any serious defection amongst the soldiers; but every section of the opposition would have been encouraged to greater activity, and the Levellers and Fifth-Monarchy men would have seized the opportunity to rise in arms. It so happened that the letter in which Thurloe announced to Henry Cromwell Pack's introduction of the Petition and Advice contained the news that the threatened invasion from Flanders was, for the time, abandoned.[1] Therefore, so far as the Royalists were concerned, the debate about the change of the constitution, which occupied the next four months, was entirely uninterrupted. They remained idle spectators of the drama played before their eyes, profoundly interested in the turns and changes of the scene, and eager to see what the *dénouement* would be, but divided in opinion about the result. Clarendon notes with astonishment that ' very many of the King's party were so deceived in their judgments, as really to believe that the making Cromwell King for the present was the best expedient for his Majesty.' For ' they thought that the army and the whole nation would then have been united rather to restore the true than to

under the Spanish colours. Charles had now five regiments instead of four, the fifth being apparently that of the Duke of Gloucester. See *Transactions of the Royal Historical Society*, 1902-3, pp. 68-75.

[1] Thurloe, vi. 74. Thurloe writes: ' I hear Charles Stewart's intention of landing forces doth somewhat coole, the Spanyarde as yet failinge him in his supplyes promised' (February 24).

admit a false sovereign, whose hypocrisy and tyranny, now being detected and known, would be the more detested.' A revolt amongst the supporters of the Protectorate, and a revulsion of feeling in favour of the exiled King, were the results they anticipated from Cromwell's acceptance of the crown.

On the other hand, ' the more sober persons ' of the King's party ' trembled ' at the proposal, ' and believed that it was the only way utterly to destroy the King, and to pull up all future hopes of the royal family by the roots.' When they considered the condition of England, and, above all, the temper of their own party, they perceived many things which favoured the foundation of a new dynasty. ' They saw all men even already tired in their hopes ; and that which was left of spirit in them was from the horror they had of the confusion of the present government ; that very many who had sustained the King's quarrel in the beginning were dead ; that the present King by his long absence out of the kingdom was known to very few ; so that there was too much reason to fear that much of that affection that appeared under the notion of allegiance to the King was more directed to the monarchy than the person, and that if Cromwell were once made King, and so the government ran again in the old channel, though those who were in love with a republic would possibly fall from him, he would receive abundant reparation of strength by the access of those who preferred the monarchy, which probably would reconcile most men of estate to an absolute acquiescence, if not to an entire submission.' For these reasons the wiser Royalists obstructed the design as much as they could, and exulted when the Protector refused the crown. ' They who at that time exercised their thoughts with most sagacity looked upon that refusal of his as an immediate act of Almighty God towards the King's restoration; and many of the soberest men of the nation confessed, after the King's return, that their dejected spirits were wonderfully raised, and their hopes revived, by that infatuation of his.'[1]

Yet it was not till ' after the King's return ' that this conclusion was generally accepted. At the moment even sagacious men were puzzled, and knew not what solution to desire. Captain Titus, writing at the begin-
ning of April, 1657, and believing that the Protector would accept the crown, held, like Hyde, that his acceptance would be detrimental to the cause of the Stuarts. ' I cannot,' said he, ' alter my old opinion that this change is not all for our advantage ; and if he does not suddenly find some disturbance from his own party, but hath a little more time given him to settle himself, I fear others will see too much reason to be of the same opinion
too.' Six weeks later he confessed that he did not know what to think. ' I cannot justify to my reason the contradictions that I find in my opinions ; now that Cromwell hath refused the title of King, though I am confident 'tis but for a time, I find myself troubled at it, and think it hath deferred his ruin that threatened him from his own party. If he had accepted it, it may be I should have been more troubled, and thought it a grand step to his establishment.'[2]

The postponement of the King's expedition had rendered action on the part of the English Royalists impossible; while, during the crisis of 1657, their doubts and divisions deprived them of all the influence which they might have indirectly exercised upon its issue. The one section amongst the opponents of the government which was troubled by no doubts, and did

---

[1] Clarendon, *Rebellion*, xv. 32, 33, 42.
[2] *Clarendon State Papers*, iii. 336, 340.

attempt to appeal to arms, was numerically the smallest and weakest. Ever since Cromwell had become
Protector he had been bitterly assailed by the Fifth-
Monarchy men. The theocratic republic which was their
political ideal was incompatible with any species of
monarchy; and the Protector's maintenance of a national
church increased their hostility to his rule. From the
first their preachers had denounced him as an apostate
and usurper, who had taken the crown from the head
of Christ to place it on his own, and whose government
was a part of that Fourth Monarchy which it was their
duty to destroy. Feake, Rogers, Simpson, Day, and
other teachers of the sect had been imprisoned for
preaching revolt; while Major-General Harrison and
Major-General Overton, whom Fifth-Monarchy men
regarded as leaders in their coming battles, had lost
their commissions, and for a time their freedom.[1] The
influence of the party had reached its height in 1653;
in the spring of 1656, when Harrison was released from
his confinement in the Isle of Wight, he found its credit
sunk to zero and its numbers much diminished. In
Wales there were still many left; but like their leader,
Vavasour Powell, they were gradually abandoning the
distinctive tenets of the Fifth-Monarchy men, and becoming peaceable Baptists.[2] In Norfolk there were
several small congregations whose ministers were
violent for the Fifth Monarchy; but their flocks

---

[1] Gardiner, *Commonwealth and Protectorate*, i. 29; ii. 71, 268, 314; iii. 5,
264; iv. 3, 42.

[2] The pamphlet called *A Word for God*, published in 1655 and written by
Powell, expresses the political views of the Fifth-Monarchy men, but in a less
extravagant form than is usual in their writings. It is reprinted in *Thurloe
Papers*, iv. 380. See also Gardiner, *Commonwealth and Protectorate*, iv. 41.
Thurloe, writing on January 1, 1656, describes Powell as 'lately rebaptised,
and several other of his partye' (iv. 373). 'His republicanism,' says Dr.
Alexander Gordon in the *Dictionary of National Biography*, 'was of the theo-
cratic type, and in this sense he was a Fifth-Monarchy man.'

CHAP.
VII
1656
were melting away, some turning Baptists like the Welshmen, others Seekers or Quakers.[1] The headquarters of the sect were in London, though even there it was dwindling.[2]

The two chief meeting-places of the London Fifth-Monarchy men were at All Hallows and in Swan Alley, Coleman Street. At the first place Feake, Simpson, and Day were wont to hold forth when they were at liberty; amongst the Swan Alley congregation the principal mover was Thomas Venner, a wine-cooper by trade. Thurloe's intelligencers reported a growing excitement amongst the members of the Swan Alley meeting in the spring of 1656. Sermons were delivered there in which the government was denounced as oppressing the saints of God, and its fall was confidently predicted. It was said that the time of their deliverance was approaching, and that the sword of the Lord was whetted and going forth against the enemies of His people.[3]

The general election of 1656 increased this fermentation. A meeting of Fifth-Monarchy men took place in

[1] Thurloe, iv. 581, 687, 698; v. 187, 220. Carte, *Original Letters*, ii. 104.

[2] ' There is another sort of men who grow somewhat troublesome ; I mean those who are named (though falsely) Fifth-Monarchy men, who have their daylye meetinges to provoake one another to blood, and professe openly that their intention is to trye for it with the sword, if they can get any convenient number together. There are some few of them in London, although I thinke their creditt declines here very much, many of their partie haveinge separated from them. Those who reteyne their principles flocke to Harrison, who continues at his father-in-lawe's house at Highgate ; where he spares not to speake his mind freely to them who come to visit hym, which I doe not heare are many. The greatest number of these people are in Norfolk. There hath been a meetinge of about thirty of them, at which they agreed of a letter to be written to his highnesse, very full of invectives against and reflections upon his person and government ; admonishinge him to lay down his protectorship, and to be generall againe, and soe governe by his officers without a counsell ; and then they say the prayers of the Lord's people will be with hym againe.'—Thurloe to Henry Cromwell, April 15, 1656 (iv. 698). See also Carte, *Original Letters*, ii. 104.

[3] Thurloe, iv. 321, 650 ; v. 60.

London during July, at which they debated, first, ' when CHAP.
the time was for destroying and pulling down Babylon VII
and its adherents ? ' and secondly, ' what are the 1656
means of doing it ? ' In the end ' they concluded the
time to be now, and the means by the sword.' For
this purpose they sought to secure the co-operation of
the section of parliamentary republicans known as
' Commonwealths-men ' ; and a discussion between the
representatives of the two parties took place, at which
Admiral Lawson and Colonel Okey met Venner and
some of his associates.[1] Vane's ' Healing Question '
was brought forward and considered as affording a
basis for union ; but it proved impossible to arrive at
any understanding as to the nature of the government
which was to be substituted for the existing one. Both
parties were zealous for the overthrow of the Protectorate; but the Commonwealths-men wished to
restore, in some shape or other, the authority of the
Long Parliament, while the constitutional aims of the
Fifth-Monarchy men were either purely negative or
absolutely vague.[2] No agreement followed ; and at
the end of July the Protector's Council, having learnt
of the conference, sent for Lawson, Okey, Venner, and
Portman, the four chief persons concerned, but released
them after they had been examined.[3] Their impunity
was doubtless due to the fact that the attempted union

---

[1] Thurloe, v. 197. The paper giving an account of the meeting is dated
at the head July 8. I take this to be the date of the meeting, rather than
the date when the information reached Thurloe's hands.

[2] 'One party was for acting under a visible authority, and for that purpose
propounded that forty of the Long Parliament should be convened in some
fitting place (for they would not have them all neither) under whom they
should act. The other were neither careful for any authority to act under,
nor that any way of government should be propounded beforehand, but were
for action with such members as they could get, and [to] wait for such issue as
the providence of God should bring thinges to.'—Thurloe, vi. 186.

[3] Carte, *Original Letters*, iii. 112. Thurloe, however, says that Venner
eluded the search made for him (vi. 186).

had proved abortive, and to the apparent insignificance of Venner and his followers.

The conduct of Venner and the Fifth-Monarchy men showed that the government under-estimated their boldness and their persistency. Unable to procure the co-operation of the Commonwealths-men, they determined to act without them, and to rise in arms at the first convenient opportunity.[1] In December, 1656, the government released Feake, Rogers, and Sir Henry Vane from their imprisonment; and, while Vane retired to the country, the other two began to attack the government again in sermons or pamphlets.[2] Preaching at All Hallows on January 5, Feake held forth for three hours on the history of his imprisonment and the ecclesiastical policy of the government. 'I am the same man still,' said he, 'not a jot changed in my principles, but as zealous as ever against Babylon, and against all her daughters. I say, the government is as Babylonish as ever; and there is as much of Babylon in the civil state, and the lawyers, and the old popish laws, and the clergy-state, as ever. This power and the old monarchy are one and the same; and this army doth as really support popery, and all the reliques of it,

---

[1] The first occasion proposed was the funeral of Pendarvis, a prominent member of the party. It took place at Abingdon on September 30, 1656; but, though there was a gathering of the sect, the appeal to arms was postponed (Thurloe, vi. 186; Wharton, *Gesta Britannorum*, 1657).

[2] The release of Rogers is mentioned in *Mercurius Politicus*, January 15–22, 1657, p. 7541. Feake's discharge, and that of Vane and Rogers, was ordered on December 11, 1656.—*Cal. State Papers Dom.*, 1656–7, p. 194.

Of the Fifth-Monarchy pamphlets published during this period the most notable are :—*A Looking Glass for, or an Awakening Word to the superior and inferior officers belonging to the Armies*, &c., E. 891, 1. This is a series of extracts from the political declarations of the army since 1647, with an appeal to the officers to remember their pledges. It is dated by Thomason October 22, 1656. See also *A Sober Admonition from some sighing souls to the officers and soldiers of the Army*, E. 902, 4. Dated February 2, 1657. *A Witness to the Saints in England and Wales, by some of the Mourners in Zion*, E. 915, 2. Dated June 15, 1657.

as ever King Charles and the archbishop of Canterbury, and the rest of the bishops did. For what means else your national church government, your corrupt state-clergy, and your college-clergy, your university-clergy, and court-chaplains ?   What are the court of Triers, but your court of archbishops and bishops, &c., that a man shall not preach the gospel without a pass-port from them ?   And what are the parish priests, and the other before-mentioned, but the same with your monks, and old Babylonish priests, and your deans and prebends ? ' [1] Some of his brethren, he continued, complained that his doctrine, instead of healing the breaches amongst the Independents, divided and separated them, but he held it needful to divide and separate them still more.   ' When the churches are gathering corruption, and striking in with the anti-christian powers of the world, and complying with the interest of Babylon, 'tis high time then to rouse them, and give them disturbance and wake those that are faithful among them, that they may see whither they are fallen, and return to their first love.   You may call it rending in pieces if you please ; but this I say, and I publish it here, as the first-fruits of my liberty among you, that till the churches be more rent and torn from the corrupt interest, and have less of Antichrist and Babylon among them, they ought to be rent.'

Feake went too far for many of the audience. His old fellow-prisoner, John Simpson, rose and contra-dicted his doctrine about the Babylonish nature of civil government, and condemned it as dangerous.   Other leading Baptist teachers followed the example, and the meeting closed in confusion. Fifth-Monarchy views had evidently lost their hold on Baptists and Inde-pendents in general. Some ministers said openly that

[1] Thurloe, v. 756.

people who tried to interpret such obscure books as
the prophecy of Daniel and the Revelation were
fools.[1]

John Rogers, who, like Feake, was addicted to the
interpretation of prophecy, was still more violent than
Feake. He published a pamphlet containing a detailed
account of his imprisonment, and a denunciation of the
Protector. Cromwell was styled a ' mis-shapen court-
monster ' and a ' bastard of Ashdod.' He was ' the
seed of the Dragon, begotten in darkness, brought forth
in weakness, nourished with unreasonableness, growing
up in wickedness, to continue with shortness, and to be
confounded with the fierceness of the wrath of God.'
The ' Little Remnant ' were exhorted to be up and
doing. ' Come, sirs, prepare your companies, for King
Jesus his Mount Sion muster-day is at hand ; his
magazines and artillery, yea his most excellent mortar
pieces and batteries be ready ; we wait only for the
word from on high to fall on, and faith and prayer to
do the execution according to Rev. xviii. 6 : " Reward
her as she hath rewarded you." Then, by the grace of
God, the proudest of them all shall know we are engaged on life and death, to sink or swim, stand or fall
with the Lord Jesus our Captain general upon his red
horse against the Beast's government, so as neither to
give nor take quarter, but according to his orders.' [2]

With such teachers it is not surprising that the
ignorant fanatics who formed the rank and file of the
Fifth-Monarchy party were eager to act, and confident
of success. They were few in number, but they com-
forted themselves with texts from the prophets. ' A
little one,' said Isaiah, ' shall become a thousand, and a
small one a strong nation ' ; and again, ' a thousand shall

[1] Thurloe, v. 755-9.
[2] *Life of John Rogers,* p. 296, from his *Jegar Sahadutha,* E. 919, 9.

flee at the rebuke of one.'[1] Venner and the Coleman
Street congregation took the lead, but other little bodies
co-operated. The first thing needful was to decide
what to put in place of the existing government, for
they found it a ' great prejudice, that they were against
everything but propounded nothing.' Accordingly ' a
declaration was penned ' and ' a form of government '
agreed upon.[2] This manifesto, which is entitled ' A
Standard set up,' began with a general denunciation
of the Protector's government.[3] In its historical
summary of events since the close of the war it
followed very closely the lines of Cromwell's narrative
in his speech to the Little Parliament, and sometimes
quoted his very words. That assembly of ' saints '
was glorified, and its resignation of authority pronounced invalid. Cromwell's assumption of power
was therefore an act of usurpation and apostasy. ' He
is guilty of high treason on the account of God and man
in the erecting this government.' His actions ' exceed
the rage, oppression and treason of the late king, for
which he was brought to justice.' ' He hath sinned
against the Lord Jesus Christ and His people.' Then

[1] Isaiah xxx. 17 ; lx. 22.

[2] Thurloe, vi. 186. According to the Secretary, the form of government
was not actually drawn up by Venner, but by some of the secret allies of the
Fifth-Monarchy men, by ' those who set all these things on foot, and will shew
themselves if the business had took as will· appear.' This points to the complicity of Harrison, Carew, and other men of mark, but confirmatory evidence
is lacking.

[3] 'A Standard set up : Whereunto the true Seed and Saints of the most
High may be gathered together into one, out of their severall Forms : For the
Lambe against the Beast, and False Prophet in this good and honourable
Cause. Or the Principles and Declaration of the Remnant, who have waited
for the blessed Appearance and Hope. Shewing, how Saints as Saints, men as
men, and the Creation shall have their blessings herein, as in the Deliverance
of the True Church out of Babylon, and all Confusion; as in the most
Righteous and Free Common-Wealth State; as in the Restitution of all things.
Subscribed W. Medley Scribe. Gen. xlix. 9. Who shall rouse him up ? Deut.
xxxiii. 27. Isai. lx. 22. Isai. lxii. 10. Rev. xix. 2. Printed in the Year
1657.' E. 910, 10.

CHAP.
VII
1657

came a sketch of the new form of government which the Fifth-Monarchy men sought to establish in England. There was no word of inherited rights or ancient laws, but a brief assertion that ' all earthly governments and worldly constitutions ' must be ' broken and removed ' to make way for ' the kingdom of Christ.' Nor was there any mention of the sovereignty of the people ; for the new state was to be a pure theocracy. ' The supreme absolute legislative power and authority to make laws for the governing of the nations, and the good and well-being of mankind, is originally and essentially in the Lord Jesus Christ, by right, conquest, gift, election, and inheritance.' The Scriptures, being ' the revealed will and rule of the legislator,' were to be the only law. There was to be a sanhedrim or supreme council—' men of the choicest light and spirit,' to represent ' the whole body of the Saints '—to conduct the government and administer the laws. The councillors were to be elected annually, by ' the Lord's Freemen,' who were vaguely defined as ' those that have a right with Christ in and according to the new covenant.' These electors were also to choose the judges of the district courts, which met every three months, and those of the towns and villages, who were to sit every month for the trial of minor cases. There were to be no tithes and no excise, no taxes at all in time of peace, and no fixed salaries for the ministers of religion. The manifesto closed with an appeal to all their brethren ' in holes and corners in the several parts of the nation,' to ' all saints that hunger after the truth,' and to ' every poor heart that desires to stand up for equity, for liberty, for deliverance from yokes and bonds,' to unite for the cause of Christ's kingdom. In their camp all ' civil and honest men ' were promised protection ; and all soldiers who still retained their 'simplicity and integrity' were summoned to separate themselves from 'the apostate and backsliding army' and enlist under the banner of the Lord Jesus.[1] The Fifth-Monarchy men had prepared a visible and tangible standard of taffeta, upon which was painted a red lion couchant in a white field, with the words, 'Who shall rouse him up?' They printed their declaration, bought pistols and saddles, horses, bags of powder, and bullets, and fixed the day for taking up arms.

As the moment for action drew near, Venner and his little band met with unexpected opposition amongst their own party. Some of the brethren held back. An objector declared that the Spirit of God was not with them, and that their design would be blasted. 'The ancient wise Christians are not with us,' he urged, pointing out that Major-General Harrison, John Carew, and Thomas Rogers all stood aloof from the projected insurrection. Still more weighty was the argument that the appointed time had not yet come. The reign of the Beast, said the Book of Revelation, was to continue for two and forty months, and it lacked as yet two months of that period. Counting from Cromwell's installation on December 16, 1654, the three and a half years were not up till June, 1657, and the rising had been fixed for April.[2]

[1] The manifesto bears the name of William Medley, to which is appended the title of 'scribe.' Medley was one of the deputation of twelve Fifth-Monarchy men who demanded from the Protector the releasing of Feake and Rogers in 1654 (*Life of John Rogers*, p. 179). He signed as secretary, but it is not likely that the manifesto was his work. Medley was the son-in-law of Venner.

[2] Revelation xiii. 5. The statement made in Thurloe, vi. 164, seems confirmed by the information printed in vi. 349. 'Col. Harrison, Mr. Pheake, Mr. Can and Mr. Rogers meet ordinarily at Mr. Daforne's house in Bartholomew-lane neer the Royal-exchange, where they profess themselves ready for an insurrection; the time being now come, as they say, wherein the three yeares and a halfe is at an end, in which the witnesses have lyen dead, and that there will be a resurrection of them.

'It is confidently believed, that upon this delusion they will ground an

CHAP.
VII
1657   These arguments for delay had no weight with Venner and his comrades. In the hope of securing aid from the Anabaptists the date was changed from Tuesday, April 7, to Thursday, April 9; but no longer postponement was accepted.[1] Their plan of campaign was extremely simple. They were to assemble at Swan Alley and two or three other places about the City, and to unite their forces at a general rendezvous at Mile End Green. What their next movement was to be is uncertain ; originally they intended to meet in Epping Forest, publish their declaration at Chelmsford, and march thence into Norfolk, where they expected to be joined by many of their sect.[2] As to arms, they had provided enough for the few score of horsemen who were to form the nucleus of the rising, and for a small number of foot.[3] Others they hoped to procure by surprising and disarming some isolated detachment of the regular forces ; and they believed that some of the common soldiers would enlist in their ranks. The spoils of the ungodly were to be employed to fill their military chest, and to be devoted to the payment of those who engaged in the work, and to the support of the families they left at home.[4]

attempt, which may be attended with some mischief, they professing it to be their resolution to destroy all, that shall oppose them ' (Information dated June 15, 1657). Compare the influence of *Pastorini's Prophecy* upon the Irish Catholics in 1823. Parker, *Sir Robert Peel*, i. 342.

[1] The first date is given in Thurloe, vi. 163.

[2] The official narrative in *Mercurius Politicus* states : ' From thence (it is said) they meant to have marched eight miles this night into Essex, and to have directed their course towards Norfolk.' But see Add. MS. 4459, pp. 111-22.

[3] Thurloe, vi. 186, 194.

[4] The resolutions of the plotters say : ' Our judgment is, that haveing a convenient place and providence, we will seize upon a troop of horse, and execute their officers, and any centinell of guard of any, and all private soldiers that do oppose us, and take their horses and arms, and horse our men withall, to take in with us such private soldiers that shall submit themselves.'

' That such gayne and spoyle as is due to the Lord, and to the treasury and work of the Lord, according to the rule and practice of the Scripture, both of

When the ninth of April came, Venner and his CHAP.
VII
followers attempted to put their design into execution.
They assembled in a house at Shoreditch during the 1657
afternoon, intending to proceed to the general rendezvous
at Mile End Green about nine. News of a suspicious
gathering at Shoreditch reached Whitehall about seven ;
and a party of horse was promptly sent to surround the
house. They found there some twenty men, armed,
booted, and spurred, bundles of declarations ready for
distribution, some money and some arms, and the
standard bearing the red lion of the Tribe of Judah. A
search revealed the fact that several hampers of arms
had been conveyed to hiding-places near the field of
their intended rendezvous ; and ten trunks of arms and
ammunition were discovered in Swan Alley.[1]

On April 11 Secretary Thurloe reported the discovery of the plot to Parliament, and laid before it the
declarations printed by the conspirators, and the
captured standard. His report implied that the government had been warned of the intended rising ;[2] and he
received the thanks of the House for his vigilance.[3] No
public trial of the conspirators took place. Venner
himself, Medley the scribe, and another of the men
taken in arms, remained prisoners in the Tower until
the end of the Protectorate.[4] Lawson, Harrison, Rich,
and Danvers, who had been arrested on suspicion of
complicity as soon as the attempted rising was discovered, were released after a few days' detention.

gold, silver, brass, and precious things, etc., be brought into a common stock
and treasury, and that officers be appointed to that charge to receive that
account.'—Thurloe, vi. 163.

[1] Thurloe, vi. 186, 291 ; *Mercurius Politicus*, April 9–16, p. 7726 ; *Cal.
State Papers Dom.*, 1656–7, p. 335 ; *Clarke Papers*, iii. 105, 106.

[2] ' It pleased God to give some light into their actions all along.'—Thurloe,
vi. 186.

[3] *Commons' Journals*, vii. 521. For the debate, see Burton, *Diary*, ii. 3.

[4] Thurloe, vi. 188 ; vii. 622.

CHAP.
VII
1657

April
22

Parliament appointed a day for the consideration of Thurloe's report, but it was too busy with the great question of kingship to spend its time in discussing an abortive plot; so the subject was first postponed and then dropped altogether.[1] The discovery of Venner's plot, like the discovery of Sindercombe's, simply increased the feeling that the Protector's acceptance of the crown would give security to the public peace. 'Both your Highness and the Parliament,' wrote Henry Cromwell to his father, 'will by this see the necessity of a closer union, and that titles and names are of little moment, in comparison of the effect which a breach or distance might produce. . . . These wild notions concerning the right of saints to reign, and the imaginary immediate government of Christ upon earth, must needs call aloud for some settlement of the government.'[2] This was the general view amongst those

---

[1] Burton, *Diary*, ii. 3. In a private letter from John Thornton to William Russell, printed in the *Life of William Lord Russell*, ed. 1820, p. 23, there is a circumstantial account of the arrest of a party of Fifth-Monarchy men near Epping, armed and mounted ready for a rising. This seems to have taken place about the beginning of May or the end of April, but I can find no other mention of this second attempt.

'Some oppositions have been made by those Fifth-Monarchy men I mentioned in my last, who were taken in time with their armes and ammunition, and standard, etc. Since which time they were attempting again, and appointed a place of rendezvous, which the Protector having secret intelligence of, sent Mr. Randall (even Joshua Randall, the sober mad-man as he called him), whom he knew to be trusty and resolute, with a party of horse to take them. 'Twas about Epping in Essex; whither he got about midnight, and found them gathering into a body well arm'd and horsed : he divides his party, and falls upon them on a sudden, firing (with powder only) in their faces, which so amazed them that they cryed quarter : and were about sixty taken (more than the party which took them; the rest escaped away), and brought to White-hall by six of the clock in the morning, with their hands bound behind them on their horse-backs; for which good service my Lord Protector hath an eye upon him that may well make him expect farther preferment. He might have had a good officer's place, if he would have gone with those forces that are sent over to help the French against the Spaniard : but his wife kept him from accepting it : and I think he would not willingly leave her for any such designe.'—This letter is dated May 7 (O.S.), 1657.

[2] Thurloe, vi. 222. Schlezer, the envoy of the Elector of Brandenburg,

who supported the Protectorate. The attempted rising
seemed more dangerous to contemporaries than it
appears to later historians. It was true that none but
inconsiderable persons—prentices, journeymen, and the
like—had actually appeared in arms, and that the
Fifth-Monarchy men were a small and decreasing sect.
But though a few desperate fanatics could effect little
against a government with so many soldiers at its
disposal as the Protector's, they could create an opportunity which more powerful opponents might utilise.
In January, 1661, the same Venner, and fifty or sixty
followers, once more took up arms for ' King Jesus ';
they beat the trained bands, threw all London into
alarm and disorder, and were not suppressed for three
whole days. In April, 1657, the conditions were far
more favourable to the prospects of such a rising than
they were in 1661 ; the number of malcontents was
greater, the government was less securely established,
and the slightest success gained by the insurgents would
have emboldened the Royalists to attempt to restore
the King, and the Commonwealths-men to re-establish
the republic. It was the perfection of Thurloe's police
system, not the military strength of the government,
which prevented the public peace from being broken.
And this vigilance was never more needed ; for, though
the Royalists were quiescent and the Fifth-Monarchy
men suppressed, the design for the assassination of the
Protector was still being carried on.

Sexby's confidence was not abated by the failure of
Sindercombe and Cecil. He attributed the discovery
of their design to the repeated postponement of its
execution. ' Poor hearts,' said he, ' they now see delays
are more dangerous than any other risk that could be

reported to his court that the discovery of the plot increased the chances that
the monarchy would be re-established.—*Actenstücke und Urkunden*, vii. 764.

CHAP.
VII
1657
run for doing the business.' Their arrest, he asserted, did not involve either the frustration of the plot for assassinating the Protector, or of the wider scheme for a rising amongst the Levellers when the assassination took place. Cecil knew too little to make dangerous revelations. Sindercombe was but a subordinate agent employed for a particular purpose, and did not know who the men were that should have seconded him. Besides, he was not the kind of man to turn informer, and would die ten thousand deaths before he would impeach anyone. ' Though,' added Sexby, ' it is to me a great grief, and to the whole a loss, to lose one gallant person by being imprisoned, yet as to the whole business this will not at all hurt, but rather quicken others to a more speedy execution of what they, as well as their friend, were at work about.' Either Cromwell would continue to bid defiance to all attempts against his person, and thus give the conspirators another opportunity ; or he would be more careful of his own safety, and thus make himself an object of contempt to his own party. Whichever course he followed, Sexby felt sure of success. ' I question not,' he boasted, ' but by the goodness of God to do his business.' [1]

Sindercombe's trial had taken place about three weeks after his apprehension. He was tried at the Upper Bench in Westminster Hall, on February 9, before Chief Justice Glyn. The recent act, rendering conspirators against the Protector liable to the penalties of high treason, facilitated his conviction, and, as his accomplices, Toop and Cecil, were allowed to turn informers, the requisite two witnesses were available.[2] He was condemned to be hung, drawn, and quartered, and ministers were sent to the Tower to prepare him

[1] Sexby to Peter Talbot, February 6, 1657. *Clarendon MSS.*
[2] An account of Sindercombe's trial is given in *Mercurius Politicus*, February 5–12, 1657. See also *State Trials*, v. 841.

for death.   The ministers found him obdurate and CHAP.
VII
unbelieving.[1]   When they tried to talk to him of peni-
tence, he refused to permit any reference to his crime. 1657
When they spoke of salvation, he replied that ' he was
for the universal point ' : held that ' all men were
brought into a saveable estate by the death of Christ,'
and ' doubted not but himself should fare as well as
others.' They spoke of his soul, and then it appeared
that he belonged to the sect which believed that, when
a man died, the soul slept with the body.   ' It may be,'
said Sindercombe, ' it shall rise again,' but he seemed
uncertain.[2]   Seeing that they could do little good, the
ministers left him to himself.

On the evening of February 13 news came to Sindercombe that he was to be executed on the morrow.   He
seemed much perturbed ; death itself did not terrify him,
but the barbarous and shameful formalities that accompanied a traitor's execution.   At midnight his warders
found him dying in his bed from some poison which he
had secretly obtained.   ' God knoweth my heart,' said
a paper he had written.   ' I do take this course because I
would not have all the open shame of the world executed
upon my body.'[3]   His admirers praised his suicide as
worthy of an ancient Roman.   Others hinted that he
had been privately poisoned by the Protector's orders.
Sexby declared that the tyrant, not daring to put him

---

[1] An account of Sindercombe's behaviour in prison, and of the manner of
his death, is in *Mercurius Politicus*, February 12–19, 1657, p. 7604.

[2] ' This is that wretched opinion of that sort of men whom we in English
call Soul-sleepers, persons so far unworthy the name of Christians, that the
ancient Heathens will rise up in judgment against them ; and in the tendencie
of it so destructive to the conveniencie of government, that it disposeth those
who embrace it, to attempt any wickedness whatsoever, any treason, sedition
or assassination, and to despise virtue, seeing it at once destroyeth both the
hope of reward and the feare of punishment, after this life is ended.'—*Mercurius
Politicus*, p. 7604.

[3] The paper is printed in *Mercurius Politicus*, and with it the verdict of
the coroner's jury and the medical evidence.

to death publicly, had ordered him to be smothered by the Lieutenant of the Tower, and promised to avenge his fate.[1]

Captain Titus informed Hyde in April, 1657, that the colonel himself would shortly set out for England, instead of leaving the business to agents. He thought that Sexby over-estimated his ability to produce a revolt in the army, but wrote hopefully about the probable results of his journey. 'I am confident that he will either procure Cromwell's death or his own; for I know he goes as much resolved to that purpose as any man can do; and I know if any man can have opportunity to effect it he will. This thing in effect is all I can persuade myself to rely upon; for that Sexby should be able by his interest to divide the army, and to get a party considerable enough to oppose Cromwell by force, I have not any proportion of faith to believe.'[2] The hostility which the proposal to make the Protector King had at first created was beginning to subside. Titus reported that 'though the opposition party in the House and army at first talked very high, yet now they are submissive enough, and begin to distrust their own strength to make any opposition.'[3] The hopes of the Royalists were based on the expectation of some movement amongst the Republicans; but the only disturbance

[1] Clarendon says that his death troubled Cromwell, who 'now found himself under the reproach of having caused him to be poisoned, as not daring to bring him to public justice' (*Rebellion*, xv. 144). He does not credit the story himself. Sexby, who speaks in *Killing no Murder* of the pillows and feather-beds with which Barkstead and his hangman suffocated Sindercombe, withdrew the charge in his subsequent confession, and said it was a foolish invention.

[2] *Clarendon State Papers*, iii. 331, 335. Clarendon came to the same conclusion as Titus in the end. Speaking of Cromwell's refusal of the crown he writes: 'The truth is, the danger was only in some present assassination and desperate attempt upon his person, not from a revolt of the army from him, which no particular man had interest enough to corrupt' (*Rebellion*, xv. 41).

[3] April 10, 1657. *Clarendon State Papers*, iii. 336; cf. Clarendon, *Rebellion*, xv. 33.

which took place was Venner's attempted rising. Sexby, however, told Father Talbot that its suppression was of no importance. ' Be not discouraged ! So long as Sexby lives there is no. danger but Cromwell shall have his hands full, and I hope his heart ere long ; for I have more irons in the fire for Cromwell than one, and he hath not cooled this, though he secured about fifty of the heads of the Fifth-Monarchy people, but not one of them dare meddle with them to take away their lives. As yet be cheerful ! It is impossible Cromwell shall carry it, if there be faith in man ; and I believe upon as good grounds as each of us have to believe one the other, two hundred thousand must fall on the ground before he carries it ; and, believe it, his own people in the army are upon the wing.' [1] He wound up with the words, ' either I or Cromwell must perish.'

In order to carry out this promise, Sexby resolved to stimulate to the highest pitch the exasperation of the Republicans against Cromwell. The excitement caused by the proposed restoration of the monarchy offered the opportunity he needed. Every Commonwealths-man regarded the Protector as an apostate and a usurper ; many held him a tyrant ; and yet very few favoured or approved the plots against his life.[2] Now, if ever, it might be possible to overcome the natural repugnance of Englishmen to political assassination, and to preach the doctrine of tyrannicide with some chance of obtain-ing a sympathetic hearing. Sexby was not a man of much literary skill or historical knowledge, but he found in the person of Captain Titus just the helper he needed. Sexby contributed to the common work a passionate

---

[1] April 26, 1657. *Clarendon State Papers*, iii. 338.

[2] Sexby confesses the existence of this objection. ' Some I find of a strange opinion, that it were a generous and a noble action to kill his Highness in the field, but to do it privately they think unlawful, but know not why.'—*Killing no Murder*, p. 23.

CHAP.
VII
1657
hatred of Cromwell, and a democratic enthusiasm which he sincerely felt, and expressed at times with a certain eloquence. Titus polished Sexby's periods, pointed his invective, supplied the necessary learning, and seasoned the whole with a satirical wit rare in the controversial literature of the time.[1] Their pamphlet, to which they gave the felicitous title of ' Killing no Murder,' undertook to prove that the assassination of the Protector was both lawful and laudable. It began by deriding the solemn thanksgiving for Cromwell's escape from Sindercombe's plot. To give public thanks for a public calamity was a mockery of God. Nobody could deny that the English were a very thankful people. As well might the Israelites in Egypt have '· cried unto the Lord, not for their own deliverance, but for the preservation of their taskmasters, and thanked God with solemnity that Pharaoh was still living, and that there was still great hopes of the daily increase of the number of their bricks.' Sindercombe had been condemned for plotting against the Protector, but he was not necessarily criminal. The question was whether he and his fellow-plotters had sought to kill a

---

[1] The authorship of *Killing no Murder* has been much disputed. In the article on Sexby in the *Dictionary of National Biography* I attributed the tract to Sexby alone. I am now convinced, mainly from internal evidence, that this was an error. Sexby never possessed the reading required to supply the classical quotations and precedents with which the argument of the pamphlet is reinforced, nor did he possess sufficient literary skill to write the dedicatory epistle or any of the more elaborately finished passages of the work. On the other hand, the conception and the scheme of the pamphlet are probably due to him. As to external evidence, both Sexby and Titus claimed the authorship: Sexby in his confession in October, 1657 (see p. 233 post), Titus after the Restoration and after Sexby's death. Evelyn describes Titus as its author in his diary for April 2, 1669, and in a copy of *Killing no Murder* now in my possession Peter Newcome, its former owner, has made the following note:—' Mem. June 17, 1697. Coll. Titus told me at his house in Bushey in Hertfordshire, on Tuesday, June 15, 1697 (as he had done the same thing some yeares before), that he writ this pamphlet at Breda ; and one Saxbie seeing it, undertooke and effected its printing.' For a fuller discussion of the question, see the *English Historical Review*, April, 1902, p. 308.

magistrate or to destroy a tyrant. That was the point to examine, for a tyrant was one ' over whom every man is naturally a judge and executioner, whom the laws of God, of nature and of nations, expose like beasts of prey to be destroyed as they are met.'

Three questions were then successively discussed : Whether my Lord Protector be a tyrant or not ? If he be, whether it is lawful to do justice upon him without solemnity, that is to kill him ? If it be lawful, whether it is likely to prove profitable or noxious to the Commonwealth ? '

The first question was easily answered. Cromwell was a tyrant because he could produce no just title to rule. ' Have not the people of England much reason to ask the Protector this question, "Who made thee a prince and a judge over us ? If God made thee, make it manifest to us ; if the people, where did we meet to do it ? Who took our subscriptions ? To whom deputed we our authority ? And when and where did those deputies make the choice ? "' Cromwell could not answer these questions. His power rested neither on God's immediate command nor on the consent of the people ; its foundations were force and fraud. Moreover, the Protector had all the outward characteristics which distinguished a tyrant. General of a free state, he had subverted liberty under pretence of defending it ; fraud rather than force had been his weapon ; he abused all excellent persons, suffered no assemblies, kept spies in all places, waged wars to divert the people, pretended a love to God and religion. According to Plato, Aristotle, Tacitus, and ' his Highness's own evangelist, Machiavel,' these were the visible signs by which a tyrant might be known, and in Cromwell they were all united.

Supposing that there was such a thing as a tyrant, was it a beast of game to be given law to, or a beast of prey to be destroyed by all means, fair or foul? Clearly the latter. 'The examples left us by the greatest and most virtuous, and the opinions of the wisest and gravest men,' agreed in holding that a tyrant might be lawfully slain by any private man. Grotius, Tertullian, Cicero, and Plutarch were quoted to prove it; and the example of the Greeks and Romans was reinforced by precedents from the Book of Chronicles and the Book of Judges. Reason as well as authority justified it. For a tyrant is 'above all other justice than that he receives from the stroke of some generous hand.' Against him the only remedy is 'Ehud's dagger, without which all our laws were fruitless and we helpless.'

Last came the third question, whether the removal of this tyrant was likely to be of advantage to the Commonwealth. Cromwell had enslaved England. Englishmen were no longer free members of an equal commonwealth, but only 'the living tools and instruments' of the tyrant. They must not think that they could continue in the condition of slaves, and not degenerate into the habits and temper natural to that condition; their minds would grow low with their fortune, and by being accustomed to live like slaves they would become unfit to be anything else. With constraint they would lose their national courage, and all other national virtues too.

'We shall not only lose our courage, which is a useless and an unsafe virtue under a tyrant, but by degrees we shall, after the example of our master, all turn perfidious, deceitful, irreligious, flatterers, and whatever else is villainous and infamous in mankind. See but to what degree we are come already: can there any oath be found so fortified by all religious ties, which we easily find not a distinction to break, when either profit or danger persuades us to it? Do we remember any engagements, or if we do, have we any shame to break them ? Can any man think with patience upon what we have professed, when he sees what we wildly do, and tamely suffer ? What have we of nobility amongst us but the name, the luxury and the vices of it ? Poor wretches, these that now carry that title, are so far from having any of the virtues, that should grace and indeed give them their titles, that they have not so much as the generous vices that attend greatness ; they have lost all ambition and indignation. As for our ministers, what have they, or indeed desire they, of their calling, but the tithes ? How do these horrid prevaricators search for distinctions to piece contrary oaths ! How do they rake Scriptures for flatteries ! and impudently apply them to his monstrous Highness ! What is the City but a great tame beast, that eats, and carries, and cares not who rides it ? What 's the thing called a Parliament, but a mock ? composed of a people that are only suffered to sit there because they are known to have no virtue, after the exclusion of others that were but suspected to have any ? What are they but pimps of tyranny, who are only employed to draw in the people to prostitute their liberty ? What will not the army fight for ? What will they not fight against ? What are they but Janizaries, slaves themselves, and making all others so ? What are the people in general but knaves, fools and cowards, principled for ease, vice and slavery ? This is our temper, this tyranny hath brought us to already ; and if it continues, the little virtue that is yet left to stock the nation must totally extinguish ; and then his Highness hath compleated his work of reformation. And the truth is, till then his Highness cannot be secure. He must not endure virtue, for that will not endure him.'

All Englishmen were bound to endeavour to rescue the liberty and honour of their country, but it was

upon the army that the duty was most incumbent.
Sexby appealed to the soldiers as a comrade in arms.
'To us particularly it belongs to bring this monster
to justice, whom he hath made the instruments of his
villainy, and sharers in the curse and detestation that
is due to himself from all good men; others only have
their liberty to vindicate, we our liberty and our honour.
We engaged the people with him, and to the people for
him; and from our hands they may justly expect a
satisfaction of punishment, seeing they cannot have
that of performance. What the people at present
endure, and posterity shall suffer, will be all laid at our
doors; for only we, under God, have the power to pull
down this Dagon which we have set up; and if we do
it not, all mankind will repute us approvers of all the
villainies he hath done, and authors of all to come.'

Not only soldiers, but every man to whom God had
given wisdom and courage, should consider it a duty to
mankind 'to endeavour by all natural means to free
the world of this pest.' Let them follow the example
of Sindercombe. He had shown 'as great a mind as
any old Rome could boast of; and had he lived there
his name had been registered with Brutus and Cato,
and he had had his statues as well as they.' Not daring
to bring Sindercombe to trial, the Protector had caused
him to be privately made away with in the Tower. But
let not this monster think himself secure because he had
suppressed one great spirit.

'There's a great roll behind, even of those that are
in his own muster-rolls, that are ambitious of the name
of the deliverers of their country; and they know what
the action is that will purchase it. His bed, his table
is not secure, and he stands in need of other guards
to defend him against his own. Death and destruction pursue him wherever he goes; they follow him

everywhere, like his fellow-travellers, and at last they CHAP.
VII
will come upon him like armed men.'[1]
This sinister threat, with a prediction that the 1657
triumph of the wicked would be short, concluded
Sexby's manifesto. The pamphlet was finished about
the end of April or the beginning of May, when all men
believed that the lengthy negotiations between Cromwell and Parliament were about to end in his acceptance
of the crown.[2] It was printed in Holland, probably at
Amsterdam or the Hague, and shipped over to England
towards the end of the month.[3] Sexby did not put his
name to it, but placed on the title-page that of his old
comrade in arms, William Allen. Allen, who was once
a trooper in Cromwell's own regiment of horse, had
been one of the leaders amongst the agitators of the
army in 1647, had obtained a commission, and became
finally Adjutant-General of the Horse in the Irish army.
He had been long suspected of disaffection to the
present government, though protesting his personal
devotion to the Protector; and about six months before
had resigned his commission on the ground of his
scruples about serving it any longer.[4]

[1] *Killing no Murder*, ed. 1689, pp. 21, 24, 26.
[2] The postscript proves clearly that it was written before May 9. ' Courte-
ous Reader, Expect another sheet or two of paper of this subject, if I escape
the tyrant's hands, although he gets (in the interim) the crown upon his head,
which he hath (under-hand) put his confederates on to petition his acceptance
thereof.'
[3] There was an English printer at the Hague, Samuel Brown, but Sexby was
at present living at Antwerp. ' It seems to me to be written on this side the
sea, by the paper and the letter,' says Hyde (*Clarendon State Papers*, iii. 343).
The books are described as Dutch print by a Custom-house officer (Thurloe,
vi. 317).
[4] See *Great Civil War*, iii. 244. There is a life of Allen in the *Clarke Papers*,
i. 432, 433. Henry Cromwell's account of his resignation is printed in Thurloe,
v. 670. It took place on November 28, 1656. Peter Newcome's note, quoted
on p. 224, describes Sexby as fathering the book on William Allen, ' who, it
seemes, was a great man for Oliver till he tooke upon him the Protectorship, and
then was as much against him. Upon the booke's comeing out Oliver sent for
Wm. Allen, and ask'd him if he was the author. Allen desired to see the booke,

CHAP.   'Killing no Murder' reached England about the
VII
1657   end of May, 1657: 300 copies of the pamphlet
were seized in London on May 25, and 1400 more two
days later, at the house of a strong-water-man in St.
Catherine's Dock. John Sturgeon, an ex-soldier of
Cromwell's bodyguard, and Edward Wroughton, one
of Venner's congregation, to whom this cargo of sedition
had been consigned, were arrested and imprisoned.[1]
Nevertheless a few copies appear to have been secretly
circulated. Samuel Morland, writing to Pell on June 4,
1657, told him that 'the most dangerous pamphlet
that ever has been printed in these times' had been
'lately thrown about the streets.' The author showed
therein 'the greatest rancour, malice and wickedness
that ever man could show—nay, the devil himself could
not have shown more.'[2] This was the official view.
To Royalist readers it seemed a masterpiece of satire
and sound reasoning. Clarendon was charmed. 'The
May   whole piece,' he told Nicholas, 'is so full of wit that I
30   cannot imagine who could write it.'[3] What pleased
him most was the humour of dedicating to the Protector himself a pamphlet written 'only to show the
lawfulness and conveniency that he be presently
killed.' He pronounced the prefatory epistle to Cromwell 'as witty a thing' as he had ever seen; and its
grave irony set the whole of the King's party laughing.

'To your Highness justly belongs the honour of
dying for the people, and it cannot choose but be an
unspeakable consolation to you in the last moments of
your life, to consider, with how much benefit to the

which Oliver lent him to read; and then Allen told him, that he knew well
enough that he had not capacity enough to be the author; but that if he had
been able to have writ it, he would with all his heart have done it.'

[1] Thurloe, vi. 315–20. Masson, Life of Milton, v. 142.
[2] Vaughan, The Protectorate of Oliver Cromwell, ii. 184, 199.
[3] Clarendon State Papers, iii. 343.

world you are like to leave it. 'Tis then only (my Lord)
the titles you now usurp will be truly yours; you will
then be indeed the deliverer of your country, and free it
from a bondage little inferior to that from which Moses
delivered his: you will then be that true reformer,
which you would now be thought; religion shall be then
restored, liberty asserted, and Parliaments have those
privileges they have fought for. We shall then hope
that other laws will have place besides those of the
sword, and that justice shall be otherwise defined than
the will and pleasure of the strongest; and we shall
then hope men will keep oaths again, and not have the
necessity of being false and perfidious to preserve themselves, and be like their rulers. All this we hope from
your Highness's happy expiration, who are the true
father of your country; for while you live, we can call
nothing ours, and it is from your death that we hope for
our inheritances. Let this consideration arm and fortify
your Highness's mind against the fears of death, and
the terrors of your evil conscience, that the good you
will do by your death, will somewhat balance the evils
of your life. And if in the black catalogue of high male-
factors, few can be found that have lived more to the
affliction and disturbance of mankind, than your Highness hath done; yet your greatest enemies will not
deny but there are likewise as few that have expired
more to the universal benefit of mankind than your
Highness is like to do. To hasten this great good is the
chief end of my writing this paper, and if it have the
effects I hope it will, your Highness will be quickly out
of the reach of men's malice, and your enemies will only
be able to wound you in your memory, which strokes
you will not feel. That your Highness may be speedily
in this security, is the universal wishes of your grateful
country; this is the desires and the prayers of the good

CHAP.
VII
1657
and of the bad, and it may be, is the only thing wherein all sects and factions do agree in their devotions, and is our only common prayer.'

Yet Sexby's malice, though it was barbed by the wit of Titus, missed its mark altogether. As a political weapon this famous pamphlet proved entirely innocuous. It came too late; Cromwell's refusal of the crown had falsified all Sexby's calculations. Instead of the swelling tide of indignation upon which he had counted, there was a general feeling of satisfaction that some kind of settlement had been arrived at. Cromwell's government was stronger than ever. The representatives of the people had ratified the dubious title which he had originally derived from the choice of the army. A republican might still regard him as an apostate, but he could not consistently argue that he was a usurper.

Sexby perceived this, and, as Titus observed, his disappointment made him morose and untractable. The confident language which he still used seemed to his coadjutor either artifice or self-deception; for Titus began to doubt whether any of Sexby's plans were likely to succeed, though convinced that their author would do all that a man could to make them successful.[1] The conviction was justified. At the end of June, Sexby, determined to see with his own eyes how matters stood, boldly set out for England. Thanks to his wariness and his skill in disguise, he was able to remain there a month, in spite of all the vigilance of the government.[2] But on July 24 he was arrested just as he was embarking

---

[1] ' Cromwell having now absolutely refused the title of King, which was a thing whereupon he founded much of his hopes, I now begin to question whether anything in his negotiations is likely to succeed, though I am still confident he will do all he can; but I know not how much that will be, though he himself be still sanguine, which is either his artifice or his disease.'—Titus to Hyde, May 23, 1657. *Clarendon State Papers*, iii. 340.

[2] *Cal. Clarendon Papers*, iii. 310; *Clarendon State Papers*, iii. 357.

for Holland again. Had he not been betrayed by one CHAP.
VII
of his associates he might have escaped; for he was
' in a mean habit disguised as a countryman, and his 1657
visage altered by an overgrown beard.' [1]

The Protector committed Sexby to the Tower, but,
like Venner, he was never brought to a trial. For
within ten days of his commitment he fell ill of a fever,
and so continued for about nine weeks. A second
attack of fever followed, and, ' having been awhile distracted in mind and being sick,' he died on January 13,
1658. In the interval between these illnesses Sexby
made a confession to the Lieutenant of the Tower, which
he afterwards confirmed before several witnesses.[2] He
admitted that he was ' guilty of the whole business of
Sindercombe,' had furnished him with five hundred
pounds and with arms, and had received money from
Spain to create confusion in England by the killing of
the Lord Protector. His other confederates he would
not name, in order ' not to cast away the lives of others.'
But they were no longer dangerous ; he was sure they
would not meddle any further in the design against the
Protector, ' having had their undertaking so frustrated,
and seeing plainly that God was against them.' As for
the book called ' Killing no Murder,' it was ' his own
work ' ; and he was still of the opinion that he might
lawfully have destroyed the Protector, ' because he was
not chosen and set up by the people.' Now, however,
' the case was altered, the Parliament having settled
the government upon him.' [3]

It was therefore true, as the promoters of the
Petition and Advice had urged, that the change they

---

[1] *Clarke Papers*, iii. 114 ; Thurloe, vi. 425 ; *Mercurius Politicus*, July 23–
30, 1657.

[2] An account of his illness and death is given in *Mercurius Politicus*, January
14–22, 1658, p. 251.

[3] Thurloe, vi. 560.

desired would make the life of Cromwell more secure.
Their view was that, by there-establishment of hereditary
kingship, his life would cease to be the only barrier
against anarchy, and, therefore, the one mark aimed at
by conspirators. Events had turned out differently
from what they had expected. Cromwell's life was
more secure, and the peace of England was more secure,
because the Petition and Advice marked the acceptance of his government by the representatives of the
nation. This is what Sexby meant when he said the
case was altered.

During the remaining period of Cromwell's rule
there were rumours of designs against his life, but
no serious plots. In August, 1657, one Gardiner was
apprehended in Whitehall ' with two pistols charged in
his pocket,' upon suspicion of intending to assassinate
the Protector. He had been making suspicious inquiries
about Cromwell's movements, loitering about Hampton
Court and St. James's Park, and asking whether it
was true that his Highness wore a coat of mail under
his clothes. Inquiry, however, did not show that he
had any very definite design, or any known accomplice
abroad.[1]

Pistols were not the only weapons thought of, and
there was also some fear of poison. On January 2,
1658, Lockhart, the English ambassador in France,
warned Thurloe to take care that no persons bearing
letters from the Queen of Sweden should be admitted
to the Protector's presence; and that any letter they
brought should be read by somebody else or burnt.
One of these messengers, an Irish priest, had boasted
that he could ' so empoison a letter that the receiver of
it should be endangered.' ' Your Lordship,' added
Lockhart, ' cannot imagine to what height the malice of

[1] Thurloe, vi. 477.

his Highness's enemies here is grown ; there is nothing
that a base and wretched spirit can be prompted to, but
it may be apprehended from them.' [1]   There was once
great excitement among the Protector's Council over
the arrival of an Italian, one Passerini, from Queen
Christina; they thought that, being an Italian, he might
bring poisoned letters, and his desire to see Cromwell in
private heightened the distrust ; but the Protector only
laughed at their cautious counsels, and saw him all the
same. [2]

Cromwell took reasonable precautions and was
properly guarded when he rode abroad, but that was all.
Of the terror of assassination which Royalist legends
attribute to him there is no trace anywhere. Heath
in his ' Chronicle,' published in 1663, is the first to give
shape to these floating reports. ' Now,' says he, ' did
the Usurper feel the thorns of his unjust acquist in the
restless fears and disquiets which measured every
moment of his time, his sleeps being disturbed with
the apprehension of those dangers the day presented
unto him in the approaches of any strange face, whose
motion he would fixedly attend ; above all he very
carefully observed such whose mien or aspect were
featured with any cheerful or debonair lineaments, for
such he boded were they that would despatch him ; to
that purpose he always went secretly armed, both
offensive and defensive, and never stirred without great
guard ; in his usual journey between Whitehall and
Hampton Court, by several roads he drave full speed
in the summer time, making such a dust with his life
guard, part before and part behind, at a convenient
distance for fear of choking him with it, that one could
hardly see for a quarter of an hour together, and always

---

[1] *Clarendon State Papers*, iii. 385.
[2] Whitelocke, *Memorials*, iv. 290 ; Thurloe, vi. 713.

CHAP.
VII
1657
came in some private way or other; he likewise never lodged above twice or thrice in one room, to which there was no passage but by twenty several locks.'[1]

Clarendon tells the same story. Cromwell, he says, after refusing the crown, ' never had the same serenity of mind he had been used to,' as if he were troubled and conscious that he had been untrue to himself, and so he was ' much more apprehensive of danger to his person than he had used to be.'[2] ' Insomuch as he was not so easy of access, nor so much seen abroad, and seemed to be in some disorder, when his eyes found any stranger in the room, upon whom they were still fixed. When he intended to go to Hampton Court, which was his principal delight and diversion, it was never known till he was in the coach which way he would go ; and was still hemmed in with his guards before and behind ; and the coach in which he went was always thronged as full as it could be with his servants, who were armed ; and he never returned the same way he went ; and rarely lodged two nights together in one chamber, but had many furnished and prepared to which his own key conveyed him, and those he would have with him when he had a mind to go to bed ; which made his fears the more taken notice of and public, because he had never been accustomed to those precautions.'

These legends were accepted by Hume,[3] and passed into English history, but in reality Cromwell feared the face of no man, and was not perturbed by imaginary dangers. At home and abroad he had more important things to think of.

---

[1] Heath, *Chronicle*, 1663, pp. 80, 731 ; cf. Heath's *Flagellum*, p. 204.
[2] *Rebellion*, xv. 143. Clarendon evidently copies Heath. •
[3] *History of England*, ed. 1841, v. 405.

CHAPTER VIII

BLAKE AT SANTA CRUZ

THREE days after Cromwell's acceptance of the Petition
and Advice, and about three weeks after his refusal of
the crown, the news of Blake's destruction of the Spanish
fleet at Santa Cruz came to England.

Blake's success was the reward of a long period of
patient vigilance and apparently fruitless labour. Ever
since Montagu left him to carry the treasure, captured
by Stayner, to England, he had been cruising off the
coast of Spain.[1] At the end of August the Protector had
ordered Blake to send Montagu home with the heavier
ships, and to keep his station with the lighter. In
obedience to this order, Blake sent to England with
Montagu the *Naseby*, the *Resolution*, the *Andrew*, and the
Rainbow. At the same time he transferred his own flag
from the *Naseby* to the *Swiftsure*, a fifty-four-gun ship,
which was the largest vessel remaining under his command. In the instructions ordering this division of the
fleet the Protector explained the reasons which led him
to keep a squadron at sea during the winter months
instead of recalling the whole of the fleet in the autumn,
according to the traditional fashion. The great object
of the Spaniards, explained Cromwell, was to carry on
their trade to the West Indies ; and therefore the chief
aim to be kept in view was to intercept their fleets either
going or coming. The squadron should also attempt to

---

[1] See chapter ii. p. 56.

prevent materials for shipping or other contraband goods from entering Cadiz, and interrupt the communication between Spain and Flanders. It would also serve to preserve English trade with Portugal and the Mediterranean, which without its protection could not be carried on with security.[1]

Before this letter reached them the two admirals had adopted a more thorough-going plan of action than the Protector proposed. On September 16 Montagu wrote that he and Blake had decided not to send the great ships home, as they had received no orders to that effect. It was unnecessary to do so, since they could now use Lisbon as a naval base. 'We have,' said he, 'this harbour to friend for shelter and provisions.' Besides this it was inadvisable to divide the fleet when there was at last some prospect of a battle. 'We now hear that Spain hath ordered to fit eighteen galleons and twelve other ships, which we judge will be out near the latter end of January; and if ever there be hopes to fight Spain this is like to be the time.'[2] Another letter, dated September 20, conveyed further intelligence, gathered from one of Stayner's prisoners, of hardly less importance. The Mexican fleet was now in the harbour of Havana—ten ships carrying no less than ten millions of plate. It would probably arrive in European waters about December, would touch at the Canaries on its way to obtain directions, and would make for one of the Galician ports, in order to avoid the English fleet.[3]

The Protector, therefore, countermanded his earlier orders.[4] 'There can be nothing,' declared Cromwell, 'of

---

[1] Thurloe, v. 364.
[2] Ib. v. 421.   [3] Ib. v. 435.
[4] Ib. v. 518. This dispatch is undated, but was evidently written after the receipt of Montagu's dispatch of September 16, and before Montagu's return—probably, therefore, somewhere about October 1.

more consequence than to intercept the Spanish fleet
going to and coming from the West Indies, for which
end our purpose is to keep a fleet in those seas, which
may be able to fight with any fleet the Spaniards can
set forth, as the most effectual means to prosecute
that war.' In case Blake had not already sent the
great ships home, as his former instructions prescribed,
the Protector left him free to keep or to send as many
of them as he might think fit. But, anticipating that
their departure had already taken place—as in fact it
had—Cromwell announced that he was dispatching two
second-rate ships and four frigates to reinforce Blake's
fleet.[1]

Blake carried out the spirit of these new instructions with admirable fidelity. When the promised
reinforcement reached him, he would have about twenty-
six ships under his command, but, even with Lisbon at
his disposal to repair and water his fleet, it would be no
light task to keep it fit for service through the coming
winter. He relied on Montagu to represent his condition
and his needs to the Commissioners of the Navy.

' What difficulties we are likely to encounter therein,
besides those which are ordinary to the season of the
year, and how hard a thing it will be to keep the whole
squadron entire together to attend all opportunities of
service for many reasons, yourself can very well judge.
Especially our trouble will be exceeding great if the
victualling ships be not hasted away, whereof we have no
small cause to be very apprehensive ; because, as you
know, the letter sent unto us touching it was so in-
definite in all the circumstance thereof, that we may
well doubt whether that due care which is promised to

---

[1] The second-rates named in the letter were the *Unicorn* and the *George;*
the fourth-rates were the *Bristol, Taunton, Phœnix,* and *Jersey.* The *George,*
Unicorn, and *Phœnix* were at Lisbon in January, 1657 (Thurloe, vi. 4). The
Bristol and *Jersey* were both present at Santa Cruz.

be taken at home will bring forth fruit in due time to
us abroad. My hopes do very much depend upon
your noble self, who I doubt not will use your utmost
endeavour to set all wheels at work to quicken an
expedition of so great consequence.'[1] Blake was
hampered not only by the delay of the English government to send supplies, but by the difficulty of providing
proper drink for his sailors, which troubled him more
than shortness of victuals. Beer, or inferior wine
copiously diluted with water and known by the name of
'beverage,' was usually served out to English seamen
in the navy of the period, but neither beer nor the
proper kind of wine could be procured at Lisbon. ' The
great anxiety,' wrote Blake on December 8, ' is how we
may be enabled to keep the sea for want of liquor.
This country is wholly drained of beverage wines. We
cannot make up above six weeks' drink at most ; and
I am forced to buy up a quantity of good drinking wine
for a reserve, to be disposed of among the seamen in
case of necessity, which is a bad, but our only, expedient.'[2] On the continent rumours exaggerated Blake's
difficulties, and it was reported that the English fleet
was in very sad condition and unprovided of all things.[3]
Nevertheless a great impression was produced by the
fact that it successfully maintained its blockade of the
Spanish coasts through the winter of 1656 ; for this
marked a new departure in naval warfare, and no other
navy had yet attempted or achieved the like. With
justifiable pride Waller celebrated the feat in his verses
on the war with Spain. The Spaniards, he said, who
aimed at the monarchy of the whole world, were now
besieged in their own ports by our ships, and saw the

---

[1] Blake to Montagu, October 10, 1656. *Lord Sandwich's MSS.*

[2] Thurloe, v. 691 ; cf. Oppenheim, *Administration of the Royal Navy*, p. 384.

[3] Thurloe, vi. 39.

red-cross flag of England flying without a rival on the
sea.

> Others may use the ocean as their road,
> Only the English make it their abode,
> Whose ready sails with every wind can fly,
> And make a covenant with th' unconstant sky;
> Our oaks secure as if they there took root,
> We tread on billows with a steady foot.[1]

The only navy which could hope successfully to challenge the English was that of Holland ; and during the autumn of 1656 and the spring of 1657 there were continual rumours that the Dutch would intervene in the war. It was certain that, for commercial reasons, their sympathies were enlisted on the side of the Spaniards ; and it was often said that Dutch men-of-war would be engaged to protect the plate fleet in its voyage from America, or to transport its cargo of silver to Spain. This belief was strengthened by the sending of Admiral de Ruyter to the Mediterranean in December, 1656. De Ruyter had six men-of-war under his command, but was to unite with the others which were already in that sea or in Spanish waters, and he was in charge of a convoy of eighty or a hundred merchantmen. Before sailing, he received secret orders from the admiralty of Holland, enjoining him not to suffer the vessels he convoyed to be searched by English men-of-war, and to resist the attempt to do so by force if necessary. He was also to take great care that the said vessels carried no Spanish goods, and to prevent Dutch ships from conveying articles which were contraband of war into the ports of Spain and its dependencies.[2] Though these instructions did not necessarily mean war with England, it was obvious that they might produce

---

[1] ' Of a War with Spain and a Fight at Sea.' *Works*, ed. Drury, p. 152.
[2] *La Vie de Michel de Ruiter, traduite du Hollandois de Gerard Brandt*, by Aubin, 1698, pp. 73-5.

that result, if the captains of English men-of-war persisted in searching vessels convoyed by Dutch ships, as they had recently been doing. However, neither the English nor the Dutch government wished for war ; and a maritime treaty between the two powers was being negotiated at the moment for the settlement of this and other outstanding subjects of dispute. De Ruyter's expedition was rather directed against France than England. His instructions told him to attack the corsairs of the Barbary states, and privateers who, under the Portuguese or any other flag, had plundered Dutch merchantmen. In particular, he was ordered to exercise reprisals against the French privateers who issued from the ports of Provence to prey upon Dutch traders. It was credibly stated that, since the last treaty between the United Provinces and France, some 328 Dutch ships had been plundered or taken by them ; and that, when sentences ordering restitution were obtained from French law courts, their execution was invariably frustrated by violence or intrigue. Tired of diplomatic representations which produced no result, the Dutch had resolved to right themselves by force.[1]

With two such serious tasks on his hands, De Ruyter was not likely to involve himself in fresh complications. Nevertheless, as soon as his squadron arrived at Cadiz—which it did about the end of January, during the temporary absence of Blake's fleet—the rumour spread that he had come to help the Spaniards against the English. The Duke of Medina-Celi, with whom De Ruyter had an interview three days after his arrival, positively informed the Dutch admiral that a treaty had been made between Don Estevan de Gamarra, the

---

[1] *Vie de Michel de Ruiter*, pp. 73–5 ; Wicquefort, *Histoire des Provinces-Unies*, ed. by Chais van Buren, ii. 435, 441, 463–74 ; Chéruel, *Histoire de France sous le Ministère de Mazarin*, iii. 58.

Spanish ambassador at the Hague, and the States General, by virtue of which the squadron was to be employed to protect the coming treasure-ships. De Ruyter could only reply that he had no such information from his government, and that, in the absence of express orders from them, he could do nothing of the kind. He left Cadiz and entered the Mediterranean with his convoy early in February.[1]

About the same time, Blake, who had been driven off his station by a storm which forced him as far south as Tetuan, returned to Lagos Bay. His health was bad ; and, though his ships were safe, the condition of flagship and fleet left very much to be desired.

' The Lord,' he wrote to Montagu, ' hath been pleased in a great mercy to provide for our safety. And in particular for myself in supporting me against the many indispositions of my body, so that by His blessing I doubt not to be enabled to continue out in the service the ensuing summer. The supply of the four months' victuals, which the Commissioners have appointed for us, I hope will be the last supplies to this voyage. I cannot imagine them so insensible of my condition as to condemn me to the durance of another winter. Neither can I conceive it advisable as to the public interest to keep out this squadron so long. The *Swift-sure*, in which I was, is so foul and unwieldy through the defects of her sheathing laid on for the voyage of Jamaica, that I thought it needful to remove into the *George;* although in regard both of necessary and honourable appointments answerable to the

Feb. 9

[1] De Ruyter arrived at Cadiz January $\frac{10}{20}$, and left January $\frac{18}{28}$. Brandt, p. 77, relates the story, placing the interview on January $\frac{13}{23}$. See also Thurloe, vi. 4. Mazarin on December 16, 1656, sent Bordeaux notice of Gamarra's plan, and of Medina-Celi's projected conference with De Ruyter to arrange its execution : Chéruel, *Ministère de Mazarin*, iii. 38 ; *Lettres du Cardinal Mazarin*, vii. 435.

CHAP.
VIII
1657

countenance and consequence of the ship [she is] much unfit to bear the standard of England, there being very few fourth-rate frigates but were better gunned in the upper and middle tier than we. I desire you will be pleased to examine the truth and grounds of these things; for indeed they are very enormous and such as make us ashamed to behold. And I believe if his Highness were thoroughly acquainted with them he would be much offended at them. . . . All the rest of our fleet are in a bad condition, and not fit to be kept out to the difficulties and hazards of another winter. Besides there is a great want of men, which cannot possibly be recruited here, and no provisions for sick and wounded, with many other discouragements. But the goodness of the Lord towards us and never to be forgotten is far greater than all the discouragements of men. Notwithstanding the great tempests of wind that we have encountered, without the Straits and within, we are all together and behold one another's face with comfort. The *George* and the *Unicorn* with the storeships are come to us in a seasonable time. And God hath vouchsafed such weather that we have got out all very near, notwithstanding much difficulty which doth usually attend such occasions, we being enforced before we can take out our provisions to provide ballast for them. . . . Sir, the indisposition of my body permits me not to be more tedious; and therefore as I began so I desire to end, wishing you all health and happiness in the Lord.' [1]

The conflicting reports which Blake received about the plans of the Spaniards caused him some perplexity. At one time it was said that they were equipping twenty or thirty ships at Cadiz, and intended to fight him; at

[1] Aboard the *George* at sea, off Lagos Bay, February 9, 1656–7. *Lord Sandwich's MSS.*

another time it was as positively asserted that they would only send out eight ships, and those with instructions to evade him and make their way to America.[1] Of the movements of the plate fleet he had for some time heard nothing. At last, on February 18, Blake ascertained the truth upon indubitable authority. He was under sail for Cadiz Bay, with twenty-nine ships under his command, when he met a merchantman called the *Catherine* of London, bound from Barbadoes to Genoa. Her commander, David Young, had fallen in with the Spanish galleons on their voyage to Europe, and kept them in sight for many days, and had left them steering a direct course for the Canaries. Young was no ordinary merchant skipper; he had once been lieutenant of the *Amity* frigate, and had lost his right hand in one of the battles against the Dutch. Realising, therefore, at once the importance of the information he had obtained, he resolved to seek out his old commander instead of pursuing his voyage to the Straits.[2] On receiving Young's news, Blake fired a salvo for joy and hastened to Cadiz. Arrived there he summoned Vice-Admiral Bourne and Rear-Admiral Stayner to a council on board the flagship.[3] Their advice was

---

[1] Thurloe, v. 556, 743; vi. 4, 18, 48, 96. *Mercurius Politicus*, p. 7486.

[2] Thurloe, vi. 153, 184; Weale's Journal (*Sloane MS.*, 1431); *Cal. State Papers Dom.*, 1657–8, pp. 243, 545. Young's owners deprived him of his command for this disobedience, and all that the English government did for him was to recommend him for a command in the Swedish navy.

[3] Stayner says the meeting took place on February 17, when Blake was lying in the Bay of Cadiz with twenty-nine sail of men-of-war. 'The generall,' he continues, 'called the vice-admirall and me on board at that time; our advice was, that he would put five or six weekes victualls into 6 or 8 sayle of the best frigatts and send them to meet them; but he would not hear of dividing the fleet, but called a councell, and imparted the intelligence to the comanders, and required their advice, which also was to send a party to the Canaries to meet them; but the Generall inquiring what provisions was in the fleet found not one monthes victualls at six to four mens allowance.' On the other hand, Weale says in his Journal under February 18: ' Under sayle with a very fayre gale for Cadiz, and hee meets with a shipp which came from the Barbadoes, commanded by Lieutenant David Young (formerly lieut. of the *Amity*

that he should pick out six or eight frigates, provision them for six weeks, and send them to meet the Spaniards. A council of captains gave the same advice ; but Blake refused to listen either to captains or admirals. With them the prospect of prize-money was the dominant motive. If the frigates could catch the galleons at sea they might be as successful as Stayner had been, and reap an even richer harvest. Some of the Spanish ships might escape, some would go to the bottom in the fight, and the bulk of the captured treasure would be claimed by the state ; but in any case a large part of the plunder would fall to the victors. Blake's strategy was dictated by less simple considerations, and he refused to divide his fleet. In the first place it was pretty certain that the Spaniards had received news of the coming of the galleons ; and it was probable that the fleet which was being equipped in Cadiz would put to sea to protect their arrival. To destroy the last war-ships which Spain could get together seemed to him an object of more immediate importance than to intercept the plate fleet on its way to the Canaries. The total destruction of the Spanish navy would make it impossible for the treasure to reach Spain, even if it did not fall into the hands of the English.

Moreover it was at present absolutely impossible to equip a squadron for such a cruise as the captains proposed. The provisions of the fleet were almost spent. Blake found upon inquiry that there were not victuals

frigate), who informed us of 12 sayle of galleounes comeing for Spayne. The generall for joy fireth 4 piece of ordnance and standeth away off on a wind and lee-haled : it bloweth indifferent fresh and wee stand off all night' (*Sloane MS.*, 1431). Weale goes on to say that they joined the rear-admiral and his squadron on February 21 ; therefore Stayner antedates the council in placing it on February 17. Stayner's narrative is addressed to Charles II, and was written some years after the events it relates (*Add. MS.*, 32,093, f. 372). John Bourne seems to have become vice-admiral when Badiley went home, and Stayner rear-admiral at the same time.

available for more than a month or so, even if rations were reduced and six men put upon the allowance of four.[1] Until the long-delayed supplies arrived from England all that the fleet could do was to remain upon its station. Accordingly Blake ordered his ships to lie between Cape Santa Maria and Cape Spartel, Bourne's squadron to the north of the line, his own in the centre, and Stayner's to the south, so as to cover as wide a space as possible.[2] The fleet kept its station till the end of March, when it put into Lagos Bay to water. There, on March 26, it was joined by the *Yarmouth* frigate, which brought with her the much-needed victualling ships from England. They carried six months' provisions for the fleet; and Blake lost no time in transferring their contents to his own ships. ' No man living,' said a letter from one of his officers, ' remembereth so much goods taken out and in, in so short a time, without the least damage either to the provisions or ships, which were board and board.' The transhipment took place in Trevila or Tavira Road, a Portuguese harbour about fifty miles north of Cadiz.[3] While the fleet lay there, news came that the treasure ships had reached the Canaries. Thereupon Blake's impatient subordinates urged him to sail direct to the islands; but he insisted on revisiting Cadiz Bay first, and, leaving Tavira on April 8, was off the bar of St. Lucar the next day. There message after message came to him from his intelligencers, all telling the same

---

[1] Stayner's narrative (*Add. MS.*, 32,093, f. 372). On October 2, 1656, the Admiralty had been instructed to send four months' provisions, for 4500 men, to the fleet under Blake and Montagu (*Cal. State Papers Dom.*, 1656–7, p. 122). These or other victuallers arrived at Lisbon early in November (*Mercurius Politicus*, p. 7502).

[2] Ib.; Stayner's narrative.

[3] Ib.; Thurloe, vi. 153; letter from aboard the *Jersey* frigate, May 6, 1657, printed in *Mercurius Politicus*, p. 7825; *Cal. State Papers Dom.*, 1656–7, pp. 193, 198, 343.

CHAP. story. The galleons, it was said, had landed the king's
VIII treasure and the best part of their cargo at Teneriffe, and
1657 lay at anchor there in the Bay of Santa Cruz, which had
been strongly fortified to protect them. On April 13
arrived one William Sadlington, captain of an English
privateer, who declared that he had seen the galleons
lying in the bay, and had marked their position.[1]

Blake delayed no longer. By this time he had also
made certain that the Spanish ships in Cadiz were in no
condition to put to sea. On the 13th he called his captains together; and told them that he had resolved to go
to the Canaries and attack the galleons in the harbour
of Santa Cruz. As before, he would not divide the fleet;
for it was confidently reported that De Ruyter had con-
tracted with the Spaniards to convoy the treasure from
Santa Cruz to Flanders, and that he had sailed for
the Canaries with sixteen men-of-war to carry out
his bargain. It might well be that a show of force
would prevent this attempt from being made; if not,
Blake would need all his ships to frustrate its accom-
plishment.[2] So, with twenty-three ships under his
command and a steady north-east wind to carry him
down to the islands, he set out upon his voyage.

The wind continued fair all the way, and on the evening of Saturday, April 18, Punto de Anaga, the north-
eastern point of Teneriffe, was sighted. By Sunday

---

[1] ' Sunday being the 12, being under sayle off Cales, came two small vessels
to the generall, one from Leghorn and the other from the Canary Island, being
in a private account, and commanded by one Saddleton' (letter from aboard
the *Jersey* frigate, May 6, 1657). Sadlington was paid subsequently a hundred
pounds for this service (*Cal. State Papers Dom.*, 1658–9, p. 74; cf. ib. p. 243).
Stayner puts Sadlington's arrival on the afternoon of April 11.

[2] Thurloe, writing to Henry Cromwell on May 5, summarises a letter of
Blake's, not now extant, in which Blake announces that he set sail from Cadiz
for the Canaries on April 13. ' He alsoe informes that de Ruyter is gone with
16 or 17 sail of ships of warre towards those islands to bringe that money into
Flanders; which hath occasioned the Generall to saile with the whole fleete'
(Thurloe, vi. 261).

night the fleet was off Santa Cruz Bay, and Blake's CHAP.
ships made ready for the battle of the morrow. Two VIII
frigates, the *Plymouth* and the *Nantwich*, were detached 1657
as scouts; and at daylight on Monday morning they
signalled that the enemy were still in Santa Cruz harbour,
though the shadow of the highlands made them in-
visible to the English fleet. About six o'clock on the
morning of Monday, April 20, Blake summoned his
captains on board the flagship to settle the details of
the attack.[1]

The Spaniards had seen the strange sails in the
offing, but felt safe and confident. A Flemish captain,
less assured, asked the Spanish commander for leave to
put to sea. The Spaniard laughed, and told him he
might go if he would. The English fleet, said Don
Diego de Egues, might come if they dared, for he would
serve them as they had been served at Hispaniola.[2]
There were good grounds for this proud security; for the

[1] The English accounts of the battle are (a) Stayner's narrative (*Add. MS.*,
32,093, f. 372). This, which is the most detailed account, has never been utilised
by historians of the battle. (b) The official narrative, ordered to be published
on May 28, 1657, ' as it was communicated in a letter from the General.' (c)
A series of letters from various officers in the fleet, printed in *Mercurius Politicus*
for May 28 to June 4, 1657, pp. 7822-6. (d) Weale's Journal, which contains
a few lines on the battle and supplies many dates for the voyage (*Sloane MS.*,
1431). (e) The autobiography of a Quaker, who was at that time boatswain's
mate on the *Bristol* frigate. This is entitled *The Fighting Sailor turned Peaceable Christian: manifested in the Convincement and Conversion of Thomas
Lurting, with a Short Relation of many Great Dangers and Wonderful Deliverances
he met withal.* Professor Montagu Burrows was good enough to refer me to
this book. The edition quoted below is dated 1813. Duro's *Armada Española*,
v. 24-7, 1899, contains an account of the battle from Spanish sources. He
states that he had published the report of Diego de Egues and other documents
in the *Bosquejo Biógrafico del Almirante Diego de Egues y Beamont, y Relacion
del Combate Naval que sostuvo con Ingleses en Santa Cruz de Tenerife* (Seville,
1892). I have used Duro's history, but have not seen these documents.

[2] Letter in *Mercurius Politicus*, p. 7822. The story is repeated in Heath's
Chronicle, and became popular. Prisoners reported that when the Spaniards
heard of the approach of Blake's fleet ' they derided us amongst themselves,
laughed our intentions to scorne, drank healthes to our confusion, and were
(of Spaniards) very jolly ' (*Mercurius Politicus*, p. 7826).

CHAP.
VIII
1657

April
20

harbour had been so strongly fortified that a successful attack seemed to be impossible. At its seaward extremity stood a strong castle of stone armed with forty guns or more. Six or seven stone forts, very near to each other and connected by a triple line of breastworks for musketeers, completed the land defences.[1] Along the curve of the shore, which lay in the manner of a semicircle, the Spanish ships were moored within musket shot of the forts and breastworks. In all there were sixteen vessels. Some seven of them were great galleons of 1000 to 1200 tons, and the rest were ships of about 300 tons.[2] The smaller ships lay close to the

[1] The harbour is well described by Glas : ' The best road for shipping here is between the middle of the town and a fort or castle, about a mile to the northward of it. In all that space ships anchor from a cable's length distance from the shore, in six, seven, and eight fathoms of water, to half a mile in twenty-five or thirty fathoms.

' In the middle of the town is a mole, built at a vast expense, for the convenience of landing. It runs to the northward, and the outermost part of it turns toward the shore. In mild weather goods are landed at a creek among the rocks, near the custom house, at the distance of a stone's cast to the southward of the mole.

' In going from the mole unto the town there is a square fort on the left hand, named St. Philip's, which is the principal one in the bay. To the northward of it, along shore, are some forts or batteries, mounted with guns, the most considerable of which is called Passo Alto. Near it is a steep rocky den or valley beginning at the seashore, and running a long way inland, which would render any attack of an enemy on that quarter extremely difficult. There is another fort along shore, to the northward of this.

' At the south end of the town are some batteries, and beyond them, close to the shore, there is a fort called St. Juan. All the seashore, from thence to the southward, is generally inaccessible, being naturally fenced with rocks, on which the surf breaks almost continually. All these forts are mounted with cannon, and joined to each other with a thick stone wall, which begins near the rocky den, and continues, with little interruption, to Fort St. Juan. This wall is only breast-high within, but higher without, facing the sea. The entry to the town from the sea is at the mole, where there is an open passage between the wall and St. Philip's castle, which commands and guards this entry.'— *Canary Islands*, 1764, pp. 235, 236.

[2] There is some difference as to the number of the Spanish ships in the harbour. Duro describes the fleet of Nueva España, which arrived at Santa Cruz in February, as composed of two men-of-war and nine armed merchantmen. He gives their names and the names of the captains. The flagship of Diego de Egues was the *Jesus Maria*, and the next in importance the *Concepcion*,

shore, but the great galleons were at anchor further CHAP.
out, with their broadsides towards the sea, and all alike ⌣VIII⌣
were covered by the guns of the batteries and the 1657
castle.

Difficult as the task was which lay before them,
neither Blake nor his captains hesitated to attempt it.
Two years before, when he destroyed the Tunisian April
fleet in the harbour of Porto Farino, Blake had learnt 1655
how little land batteries could avail against skilled
gunnery and disciplined crews.[1] He was now about to
repeat the experiment on a larger scale, and the only
question the council was asked to discuss was the
manner of attack. Should the whole fleet or part of it
be sent in to destroy the galleons; and if only part,
should Blake command it himself or entrust the duty
to one of his subordinates ?

At a previous consultation Stayner had suggested
that twelve of the best frigates should go into the bay,
and the rest of the ships stay outside, but he had not
succeeded in persuading his commander. Blake now
adopted Stayner's plan, which was supported by the
judgment of the captains in general, and selected for
its execution four frigates out of each of the three
squadrons forming the fleet.[2] The captains asked that

on board which was Don José Centeno, his second in command. The English
official narrative and other accounts agree that the fleet attacked consisted of
sixteen ships, and the narrative gives the names of the commanders. The
discrepancy is caused by the fact that Duro makes no mention of any but the
treasure ships. 'The Spaniards,' says one of the accounts in *Mercurius
Politicus*, 'were sixteen great ships : thirteen of them came from the West
Indies; the other three were outward bound' (p. 7824). The English official
narrative confirms this, saying, 'These commanders with their ships were in
Santa Cruz before their fleet arrived from the Indies,' and giving three names
not in Duro's list. It also mentions a ship that came from Santo Domingo,
whose commander's name is not to be found in Duro's list. This brings the
total up to fifteen ships.

[1] Gardiner, *Commonwealth and Protectorate*, iii. 383 ; Corbett, *England in
the Mediterranean*, i. 306.

[2] The ships selected were the *Speaker, Lucie* (? *Lyme*), *Lamport, Newbury*,

CHAP.
VIII
1657

April
20

Stayner might command them, and Blake inquired if he was willing to do so. ' With all my heart,' answered Stayner, and the command of the frigates was formally entrusted to him. One important modification, however, was made in the original plan. Blake was resolved to strike with his whole force, and did not intend that any of his vessels should remain idle spectators of the battle in the harbour. He told Stayner that he, with the rest of the fleet, would follow the first division, and batter the castles while they destroyed the ships. No detailed instructions were given either to Stayner or his captains, but he was left free to give them whatever directions he thought fit. Stayner's own orders were very simple and clear. He told the eleven captains to follow him in a line, observing the order in which Blake had named them. He himself would lead them, and would go wherever he saw the greatest danger. They were to anchor three or four cables' length from the shore, so that they might have room to veer their ships, if necessary, during the fight, and to heave them off after they had done their business. Finally, not a gun was to be fired until they were at anchor.

Save that two shots were fired as the ships sailed into the bay, these orders were punctiliously observed. Stayner, as he had promised, led the way in the *Speaker*.

' I stood,' says he, ' upon the forecastle of our ship to seek a good berth for the better doing of our work. I perceived I might get in between the admiral and the vice-admiral, to our great advantage, which I did. . . . We went as near as we could with safety, and were within pistol shot of the admiral and vice-admiral and little more of the rear ; they were all great ships that rode

Bridgwater, Plymouth, Worcester, Newcastle, Foresight, Centurion, Winceby, and *Maidstone.* Stayner gives their names in the margin of his narrative.

near the castle, a thousand and twelve hundred tons apiece.'

The rest of the frigates imitated the action of the *Speaker* as well as they could, though not without disorder; for the Spaniards fired furiously from the shore, and some of the English commanders were less careful than they should have been. Nevertheless, between eight and nine o'clock all Stayner's division were anchored alongside the Spaniards, and the battle began.

During the first stage of the fight the position in which the Spaniards had placed their ships was so far from increasing their security that it positively assisted their assailants. The English frigates were to some extent protected from the fire of the batteries along the shore by the lofty hulls of their opponents, and their loss was very slight. 'They were my barricadoes,' said Stayner of the two vessels he engaged; the vice-admiral's ship covered the *Speaker* from the fire of the nearest fort, the admiral's from that of the great castle. Under these conditions the superior gunnery of the English frigates rapidly produced its natural results, and ship after ship struck or was silenced.

Between eleven and twelve, Blake and the rest of the English fleet entered the harbour, and stationed themselves to seaward of the first division. By that time some of the frigates, having disposed of their immediate opponents, were already trying to warp themselves off; others were attempting to take possession of their prizes or to set them on fire. The greater galleons still resisted, but it was evident that they could not long defend themselves, and the arrival of the second division sealed their fate.[1] Between twelve and

---

[1] All these details are from Stayner's narrative. The official account says nothing of the division of the fleet, but the fact is confirmed from several sources. Weale's Journal says, under April 20 : ' In the morning under sayle

one, the ship of the Spanish vice-admiral was seen to be in flames, and immediately afterwards it blew up. A few minutes later the galleon of the admiral blew up also, and in a moment nothing was to be seen of her but the carved work of the stern floating on the waters.

So far as the Spanish fleet was concerned the battle was over ; what remained was a contest between the English ships and the forts. The fire of the Spanish batteries, hitherto partly masked by their own vessels, increased in vigour, but ere long the guns of Blake's ships asserted their superiority. Some of the works on the shore were deserted by their defenders, and others temporarily silenced. Meanwhile the boats of the squadron completed their destruction of the Spanish fleet. Sometimes the Spaniards had entirely abandoned their ships ; in other cases a few men remained behind, who fired an ill-aimed broadside as the boats approached, and then dropped over the side and escaped to the shore. The smoke of the guns and the burning ships usually protected the assailants from serious loss, and their chief danger came from the musketeers in the breast-works. The boatswain of the *Bristol* gives an exact and vivid picture of the process. The first galleon he attempted to board seemed to have no men in it.

' They lay close on board until we came within two or three ships' lengths of them, and then they rose up

off Neger point, the Gen[ll] calleth a Counsell of Warr, 12 frigotts are ordered to fall on first of whom the *Speaker* is chiefe ; about 9 in the morning the Gen[lls] gunnes begin to worke, and the bulletts to fly, by that time wee come in some are warping off and others fyring, some sunke, as neere as I can guesse thus : there Admirall fired accidentally, there Vice admirall and reare admirall were burnt and about 12 more, with the 4 prizes that were warped off ; soe that there were in all 16 sayle fiered and sunk, besides some small vessels, viz. 14 burnt 3 sunke : in the evening we are under sayle, and all get off God be praised, but as soon as off the *Speaker's* foremast and mainmast goe by the board, and she is like a wracke in the sea very leake and much toren ' (*Sloane MS.*, 1431). Weale in the *Jersey* and Lurting in the *Bristol* both came in with the second division.

and fired several guns at us, but being so near their ships all their shot went over us.'

The next ships to which he turned his attention were really occupied.

'I saw,' says he, 'three galleons on shore, all on board one another, one of them along the shore, and one across her hawse, and the other across her stern, about a musket shot from our ships; and there was a castle on one side of them and a breastwork on the other with about fifty or sixty men in it, as was supposed; and the galleons lay about half a cable's length from the castle, and the same distance from the breastwork, about fifty yards from the shore. Then I took the pinnace and two men with me, and was going to set them on fire; but the captain saw me, and called me back, and sent five men more with me; and on our setting forward our ship fired a gun, and in the smoke thereof we got on board the galleon, receiving no harm (the Spaniards having left them), and I instantly set one of them on fire, which burnt the other two galleons. And when we could stay no longer by reason of the fire, and our ship's crew not being, as formerly, mindful of us to fire some guns, that in the smoke thereof we might have retired from the galleons without the discovery of any from the breastwork . . . the breastwork having full sight of us, discharged a volley of fifty or sixty small shot, and killed two of our men, and shot a third in the back, and I sat close to one that was killed, between him and the shore, and received no harm.' [1]

In this manner all the Spanish ships which had not been sunk were successively fired. Blake regarded it as useless to make prizes, thinking, no doubt, that it would be dangerous, if not impossible, to carry them out of the bay. The *Swiftsure* and four frigates belonging

[1] Lurting, *The Fighting Sailor*, pp. 8, 9.

to Stayner's division had each a captured vessel at her stern, which they confidently hoped to bring off. Blake sent peremptory orders that these prizes should be burnt, and had to repeat his orders three times before their reluctant captors obeyed.[1]

By three o'clock the business of destruction was complete, and nothing was left for Blake to do but to effect a safe retreat from the bay. This was the most critical part of his task. 'It remained to complete this mercy,' says the official narrative of the victory, 'that our own ships should come off well, wherein the greatest hazard and difficulty lay; for some, riding near the shore and being sorely maimed, did require to be warped off; others, when we came to weigh, drove with the wind, [which was] the while blowing right into the bay, and one of our best frigates struck. The enemy in the meantime supplied fresh men into his forts for those we had killed and beaten out, in the heat of the action; and from them and the castle continued playing upon us, till about seven of the clock at night every ship and vessel belonging to the fleet were by the good hand of God got safe out of command.'[2]

The last ship to leave the bay was the *Speaker*. While the whole fleet had lost but fifty men killed and

---

[1] Stayner's narrative. 'Seven or eight of their ships we had possession of, but they were either disabled by shots or by them set on fire, so that we could not get any of them off.'—*Mercurius Politicus*, p. 7824.

[2] The castle, which is evidently the fort called by Glas St. Philip's, is described by Lurting as having '40 guns at least,' but its batteries did little damage. 'As for the castle of 40 guns,' says he, 'we were got so far into the bay that they could not bring upon us above two or three guns.' The same cause, no doubt, protected other ships from its fire. The danger was during their return. 'Coming out of the bay we came within three or four ships' length of the castle, that had 40 guns, and they kept their guns in readiness, until we came directly over against the castle; then they fired, but we were so near that most of the shot went over, and did us little harm, only in our rigging.' —Lurting, pp. 7, 9.

about 120 wounded, Stayner's ship had five men killed, ten mortally wounded, and thirty others seriously injured. She was so battered and damaged by Spanish shot that she was scarcely seaworthy. Her crew warped her off for about half a mile, but it was all they could do to keep her afloat. ' We had now no shift to keep her from sinking,' says Stayner, ' but by nailing hides over the holes, and butt staves along the sides of the hides, for we had eight or nine foot of water in the ship.' Her masts were tottering, her mainyard and foreyard shot away, her maintopmast by the board. ' We had not one whole rope overhead, nor sail, but spritsail and spritsail-topsail.' Blake appointed Vice-Admiral Bourne to tow the *Speaker* out, but Bourne cast off the tow rope in his haste to get away with the rest of the fleet, and left her still within range of the Spanish batteries. The solitary ship became the mark of every gun the Spaniards could bring to bear upon her. ' They paid us extremely,' says Stayner. ' So we rid till the sun went down ; then the wind came off shore, and we set those pieces of sail we had, and cut away her anchor.' [1] Thus at last the *Speaker*, keeping her guns going as she went, forged slowly out of the harbour. As soon as she was outside her foremast fell, and mainmast and mizen-mast speedily followed, but the *Plymouth*, standing in to her aid, took her in tow, and the boats of the fleet brought carpenters and seamen to repair her damages.

---

[1] ' The sea breeze in Teneriffe generally sets in about ten o'clock in the morning, on the east and north-east sides of the island, and blows till five or six in the evening, when it falls calm till midnight ; then the land wind begins, and continues till seven or eight in the morning, when it is succeeded by a calm, which continues until the sea breeze begins again to blow.

' The sea breeze in the bay of Santa Cruz, and on all the east side of the island, blows commonly at east, and the land wind at west. On the north side the sea breeze blows at north-east by east, or north-east, and the land wind directly opposite to it.'—Glas, *Canary Islands*, 1764, p. 260.

To contemporaries there was something so like miracle in the successful withdrawal of Blake's fleet that a legend was at once invented to explain it. ' The wind,' said a popular historian of those days, ' blew so strong into the bay that many despaired of getting out again. But God's providence was miraculously seen in causing the wind upon the sudden to veer about to the south-west (a thing not known in many years before), which brought Blake and his fleet safe to sea again.' [1] Clarendon repeated the story, and gave it currency among the historians of the next two centuries.[2] It gained credence even with seamen. Nelson, writing in 1797, just before his own unlucky attempt on Santa Cruz, and weighing the chances of success or failure, alluded to the story as if it were a well-known historical fact. ' I do not reckon myself equal to Blake,' said he, ' but, if I recollect aright, he was more obliged to the wind coming off the land than to any exertions of his own : fortune favoured the gallant attempt, and may do so again.' [3] Yet, as in most cases, there was a basis of fact underlying the fiction, and a passage in the official narrative of the victory was the origin of the popular error. The two days following the battle were spent in patching up the damaged vessels, which were during that period ' indifferently well repaired for present security.' Then, and not till then, the north-east wind ceased. ' The wind veered to the south-west (which is rare among those islands), and lasted just enough to bring us to our former station near Cape

---

[1] *The Perfect Politician : or a full View of the Life and Actions of O. Cromwell*, 1660 (attributed to Henry Fletcher), p. 300. The passage is copied verbatim in Heath's *Chronicle*, ed. 1663, p. 722. See also Edward Phillips's continuation of Sir Richard Baker's *Chronicle*, ed. 1670, p. 648.

[2] *Rebellion*, xv. 55.

[3] *Despatches and Letters*, edited by Sir H. Nicolas, ii. 379 : cf. Mahan, *Life of Nelson*, 2nd edition, p. 253.

Maries, where we arrived the second of May following.'[1] CHAP.
A careless reader transferred the incident from the VIII
voyage to the battle, and it became one of the conse- 1657
crated fictions of history.

Blake once again selected Captain Story to bear
the news of his victory to England. On May 28 Secretary Thurloe read the relation of the battle to the
Parliament.

'The captain that brought the news,' said the
Secretary, ' was in the action and said it was the hardest
service that ever was. The enemy thought themselves
so secure that they wished the whole cause between us
and Spain had depended upon this. The silver was all
unladen and on shore, but some of the goods were
taken. Not a ship was left, but all were burnt or sunk.
Though we had received no benefit from it, yet certainly the enemy never had a greater loss. It is the
Lord's doing, and the glory be His.'[2]

For a moment joy or surprise made the members
silent ; a success so sudden and overwhelming was more
than they had dreamed of or hoped for. Then Walter
Strickland, one of the Protector's Council, moved for a
day of thanksgiving; and Wednesday, June 3, was
appointed for that purpose in London, and a day, a fortnight later, for the rest of the three nations. The house
proceeded to vote Blake a jewel worth five hundred
pounds as a testimony of the national gratitude. Some
suggested a large sum of money in addition, and one
member said that he had heard from Blake's kinsmen
that the admiral had saved nothing by the service, but
spent of his own estate in it. The Speaker stopped all
argument by reminding the House that Fairfax had
been given a jewel of just the same value for his victory

[1] Official narrative, p. 4.
[2] Burton, *Diary*, ii. 142–6 ; *Commons' Journals*, vii. 541.

at Naseby.[1]   The question of rewarding Blake's subordinates was next discussed.   Captain Story, as
bringer of the good tidings, was voted a hundred pounds.
A member proposed that every captain in the fleet should
be given a medal worth ten pounds, ' but the motion
relished not ' and was accordingly dropped.   Another
moved that a jewel worth two hundred pounds should be
conferred upon Stayner; to which several persons objected
that this would seem to slight the rest of the officers,
and might cause a quarrel in the fleet, so Stayner
received nothing.   No such timid scruples restrained the
Protector from conspicuously rewarding distinguished
merit, and Stayner was knighted as soon as he returned
to England.[2]   Cromwell also wrote to Blake, thanking
him for his services, and saying, ' We cannot but take
notice, how eminently it hath pleased God to make use
of you in this service, assisting you with wisdom in the
conduct and courage in the execution.' [3]

To Spain the consequences of the battle of Santa
Cruz were not to be measured by its losses in men and
money.   Its existence as a great power depended on its
free intercourse with its American colonies, on its
monopoly of colonial trade, on the uninterrupted flow
of gold and silver from the colonies to the mother
country.   The colonies, on the other hand, depended
entirely upon Spain for their supply of the simplest
necessaries and for all the manufactured goods which
they consumed.   Therefore the blow which Blake
struck was felt at once on both sides of the Atlantic.

[1] The jewel cost £565, and consisted of a portrait of the Protector set in
gold, with four large diamonds and about forty small.   The jeweller's bill has
been printed in *Notes and Queries*, December 2, 1876.

[2] On June 11, 1657.   He was knighted over again by Charles II on September 24, 1660.   The *Speaker* and the *Fairfax* were sent home by Blake on May 6,
and arrived June 10.

[3] Carlyle's *Cromwell*, Letter ccxviii; Thurloe, vi. 342.

Throughout Spanish America there was a sudden rise CHAP.
VIII in the prices of all things which came from Europe. Cloth worth about a shilling a yard in England, now cost 1657 five pieces of eight, a pair of shoes fetched five pieces of eight, and all other things rose in proportion. ' Unless,' it was said, ' they have a speedy supply, they will be constrained to trade with any nation that will bring them the necessaries that they want.' [1] The galleons which Blake destroyed at Santa Cruz were in a few days to have returned to America laden with European goods; but now it would be necessary to freight Dutch ships for the purpose, and Spain might be constrained in the end to let the Hollanders share in the monopoly which had hitherto been so jealously preserved. Hopes of this favour were held out to the Dutch by the Spanish ambassador at the Hague.

Above all, the non-arrival of the expected treasure disorganised the finances of Spain, and fatally hampered all the military operations of the government. At the commencement of 1657 the Spaniards bade fair to conquer Portugal. At the end of May, Olivenza, the strongest fortress on the border, had fallen into their hands, and Spanish troops entered Portugal from two sides ; [2] but their further progress was prevented by the incapacity of Spain to feed or pay its armies. By July the Spanish infantry had melted away ; not 3000, reported deserters, were still with the colours ; many had died for want of food, and others had fled. But for the financial exhaustion of Spain, Portugal, with a child for its monarch and a woman for its regent, could hardly have maintained its independence.

' 'Tis God's great goodness to these people,' wrote the English consul at Lisbon, ' that preserves them from

---

[1] Thurloe, vi. 312, 387.
[2] Ib. vi. 184, 212, 312.

CHAP.
VIII
1657

the fury of the Spaniards, for they have hitherto taken no course to oppose them ; for here hath been nothing but emulations amongst the nobility, and thwarting and contradicting one another.'

He concluded by terming the Portuguese ' a petty people, who could not have subsisted, but would all have been trampled under their enemies' feet this summer, if His Highness's fleet had not kept them from invasion by sea.' [1]

The same want of money hampered the operations of the Spaniards in Flanders. During the campaigns of 1657 and 1658, their army was notably inferior in numbers to that of the French. Spain, moreover, was unable to fulfil its promises to Charles II, either with regard to the payment of his troops or to the provision of men and money for his expedition to England.[2]

Meanwhile the treasure which should have paid Spain's soldiers was lying useless at the Canaries. In order to preserve it from Blake it had been conveyed five or six miles into the hills—probably to the town of San Cristobal de la Laguna—and there it still remained. Report said that it was worth five million pieces of eight, but its nominal value mattered little so long as it was inaccessible. The silver might as well have been still in the mines of Mexico, for the Spaniards had no means of bringing it away.[3] The fleet which had been so long preparing at Cadiz was still incapable of putting to sea, and the sailors collected to man it had been drawn off to serve in the invasion of Portugal. Rumours

---

[1] Thurloe, vi. 386–8.
[2] Ib. vi. 423 ; *Cal. Clarendon Papers*, iii. 355, 362.
[3] Duro states that it had been landed. A letter from an English officer says : ' Their treasure was conveyed ashore, and the major part of it is reported to be at a town about five or six miles up in the country, called Arragona ' (*Mercurius Politicus*, p. 7826).

were still circulated that a squadron of Dutch men-of-war was to transport the treasure to Spain or the Low Countries; but no agreement for the purpose had yet taken place, nor was it likely to take place. De Ruyter had quite enough on his hands without that; for he was now in the Mediterranean on his mission of punishing depredations on Dutch trade, and the vigour of his reprisals had created an international crisis. At the beginning of March he had captured two French privateers, and during June he blockaded a small squadron of French ships in Spezzia. France and the United Provinces were for three months on the brink of war, and the Dutch government was not inclined to quarrel with England. It needed the Protector's mediation in its dispute with France, which Cromwell was not slow to offer.[1]

The Spanish government found it impossible to transport the Santa Cruz treasure in neutral merchantmen. The Protector would not hear of abandoning the right of search. Montagu, who in July took up the command of the fleet in the Downs, received orders to search any Dutch ships said to have on board them bullion and other goods belonging to the Spaniards. Such a search, declared the Protector, was unquestionably 'agreeable both to the laws of nations and the particular treaties which are between this commonwealth and the United Provinces.'[2] Blake acted upon the same principle, and even went further. In June, 1657, his frigates captured a ship called the *Flying Fame*, of Amsterdam, which was coming from the Canaries to Cadiz. It contained 300 Spanish sailors,

CHAP.
VIII

1657

and, though the ship was released, the sailors were made prisoners of war. With the Atlantic and the Channel both watched in this way, any attempt to transport the silver would result in its capture, or its total loss.[1]

Thus the sea power of England undermined the position of Spain as a continental power; for that position was mainly founded on the wealth it derived from its American colonies and used in the interests of the Catholic cause and the Hapsburg house. For a century Spanish kings had employed the treasure of the New World to disturb the balance of the Old. As Waller put it :—

> From the New World her silver and her gold
> Came, like a tempest, to confound the Old ;
> Feeding with these the bribed electors' hopes,
> Alone she gave us emperors and popes ;
> With these accomplishing her vast designs,
> Europe was shaken with her Indian mines.[2]

Blake had effectively put a stop to this process ; and his work was so far complete that the Protector thought it safe to reduce the strength of the fleet in Spanish waters. On June 10, 1657, Cromwell sent Blake instructions to return to England with part of the fleet, as several of his ships were so defective that they could not stay out another winter without great hazard. The admiral himself was to come home with the returning ships, leaving nineteen behind him. Out of these nineteen, fourteen, under Captain John Stoakes, were to continue off Cadiz, and five frigates were to be sent into

---

[1] Thurloe, vi. 364, 399, 425, 454, 485 ; *Cal. State Papers Dom.*, 1657–8, p. 395.

[2] ' Of a War with Spain and a Fight at Sea.' *Poems*, ed. Drury, p. 151. As to the political importance of the annual fleets to Spain, see Mr. Oppenheim's remarks, *Naval Tracts of Sir William Monson*, i. 25.

the Mediterranean to put down Spanish or Turkish pirates.[1]

Before returning to England, however, Blake thought it advisable to pay another visit to Sallee. He was there about the end of June, and concluded a treaty with its governor by which he redeemed all the English sailors then in captivity.[2] On July 11 he was back in Cascaes Road, and handed over the command of the fleet to Stoakes. On the 17th he himself set sail for England with eleven ships. All eleven were in bad condition from having been too long at sea, but their commander was more battered and more weatherworn than the worst of them. Blake's health was broken, and all his strength expended. ' The general,' wrote the English consul at Lisbon, ' is very weak. I beseech God to strengthen him.' It was said that for twelve months past he had been ' only nourished with broths, jellies, and cordials.'[3] During the voyage Blake grew daily weaker, and by the time that the Lizard was sighted he knew that his end was near. All he hoped for was some respite and to die at home. ' He was very desirous,' we are told, ' to be ashore, and, if God saw it fit, to add some days to his life for settling his affairs.' For this reason his flagship, the *George*, separated from the rest of the ships, which were bound for the Downs, and bore up for Plymouth, in order to land him there. She reached Plymouth on the morning of August 7, but Blake died in sight of the harbour an hour before she entered Plymouth Sound.[4] To the

[1] Thurloe, vi. 342.
[2] Ib. vi. 364, 388, 401.
[3] Ib. vi. 401 ; *Clarke Papers*, iii. 115.
[4] ' Whitehall : 10 Aug. Last night came news that some of our ships, more foul than the rest, were returning home, together with General Blake himself, from the coast of Spain, he being sick nigh unto death.
' This morning came the unwelcome news of the death of that gallant general ; a man of great honor, that had wholly devoted himself to the service

last he was mindful of the welfare of the men who served under him, and on the night before he died he called Rear-Admiral Bourne and other captains round him, and charged them to represent to the government the necessities of the ships left behind at Cadiz. ' As he had lived,' wrote one of his captains, ' so he continued to the end, faithful. The Lord grant that a supply of his great loss may be made up for the good of his people.'[1] All felt that he could not be replaced. ' I am sorry,' wrote the stolid Monck, ' to hear the ill news of the death of my old friend General Blake, and doubt his Highness will find a want of him.'[2] The government gave Blake the public funeral which befitted his services, as it had done to Admiral Deane, killed fighting the Dutch in 1653. Blake's body was embalmed and lay in state for some days at Greenwich House. It was then borne by water to Westminster, with a train of barges following it and with minute guns firing from the Tower. Finally it was interred in Westminster Abbey, to the sound of volleys of musketry from all the regiments in London.[3] His body rested there till

of his country, and who gave many proofs of an extraordinary courage and conduct, in actions both by sea and land. He hath been a long time decaying, and in his return being come to the Lizzard Point, finding himself to fail, he called several of the commanders of the other ships aboard his own, to confer with them ; afterwards, drawing on towards his last, he willed them to bear up with all speed for Plimouth, hoping to have reached land before his death ; but in the very entrance into the Sound of Plimouth he expired. His body being imbowelled, and closed in a sheet of lead, the bowels were interred there in the cathedral church, and his corps were (sic) sent along with the ships toward the Downs. The fleet remains still upon the Spanish coast.'—Mercurius Politicus, No. 375, August 6–13, 1657, p. 7988.

[1] Cal. State Papers Dom., 1657–8, p. 57.

[2] Thurloe, vi. 467.

[3] Clarke Papers, iii. 118. Blake's body was brought to Greenwich on August 19. The funeral took place upon September 4, and was described at length in the newspapers. The cost of it amounted to £550 (Cal. State Papers Dom., 1657–8, pp. 60, 68, 179). An elegy on Blake's death was printed at the time, written ' by George Harrison, gent. on board the Dunbar in the Downs ' (Naval Songs and Ballads, ed. by C. H. Firth, 1908, p. 48). A long poem on his life and actions is to be found in Poems on Affairs of State, pp. 274–90.

the Restoration. On September 9, 1661, Charles II CHAP.
issued a warrant for its disinterment, and Deane's body $\overbrace{\qquad}$
shared the same fate. Both were taken up and flung 1657
into a pit somewhere in the green on the north side of
the Abbey, between the north transept and the west
end.[1]

At the same time as Blake—perhaps on the same
day—died another of the naval heroes of the Commonwealth, Blake's comrade in arms, Vice-Admiral Richard
Badiley.[2] As faithful as Deane or Blake in his service
to the state, he had earned less conspicuous rewards,
and escaped public honour and public shame.

[1] The warrant is printed in Chester's *Westminster Abbey Registers*, p. 521 ;
see also Stanley, *Westminster Abbey*, ed. 1886, p. 209 ; Kennet's *Register*,
p. 534. 'Reinterred in a pit dug at the back door of one of the two prebendal
houses in St. Margaret's churchyard which then blocked up the north side of
the Abbey.'

[2] *Mercurius Politicus* for August 6–13 announces the death of both. Under
August 11 it says : 'This day we had an account also touching the death of
Vice-Admiral Badiley, who hath been some time absent from sea, by reason of
indisposition of body ; and of late going to the waters in hope of recovering
health, he decayed more and more, and hath exchanged this life for a better.'
Mr. T. A. Spalding, in his *Life and Times of Richard Badiley*, gives August 7
as the date of his death.

CHAPTER IX

CHAP. IN the same month of May, 1657, in which Cromwell
IX refused the crown (May 8) the contingent which the
1656-7 Protector sent to the assistance of Louis XIV against
Spain landed in Flanders.

During the troubles of the Fronde France had lost
the conquests which she had previously made in Flanders,
and was now painfully and slowly winning them back.
In 1656 negotiations for a peace between France and
Spain had been commenced; but they definitely failed,
as France refused to restore the Prince of Condé to the
estates and offices he had forfeited by his rebellion.
During this negotiation warlike operations had not
been intermitted in the Low Countries, but the fortune
of war seemed to have turned against France. In
July, 1656, the Spaniards defeated the French army
which was besieging Valenciennes; in August the
fortress of Condé fell into the hands of the Spaniards.
Mazarin, unable to conclude a satisfactory peace with
Spain, and worsted in the campaign, needed an ally,
and the only ally who offered himself was the Protector. Much against his will he was obliged to
promise the cession of Dunkirk in return for English
aid; and Lockhart, Cromwell's ambassador, came to
an understanding with Mazarin on the subject in
November, 1656.[1] The terms of the treaty were not

[1] Gardiner, iii. 484; Chéruel, iii. 9–36.

definitely settled until March, 1657. There were various difficulties in the way on both sides. The Protector, whilst willing to assist the French with ships as the price of Dunkirk, demurred for some time to the demand that he should supply a contingent for service on land.[1]

When Cromwell had agreed in principle to the supply of a land force, the French government on military grounds refused to begin by attacking Dunkirk. Turenne urged that Gravelines must be taken first, and adduced sound strategic reasons for defeating the Spanish field army before beginning the siege of any seaport.[2] Besides this there were differences as to the scope of the intended alliance. The Protector continually returned to the plan of a general confederation. Thurloe proposed a league between France, England, Sweden, Denmark, and the United Provinces, apparently to attack the House of Austria. Mazarin wisely pointed out in reply that Holland was little inclined to any such league, and visibly favoured Spain against Cromwell. He succeeded in the end in keeping the Protector to the point and restricting the treaty to a simple alliance between England and France against Spain.[3]

The treaty was signed on March $\frac{13}{23}$, 1657.[4] Its preamble recited that the late negotiations, conducted by Lionne, had conclusively proved that Spain, by rejecting the honourable and advantageous conditions

---

[1] Thurloe, v. 574, 585 ; Guizot, *Cromwell and the English Commonwealth*, ed. 1854, ii. 556.

[2] Thurloe, vi. 21, 32.

[3] Chéruel, iii. 35–40 ; *Lettres de Mazarin*, vii. 434. See also Bourelly, *Cromwell et Mazarin : Deux Campagnes de Turenne en Flandres*, 1886, p. 12.

[4] The Latin text of the treaty is printed by Guizot, ii. 562. For comments, see Chéruel, iii. 52–8 ; and for Lockhart's explanations, Thurloe, vi. 115.

CHAP.
IX
1657
offered, intended to keep Christendom in a perpetual state of discord, and must be brought to more moderate counsels by force of arms. In April, therefore, England and France were to make a joint attack on the fortresses of Gravelines, Mardyke, and Dunkirk, by sea and land. England was to provide a fleet of ships, great and small, for blockading those ports and assisting in their siege. France was to supply 20,000 men, horse and foot, for the land operations. In addition to this, England was to furnish 6000 infantry for the said sieges, being six regiments of 1000 men each. Half of them were to be pikemen, half musketeers, and all were to be Englishmen without any admixture of Scots or Irish.[1] Three thousand of these auxiliaries were to be raised and transported at the expense of France ; the other 3000 at the expense of the Protector. During their service all the 6000 were to be paid and fed by France.

Next came some stipulations about the division of the spoils. Dunkirk and Mardyke were to fall to the share of England, Gravelines to go to France. But in case Gravelines should be captured first it was to be handed over to the Protector until he obtained possession of Dunkirk. The Protector was to garrison the conquered towns with his own forces, but half the 6000 auxiliaries were to serve the King of France as long as he wished to make use of them. The English contingent, however, was to be always regarded as a separate corps under the command of its own general.

Article eleven of the treaty was of some political

[1] Scots and Irish were excluded as likely to desert to Charles II, and not to be trusted to fight against the ally of the House of Stuart. As a rule an English regiment was composed two-thirds of musketeers and one-third of pikemen, but the French army was weak in pikes, and the Spanish pikemen were renowned for their steadiness and skill. Hence, no doubt, this stipulation.

interest. It bound the Protector to preserve the free
exercise of the Catholic religion in any Flemish towns
which came into his power. In Dunkirk, Mardyke, and
Gravelines, ' he shall leave all things so far as concerns
the Catholic religion in the same state in which he
finds them, and he shall maintain the ecclesiastics, either
regular or secular, in the enjoyment of their revenues
and the possession of their churches.'[1]

Besides this a secret article of considerable importance was appended to the treaty. For a whole
year from March 23, 1657, France and England engaged
to conclude no truce or treaty with Spain save by
mutual consent. All propositions which one of the
allies might receive from Spain were to be communicated
to the other, and in case the King of Spain at the persuasion of the Pope or the Venetian republic should
consent to the meeting of a conference to treat of a
general peace, English plenipotentiaries should be
invited and empowered to take part in it.

Both the King of France and the Protector promptly
ratified the treaty, but its execution was retarded by
numerous difficulties. The campaign should have begun
in April with the siege of Gravelines and Dunkirk, but
neither the French nor English were ready. Lockhart
had warned his government to raise troops and name
officers, and make other preparations without waiting
for the formal conclusion of the treaty, but his advice
was not followed.[2]

Consequently the Spaniards were in the field first.
They besieged the small fortress of St. Ghislain, which,
thanks to the revolt of the Irish troops amongst its
garrison, fell into their hands on March 23, 1657.[3]

---

[1] Guizot, ii. 566. The Latin original is quoted on p. 211, vol. ii. post.
[2] Chéruel, iii. 58 ; Bourelly, pp. 7, 11, 12 ; Thurloe, vi. 87, 108.
[3] Carte, *Life of Ormond*, iii. 657 ; Clarendon, *Rebellion*, xv. 80.

Turenne by the beginning of May had 24,000 men under his command on the borders of Picardy, but it was already too late. The Spaniards, informed of the terms of the treaty, had thrown 2000 picked infantry into Dunkirk, and as many more into Gravelines, while a mobile force of 4000 under the Prince de Ligne was ready to succour whichever of those places the French might attack. Under these conditions an attack on the seaports offered little chance of success; so Mazarin and Turenne resolved to attack some inland place of importance.[1] Cambray, which had a weak garrison of but 400 men, was chosen for this diversion. On May 29 Turenne suddenly appeared before Cambray with his whole army and invested the place. But the Prince of Condé with equal decision made a forced march to its relief, and, breaking through Turenne's lines, threw himself into Cambray with 4000 cavalry.[2] Turenne's stroke was thus frustrated; and, since the capture of the city was now impossible, he raised the siege and retired to St. Quentin. There, on the plateau between Oise, Scheldt, and Somme, he could bar the march of the Spaniards upon Paris, whether they sought to advance by the valley of the Oise or by that of the Somme. In this camp, early in June, the English contingent joined him.[3]

The 6000 Englishmen sent by the Protector to serve in Flanders were levied and organised in very great haste. About a quarter of their number consisted of soldiers drafted from the standing army in England; the remainder were volunteers, raised by beat of drum

---

[1] Chéruel, iii. 62, 64.
[2] Ib. iii. 58; Bourelly, pp. 15–18; Thurloe, vi. 304. Mazarin apologised to Lockhart for the attempt on Cambray, saying it would draw the Spanish forces away from the coast (Thurloe, vi. 298; cf. Lettres de Mazarin, vii. 493).
[3] Bourelly, p. 18.

for this special service, and in many cases must
have been raw recruits who had never seen service
before.[1]

Yet many of these volunteers were doubtless
old soldiers. England was full of men who had
learnt during the civil war how to handle pike and
musket, and were willing to take up their old trade
again when opportunity offered. The 6000 men could
hardly be described as veterans, but probably at least
half of them had seen service before. They were given
the red coats worn by the New Model, ' for the terrible
name thereof ' as a contemporary historian tells us, and
they were not likely to disgrace their uniform.[2] Like
the men, the officers were rather a heterogeneous body.
Of the six colonels three, Reynolds, Morgan, and Alsop,
had served or were serving in the regular army; two,
Clark and Lillingston, had held commands in the English regiments in the Dutch service; and the sixth,
Bryce Cochrane, was a soldier of fortune who had
served in the Scottish forces in Ireland and under David
Leslie in Scotland. Some of their subordinates had been
captains or lieutenants in the regular army who were
now promoted to higher posts in the new regiments;
but a good many seem to have possessed little experience and to have been chosen with very little care.[3]
However, the two generals were both carefully selected.
For general, the Protector pitched upon Sir John
Reynolds, who had fought throughout the civil war as
a cavalry officer, and had risen to be Commissary-
General of the Horse in Ireland. No doubt the choice
fell upon him because he was a man of some political
and administrative ability as well as a soldier, and

[1] See ' Royalist and Cromwellian Armies in Flanders.' *Transactions of
the Royal Historical Society*, 1902–3, p. 76.

[2] Heath, *Chronicle*, p. 720.

[3] See ' Royalist and Cromwellian Armies in Flanders,' pp. 77, 78, 111.

CHAP. qualified both by birth and education for a post which
IX involved something more than purely military duties.
1657 The fact that he was Henry Cromwell's brother-in-law
seemed a guarantee of his fidelity to the government,
whatever temptations the chance of war might bring.
Henry Cromwell trusted him completely, had employed
him in delicate missions to the Protector and his Council,
and regarded him as his right hand in the government
of Ireland. Reynolds was reluctant to leave Ireland;
but the Protector's commands were so ' express and
positive ' that he finally accepted a commission as
April, ' captain - general and commander - in - chief ' of the
25 English contingent.[1]

The second in command was a man of very different
character to Reynolds. Major-General Thomas Morgan had served in the wars of the Low Countries and in
the Thirty Years' War, at one time under the French
flag, at another under that of Bernhard of Saxe-Weimar.
He had fought for the Parliament throughout the civil
war. Sometimes he had commanded a regiment of
foot, sometimes a regiment of dragoons, and he was
also held to be a skilful artilleryman and very expert in
sieges. Morgan had been Monck's chief assistant in
the subjugation of Scotland, and there was no one of
whose military judgment and trustworthiness Monck
had a higher opinion. The little, active, shrill-voiced,
choleric man knew his business thoroughly, and played

---

[1] Thurloe, vi. 223, 230, 347. There is a life of Reynolds in the *Dictionary
of National Biography*, xlviii. 47. His commission is as ' captain general and
commander in chief,' but at first he was only offered the post of second in
command. He wrote to Henry Cromwell on April 14, saying that he regretted
to exchange his present post in Ireland ' for the second command of 6000 foot
on foreign service, which is the employment now to be conferred upon me, but
I have not accepted my commission and do hope it will not be proffered. I
have offered to go with the title of Major-General of the said 6000 under your
Excellency or the lord Richard, but I am not willing to serve under another
nation and a foreigner, or at best a general but half an Englishman.'—*Lansdowne
MSS.*

a far more important part in the campaign than his nominal commander.[1]

The new levied forces were hastily organised, for time pressed and the campaign in Flanders had begun. On May 1, 1657, whilst Morgan was still on his way from Scotland, the six regiments were reviewed on Blackheath, ' stout men and fit for action, as was manifest from their appearance,' says a spectator. Hugh Peters preached a sermon to the soldiers, ' exhorting them that when they come abroad they be sure to avoid the vices of other places, and to remember the virtuous and victorious military discipline of England, by which, through God's blessing, so many great actions have been performed at home. This wrought upon the soldiers so that they declared themselves with alacrity resolved to uphold the honour and renown of England abroad.' [2] No time was lost; 3000 or 3500 men embarked on the 8th or 9th of May and were landed near Boulogne; the remainder followed a week later.[3]

The soldiers of the English contingent were very well satisfied with their reception by their allies. ' We are nobly treated in all places,' says a letter from the camp.[4] For the first few days at all events they were well lodged and regaled with wine and beer at each town they came to; and their only complaint was that the French rate of pay was much lower than that which

[1] For a life of Morgan, see *Dictionary of National Biography*, xxxix. 33. He was summoned from Scotland by Cromwell on April 23, 1657.

[2] *Mercurius Politicus*, April 30–May 7, p. 7769. See *Royalist and Cromwellian Armies in Flanders*, p. 78.

[3] According to *Mercurius Politicus*, 3500 were embarked on May 8 and May 9, the rest on May 16 (ib. pp. 79, 80). See also *Clarendon State Papers*, iii. 340, and Thurloe, vi. 287, 291. Bourelly, referring to the Letters of Mazarin, gives May 18 to 24 (N.S.) as the dates during which the English troops were transported (*Lettres de Mazarin*, vii. 453, 470–2, 497).

[4] See *Royalist and Cromwellian Armies in Flanders*, p. 81; Thurloe, vi. 297; *Clarke Papers*, iii. 110; and *Mercurius Politicus*, May 21–28.

CHAP. they had been accustomed to get in England.[1]
IX About the eleventh of June, Reynolds and the Eng-
1657 lish contingent joined Turenne at St. Quentin.[2] At
June
6 Ribemont-sur-Oise, on June 16, Louis XIV and Car-
16 dinal Mazarin reviewed the six regiments, and were
highly pleased with their appearance.[3] 'They are all
well-made soldiers and look as if they would do good
service,' wrote Mazarin, while Turenne described them
as the finest troops that could be seen.[4]

Immediately after their arrival the French government, in the hope of inducing the Spaniards to withdraw
their forces from the Flemish coast, resolved to attack
Montmédy in the duchy of Luxemburg. While Marshal
de la Ferté with part of the army laid siege to it, Turenne
with another part covered the siege and protected the
French frontier from attack. The siege began on
June 11, lasted a couple of months, and ended on
August 7.[5] During these two months the English
contingent formed part of the covering army under
Turenne, was part of the time stationed at Guise, and
was generally under the immediate command of the
Marquis de Castelnau. When Montmédy fell, Turenne
turned his course westwards, and made a sudden attack

[1] On the question of pay, see *Clarke Papers*, iii. 110, and Thurloe, vi. 287,
290, 297. Half of the 6000 were to have been armed by the French government, but this stipulation was very imperfectly carried out. However, the
Cardinal provided eighty tents for the officers, and a couple of wagons for the
baggage of every regiment (ib. 290, 297, 301).

[2] Their march is traced by Bourelly, p. 18, note 1. Cf. *Lettres de Mazarin*,
vii. 482, 488, 500.

[3] Ribblemont, Lockhart terms it (Thurloe, vi. 337). See Bourelly, p. 21.
Mercurius Politicus, June 18–25, p. 7874, gives a description of the review, and
says it took place on June 6. At Tupigny, on June 8, says Bussy-Rabutin,
Mémoires, ii. 30.

[4] Bourelly, p. 22 ; *Lettres de Mazarin*, vii. 475, 507. Mazarin also praised
their good behaviour, and hoped the King's troops would take example by it
(ib. vii. 488, 514, 731).

[5] Bourelly, pp. 19–26 ; cf. Thurloe, vi. 351, 383, 385, 397, 423–6 ; *Mercurius Politicus*, pp. 7907, 7916, 7926, 7969, 7978, 7985.

on St. Venant, which surrendered after a ten days' CHAP.
investment.[1] All these operations received little hind- IX
rance from the Spaniards. Don Juan and Condé 1657
marched to raise the siege of Montmédy, but avoided
giving battle ; and an attempt to surprise Calais, in the
hope of inducing the French to abandon the attempt
on Montmédy, failed. In the same way, when Turenne
besieged St. Venant, the Spaniards responded by a
sudden attack upon Ardres, and would have succeeded
in taking the place, which was but weakly garrisoned,
had not the fall of St. Venant enabled Turenne to
march to its relief. August

In these operations the English troops and their $\frac{17}{27}$
leader justified the good opinion which Turenne and
Mazarin had expressed of them. The English officers
were somewhat surprised by the strategy of the Spanish
and French leaders. The elaborate manœuvring for
strategic positions, the time spent in the sieges of unimportant fortresses, the deliberate avoidance of battle
on the part of the Spaniards, and the fact that the
French made no attempt to bring about a general engagement, seemed strange to soldiers bred in the school
of Fairfax and Cromwell. ' Fighting,' said Reynolds
contemptuously in one of his letters, ' is not the fashion
of the country.' [2] When Don Juan and the Spanish
army came to the relief of St. Venant, and established
themselves at Calonne on the Lys, about a mile from
the besieged town, Reynolds urged Turenne to attack.
If he would let him have but 2000 French horse, said
Reynolds, he would with them and his 6000 English
foot fall upon the Spanish camp ; ' thinking that
number of horse sufficient in that enclosed country, and

---

[1] See *Mercurius Politicus*, August 27–September 3, and Thurloe, vi.
462, 467, 479.
[2] September 1, 1657 ; Reynolds to H. Cromwell. *Lansdowne MSS.*

relying on the bravery of his English foot who had been accustomed to hedge fighting to supply their want of numbers.' But Turenne thought the undertaking too desperate and refused his consent.[1] Nevertheless, during the course of the siege, the English infantry found opportunity to show their quality ; and the desperate courage with which 600 of them stormed the outworks of St. Venant not only gained them great praise, but, by hastening the surrender of the town, enabled Turenne to march to the relief of Ardres. ' I rejoice to tell your lordship,' wrote Lockhart to Thurloe, ' that the taking of St. Venant and the raising of the siege of Ardres, is wholly imputed to the good service of our English forces, of whom there is so high an esteem as is scarcely credible.' [2]

In other respects the French generals found the English soldiers less satisfactory. They behaved much better in the towns and villages in which they were quartered than the French soldiers did.[3] On the other hand, they were somewhat exacting, and inclined to mutiny when they were not paid with due regularity. At this same siege of St. Venant, Turenne, in order to appease them, was forced to cut up his own plate and distribute it amongst them by weight in place of coin.[4] The brown bread, composed largely of rye and bran, upon which the French soldier was fed, was distasteful to men accustomed to a liberal

---

[1] *Life of James II*, i. 305, 309.

[2] Thurloe, vi. 487. There are three accounts of the exploit of the English at St. Venant : *Clarke Papers*, iii. 116 ; *Harleian Miscellany*, iii. 342 (' A Relation of Major-General Sir Thomas Morgan's Progress in Flanders ') ; *Mercurius Politicus*, August 27–September 3, 1657, pp. 1590, 1597. French narratives do not seem to mention it.

[3] Thurloe, vi. 337.

[4] Bourelly, p. 27 ; Chéruel, iii. 70. Lockhart says, speaking of the delay to pay the money : ' The forces endured much hardship before it came, though M. Turenne had the kindness to cut his plate, and give it out by weight to them.' Thurloe, vi. 487 ; *Lettres de Mazarin*, viii. 46, 111, 132.

allowance of cheese and biscuit. They relied upon the chap. five sous a day, which the French government was ⁱˣ pledged to pay them, to supplement their rations with 1657 more palatable and familiar food ; and when they did not get their money, not only grumbled, but fell ill. 'Since our coming into France,' wrote Major-General Morgan August to General Monck, after the relief of Ardres, 'we have $\frac{21}{31}$ had many hard marches, and being run in arrear of pay for six weeks together, our men being forced to subsist only with their ammunition-bread, water, and fruit, it hath brought them into a great weakness and much discouraged them, insomuch that they make all the shifts they can to get into England, notwithstanding we take all the care possible.' [1] Sickness and desertion rapidly reduced the number of the English contingent. At the beginning of September, Sir John Reynolds wrote to Henry Cromwell, pressing to be recalled from Flanders, and saying that his 6000 men were now less than 4000. 'Howsoever,' he added figuratively, 'if I must fight on until my dagger, which was a sword, become an oyster knife, I am content and submit.' [2]

The Protector was not content to see his troops spent in marches and sieges far away from the ports against which he meant them to be employed. He refused to accept the reasons by which Mazarin and Turenne proved the necessity of the operations in

[1] Clarke Papers, iii. 116. 'We find a great want of cheese, which I hope will be supplied, bread and water being strange to our soldiers,' says another officer. Ib. iii. 111 ; cf. Guizot, ii. 575. See Cromwell's Army, pp. 212, 225, for additional information on the question of provisions. The desertions were numerous, and sufficient care was not taken in England to arrest those who returned home. A certain number of men deserted to the Spaniards and swelled the regiments under the command of the Duke of York. Thurloe, vi. 480 ; Clarendon State Papers, iii. 344, 407 ; Clarke MSS., xxxix. 110.

[2] Reynolds to Henry Cromwell, September 1, 1657. Lansdowne MSS. Guizot, ii. 577. See also Lettres de Mazarin, viii. 149, 151, 161.

the interior of Flanders and the impossibility of attacking Dunkirk or Gravelines.[1] Lockhart represented his
master's views to the Cardinal with great persistency.
As soon as he heard of the siege of Cambray he
protested against it. While thanking the Cardinal
for the unusual favours granted the English troops,
he told him that the good usage of his soldiers was
not all that his Highness expected ; and that unless the more material part of the treaty were kept,
the Protector's service would require their presence
elsewhere.[2] During the siege of Montmédy, Lockhart
renewed his remonstrances. He pointed out to the
Cardinal ' the ill consequences that were like to follow
upon their delays,' and told him ' that the remissness
of their procedure, in what concerned the keeping of
their promises, did very much lose the affections of
many persons of interest in England, who had hitherto
always expressed great zeal for the alliance with
France.'[3]

The Protector urged Lockhart to still greater vigour.
' I desire you,' he said, ' to take boldness and freedom to
yourself in your dealing with the French on these accounts.' In another letter, dated August 31, he ordered
him to present what was practically an ultimatum to
the Cardinal. Unless an immediate movement was
made against Dunkirk and Gravelines the English
forces were to be withdrawn. ' I am deeply sensible,'
said Cromwell, ' that the French are very much short
with us in ingenuity and performance. And that which
increaseth our sense of this is, the resolution we for our
part had, rather to overdo than to be behindhand in
anything of our treaty.

---

[1] Chéruel, iii. 64, 67.
[2] Thurloe, vi. 298, 301, 346.
[3] Ib. vi. 345, 421, 437.'

'To talk of giving us garrisons which are inland, as CHAP.
caution for future action ; to talk of what will be done XI
next campaign—are but parcels of words for children. 1657
If they will give us garrisons, let them give us Calais,
Dieppe, and Boulogne ; which I think they will do as
soon as be honest to their words in giving us any one
Spanish garrison upon the coast into our hands. I
positively think, which I say to you, they are afraid
we should have any footing on that side, though
Spanish.

'I pray you to tell the Cardinal from me, that I think,
if France desires to maintain its ground, much more to
get ground upon the Spaniard, the performance of his
treaty with us will better do it than anything appears
yet to me of any design he hath. Though we cannot
so well pretend to soldiery as those that are with him ;
yet we think that, we being able by sea to strengthen
and secure his siege, and to reinforce it as we please by
sea, and the enemy being in a capacity to do nothing to
relieve it, the best time to besiege that place will be
now. Especially if we consider that the French horse
will be able so to ruin Flanders as that no succour can
be brought to relieve the place ; and that the French
army and our own will have constant relief, as far as
England and France can give it, without any
manner of impediment, especially considering the
Dutch are now engaged so much to the southward as
they are.

'I desire you to let him know, that Englishmen have
had so good experience of winter expeditions, they are
confident, that if the Spaniard shall keep the field, as
he cannot impede this work, so neither will he be able
to attack anything towards France with a possibility
of retreat. And what do all delays signify but the
giving the Spaniard opportunity the more to reinforce

CHAP.
IX
1657

himself; and the keeping our men another summer to serve the French, without any colour of a reciprocal, or any advantage to ourselves!

'And therefore, if this will not be listened unto, I desire that things may be considered of to give us satisfaction for the great expense we have been at with our naval forces and otherwise; which out of an honourable and honest aim on our part hath been done, that we might answer our engagements. And that consideration may be had how our men may be put into a posture to be returned to us; whom we hope we shall employ to a better purpose than to have them continue where they are.'[1]

Lockhart lost no time in carrying out these instructions, though doubtless he softened the expressions used by Cromwell when he delivered his message to the Cardinal.[2] But his previous remonstrances had produced their effect. Turenne, after the capture of St. Venant, had turned his course westwards and drew down towards the coast, intending to force the Spaniards to give battle, if it were possible, and to commence operations against the Flemish seaports.[3] On September 13 Sir John Reynolds announced the movement to the Protector, writing at the same time to Admiral Montagu, who commanded the English fleet in the Downs, to assist in the enterprise by approaching the Flemish coast with his fleet, and by lying before Dunkirk and Mardyke. The English government was asked to supply heavy artillery and mortarpieces for a siege, biscuit in case the communications of the besiegers with France should be interrupted, and hay for the cavalry. At the desire

Sept.
$\frac{3}{13}$

---

[1] Thurloe, vi. 490 ; Carlyle's *Cromwell*, Letter ccxxii.

[2] Lockhart's account of this interview is not to be found, but he refers to it in a later letter (Thurloe, vi. 618). For French accounts of it, see Chéruel, iii. 69, and Bourelly, p. 33 ; *Lettres de Mazarin*, viii. 79.

[3] Thurloe, vi. 437.

of Turenne, Reynolds also asked for two or three thousand fresh foot to fill the gaps in the English contingent.[1] Later in the month Talon, the intendant of Turenne's army, came over to London in company with Reynolds to discuss the plan of operations, and to arrange for the necessary supplies and reinforcements. According to Turenne, all that was possible at this late season of the year was to attack Mardyke. The Protector was reluctant to accept this view; and in a stormy interview with Bordeaux he reiterated his complaints about the time which had been wasted in inland sieges. Mardyke, he said, could not be held without great expense, and was not a sufficient compensation for the money spent in keeping the fleet constantly ready to co-operate with the French army. Bordeaux recapitulated all the reasons which had prevented the French from attacking the coast fortresses at the beginning of the campaign. The siege of Montmédy had been undertaken, he said, in order to draw the Spanish forces away from the coast and leave Turenne more free to approach it. The taking of St. Venant had secured the passage of the Lys. Since then he had turned the line of the Colme and taken Bourbourg, which rendered an attack on one of the ports possible; but both Dunkirk and Gravelines were too strong to be safely attacked while a Spanish army was stationed behind the canal which ran from Bergues to Dunkirk. As Mardyke was a fort which must be captured before the siege of Dunkirk could be thought of, Turenne had thought that he would be doing the Protector agreeable service if he put the place in his hands.[2] Cromwell was probably not convinced by these arguments, but he calmed down and agreed to furnish

---

[1] Thurloe, vi. 497, 508, 516, 517, 523.

[2] This interview is related by Bordeaux to Brienne in a letter dated September 17, 1657. Guizot, ii. 575.

CHAP.
IX
1657

the artillery and some of the supplies demanded. He promised to send 2000 men to recruit the English contingent.[1] Moreover, in accordance with Turenne's wishes, an English fleet of twenty-five sail prepared to take part in the attack on Mardyke.[2]

Mardyke, now only a village, was important then because it commanded one of the best harbours on that coast. Its defences were the fort proper, a small work of earth and stone, and a wooden fort built upon piles, communicating with the more important work and serving to defend the road. Both were taken without any difficulty. Turenne appeared before Mardyke on September 29, drew a line of entrenchments between the fort and Dunkirk to prevent the Spaniards from assisting the garrison, battered and took the wooden fort on the third day, and obliged the main fort to surrender on the fourth. Ten guns, about 400 soldiers, and a surprising number of officers fell into the hands of the victors.[3]

Sept.
19
29

As the terms of the treaty required, Mardyke was immediately handed over to the English; and the Protector seemed to the French ambassador to be highly delighted at its capture.[4] What Cromwell hoped was that the French army would immediately proceed to take Dunkirk; and he now offered to send over 5000 men of the regular army if Turenne would proceed to attack it. Turenne preferred to attempt Gravelines, which was less strongly garrisoned than Dunkirk, and was said to be insufficiently provisioned. But when he

---

[1] *Clarke Papers*, iii. 119; *Mercurius Politicus*, pp. 1639, 1648; Thurloe, vi. 526, 553; Bourelly, p. 35.

[2] Thurloe, vi. 503, 526.

[3] Bourelly, pp. 35–9; *Mercurius Politicus*, September 24–October 1, pp. 1652, 1664. Mardyke was taken $\frac{\text{September 22}}{\text{October 2}}$.

[4] Bordeaux to Brienne, October 11, 1657; Guizot, ii. 579.

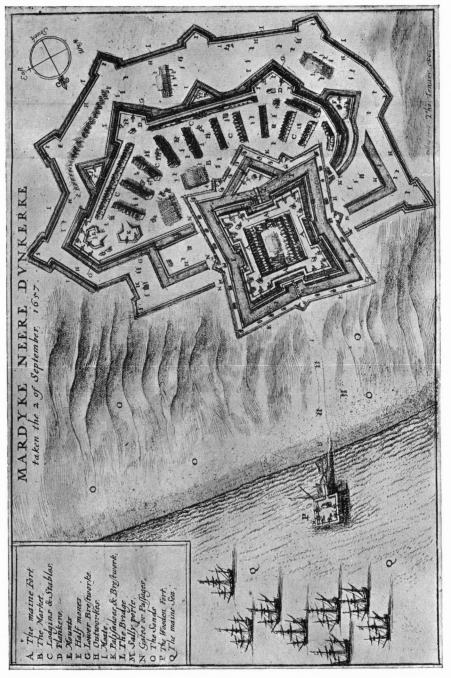

MARDYKE NEERE DVNKERKE
taken the 2 of September, 1637.

A. The maine Fort.
B. The Market.
C. Lodgins & Stables.
D. Flankers.
E. Mounts
F. Half-mones
G. Lower Brestworkes.
H. Outworkes.
I. Moate.
K. Palissadoes, & Brestwork.
L. The Bridge.
M. Sally portt.
N. Gates or Passages,
O. The Sands
P. the Wooden Fort,
Q. The maine Sea,

FACSIMILE OF A PLAN OF MARDYKE, BY HOLLAR.

[To face p. 285, Vol. I.

approached to invest it, the garrison of Gravelines cut CHAP.
the dykes and flooded the country round, so that he IX
was obliged to draw off his army. Accordingly he 1657
took up his position at Ruminghen, on the left bank
of the Aa between St. Omer and Ardres, leaving some
800 English in Mardyke and a mixed garrison of a
couple of thousand men in Bourbourg.[1]   The English
contingent was divided ; three battalions were put in
Mardyke, three in Bourbourg, and six marched with
Turenne.

Mardyke was a place easier to take than to keep.
The principal fort would not hold more than 500 or 600
men ; and so small a garrison was not sufficient to maintain it against the Spanish forces at Dunkirk, only a
league away. It was resolved, therefore, to repair
some old and ruinous outworks once attached to the
fort, so as to make it capable of containing a garrison
of 2000 foot and 500 horse.[2]   Turenne promised to
remain within supporting distance of Mardyke for ten
days, in order to enable this extension of the works
to be made.[3]   On the other hand, the Spaniards
resolved to recapture the place before the new
fortifications were completed.   Accordingly Don Juan,
accompanied by the Duke of York and Charles II,
marched from Dunkirk with 4000 or 5000 men, and made
a night attack on Mardyke.   Some of the new entrenchments were levelled, but the assault was not pushed

---

[1] Bourelly, p. 40 ; Thurloe, vi. 542, 547, 548. Fleetwood, writing to Henry
Cromwell on October 6, says : ' We have now the care of Mardyke upon us,
the French being risen from before Gravelines through the violence of the
waters which came down upon them from the drawing up of the sluices.'
Lansdowne MS., 821, f. 339.   See also *Mercurius Politicus*, October 1–8, p. 7,
and *Clarke Papers*, iii. 121.

[2] A broadside relating the capture of Mardyke (which is wrongly dated
September 2) is in the Thòmason collection.   It contains a plan engraved by
Hollar showing the fort and outworks.   The British Museum press-mark is
669, f. 20 (67).   On this plan see Thurloe, vi. 654.

[3] *Clarke Papers*, iii. 120, 126.

CHAP.
IX
1657
Oct.22
Nov. 1

home.   Aided by the fire of the English ships in the harbour, the garrison easily repulsed the attack; and the Spaniards retreated, leaving behind them their fascines and scaling-ladders, and losing perhaps a few score of men.   The Marquis of Ormond had his horse killed under him; a captain in the Duke of Gloucester's regiment was killed, and Charles II exposed himself a great deal more freely than his advisers approved.[1] Hyde entreated him to be more careful of his person for the sake of those whose interests and hopes were bound up with him.   'I am none of those,' he said, 'who think that you are like to recover your three kingdoms without being in danger of your life, but let it be when the adventure is of use and there is a recompense in view; truly, Sir, you ought to take some compassion of us.'[2]

Charles had the good sense to recognise the justice of Hyde's expostulations, and to be more cautious in future.   Some months before he had been petitioned by Lord Bristol to chide the Duke of York for too recklessly exposing himself to danger at the siege of Ardres, and he was content to leave his younger brother to maintain the military reputation of the family.

One result of the attack on Mardyke was to cause a serious dispute between the allied powers.   Turenne had been at once informed of the attempt of the Spaniards on the place, and had marched ' with incredible speed ' to its relief.   He arrived at daybreak the next morning,

---

[1] A good account of the attack is given in the *Life of James II*, i. 323 ; there are also accounts in Thurloe, vi. 578, 580 ; *Clarke Papers*, iii. 122, 124 ; *Mercurius Politicus*, October 22–November 5, pp. 54, 65, 70, 80.   Newspaper accounts grossly exaggerate the loss of the Spaniards.   A second attack, from the sea this time, took place about ten days later.   *Life of James II*, i. 325.

[2] *Clarendon State Papers*, iii. 359, 374 ; Clarendon, *Rebellion*, xv. 132.

a few hours after the Spaniards had been repulsed, and resolved to remain within supporting distance until the new works were finished. In his opinion, however, Mardyke was too isolated and too weak a post to be safely held after his army had with-drawn—as it must soon do—into winter quarters. He originally proposed that the works at Mardyke should be razed to the ground or blown up, to avoid the dis-grace of losing what seemed almost impossible to keep. But this suggestion caused the liveliest disgust and anger in the minds of the Protector, Lockhart, and the English leaders.[1] It was regarded not as a strategic necessity, but as a proof of the bad faith of the French. Lockhart and the Cardinal had several angry interviews on the subject, and the Protector told Bordeaux that he would bid his troops evacuate Mardyke if Turenne ordered them to do so, but should consider the alliance at an end if it were done. Under these circumstances the proposal was naturally abandoned, as Mazarin had foreseen it must be.[2]

The Protector was not content with its abandon-ment : Lockhart demanded that France should bear the expense of holding Mardyke until Dunkirk was taken, arguing that by the treaty both were to be ceded, not one without the other. He said that though there was an English garrison in Mardyke it was there in the name of the King of France, and under the command of any officer he chose to send there if he was above the rank of a colonel, advancing this as a proof that the responsibility of keeping the place was incumbent on the French government.

---

[1] Thurloe, vi. 578, 618 ; Guizot, ii. 580 ; *Clarendon State Papers*, iii. 375 ; Bourelly, p. 41 ; *Clarke Papers*, iii. 124.

[2] See Bordeaux's dispatch to Brienne describing his interview with the Protector, November 5, 1657. Guizot, ii. 580.

Thurloe reiterated the old complaint that England had gone to the expense of sending a contingent to Flanders and maintaining a fleet to assist its operations, and that all the profit of the campaign had fallen to the share of France.[1]

Neither Bordeaux nor Mazarin had much trouble in showing the inanity of the demand that the cost of keeping Mardyke should fall upon France; the real difficulty was to overcome the rooted feeling of distrust which lay at the root of these recriminations. It was not easy to convince the Protector, and the English in general, that France meant to carry out honestly a treaty which would give England a foothold on the continent. Mazarin bitterly complained to Lockhart 'that there was that jealousy of him and the sincerity of his proceedings,' and that he had formerly flattered himself with the 'hope of having some share in his Highness's good esteem.' He added, 'in a way of earnestness that is not usual to him, that except there were mutual confidence between persons that pursued a joint interest, their common undertakings would never have good success.' He concluded by expressing, 'in very passionate terms, the great desire he had to be in his Highness's good opinion, which he should be ready to purchase at any rate.' [2] In the end Lockhart succeeded in mollifying Mazarin, and Bordeaux in appeasing the Protector. There was no good ground for suspecting the Cardinal's sincerity; his correspondence conclusively proves that he was resolved to carry out the treaty with perfect honesty. Moreover, the Protector did not fully appreciate either the military position in Flanders or the merits of Turenne's

---

[1] Bourelly, p. 41; Thurloe, vi. 614; *Lettres de Mazarin*, viii. 196, 217, 268.

[2] Thurloe, vi. 618.

generalship. He was convinced that the French might CHAP.
IX
1657
have taken Dunkirk if they had attacked it earlier, or
even if they had vigorously besieged it after the fall of
Mardyke. Lockhart told him so, but the ambassador's
military experience was too slight to justify the positive-
ness of his assertions, and the Protector believed him
too readily.[1] Besides this, Cromwell's political position
made him exacting. In a few weeks Parliament would
meet again, and he had to face it with nothing to show
for his expenditure on the Flemish campaign but a
barren and costly trophy. Thurloe told Bordeaux that
the majority of the Protector's Council disapproved of
this conquest, and regarded it as an occasion for drain-
ing England of men and money. When the Protector's
foreign policy came to be discussed, it was certain that
this opinion would find many voices to express it in
Parliament.[2]

The dispute was settled by a compromise. Reynolds
received a commission from the King of France as
governor of Mardyke, taking it with some fear lest the
English government should disapprove his action.[3]
The Cardinal promised every kind of assistance in keeping Mardyke and Bourbourg, which latter place was
also occupied mainly by English troops. Money was
sent for the subsistence of the English forces, and for
completing the fortifications, with some able engineers
to assist in the work. To show that the honour of
France was engaged in the retention of the places, the
garrisons were reinforced by eighty of the King's own
guards, and eighty of the Cardinal's, while French
officers of distinction volunteered to take part in the
defence. Turenne stayed near Mardyke as long as he

[1] Thurloe, vi. 618 ; Guizot, ii. 580.
[2] Guizot, ii. 583.
[3] Thurloe, vi. 579, 605, 614, 618 ; *Clarke Papers*, iii. 124.

CHAP.
IX
1657

could. When he was forced to retire into winter quarters by lack of forage for his numerous cavalry, he promised to leave 300 horse at Mardyke; and stationed the French and Swiss guards with some of the best of the old regiments about Calais and Boulogne, so that Mardyke could be relieved in twenty-four hours if it was again attacked.[1]

Nevertheless, throughout the whole winter of 1657-8, it seemed doubtful whether it would be possible to maintain the place. The work of refortifying it went on very slowly. Turenne and the French engineers repeatedly complained of the laziness of the English soldiers. They found them, as Monck found his men in Scotland, excessively reluctant to dig, even if it was necessary to defend themselves from attack. ' They were very lukewarm in the business and not very docile,' complained one engineer. Another said that the men under his orders were not only very lazy, but that some of them left their work and used their shovels to dig out rabbits in the sandhills they were charged to fortify.[2] One great difficulty was that there was no wood to be had anywhere near Mardyke, and timber for the palisades had to be either fetched from about seven miles off, or sent from England.[3] Wood was also needed to build barracks for the accommodation of the soldiers. ' I have been here now this seven weeks,' wrote an officer at the end of November, ' waiting for timber and boards, wherewith we are to erect houses and lodging for our soldiers, but besides empty promises we have got but little hitherto ; which neglect makes the condition of the soldiers very miserable, and so destructive that we send every day no less than ten, twelve, or more to the

[1] *Clarke Papers*, iii. 124, 127 ; Thurloe, vi. 624 ; Bourelly, pp. 48-54 ; *Lettres de Mazarin*, viii. 234, 268, 308.
[2] Bourelly, pp. 51, 92.
[3] *Clarke Papers*, iii. 124 ; Thurloe, vi. 637.

grave; for we have about 2000 men, but have not
accommodation for above 600 of them; hence the shifts
we make for lodging are very hard and unwholesome,
tending to the destruction of many every day.' [1]
Another letter from Mardyke says : ' We have abundance of sick men, and are likely to be more, for sickness
is here very rife ; it takes them with giddiness in the
head and distractions, many swellings in the legs and
joints, violent fevers and agues of all sorts.' [2]   ' The
sick of all the army are a very sad spectacle to behold,'
says a third letter ; ' the Lord comfort them, for we
have neither firing, straw, or covering, save what we
pay for ; yet in regard it is for his Highness's service
and the interest of England we will cheerfully embrace
the greatest hardships, and by God's assistance wade
through all difficulties.' [3]   The situation of Mardyke was
unhealthy, and the inundations made by the Spaniards
for the defence of Gravelines made the whole district
still more unwholesome.   The English Royalists quartered at Dunkirk suffered almost equally severely;
and the Duke of York says that he never had half his
men fit for duty.[4]

Cromwell's government attributed the sufferings of
the garrison of Mardyke to the neglect of the French
government to supply them with necessaries, and complained loudly.   ' If the Cardinal,' wrote Thurloe, ' do
not give some effectual order for supplying their wants
that they may live, I do not see what other course can
be taken but to call our men home, which is much
better than to have them die or at last run away to the
enemy.' [5]   The letters of Reynolds to Thurloe are full

---

[1] *Clarke Papers*, iii. 128.   [2] Ib. iii. 122.
[3] Ib. iii. 123.   [4] *Life of James II*, i. 317, 322.
[5] Thurloe to Reynolds, November 22, 1657.   Thurloe, vi. 626 ; cf. pp. 614,
637, 653, 659, 677.   The Cardinal declared that what was due in provisions
and money to the garrison of Mardyke was punctually paid.   Lockhart did not

CHAP.
IX
1657

of similar complaints. Nor was it only the garrison of Mardyke who suffered ; those regiments of the English contingent which were quartered at Bourbourg and the posts occupied by the French lost almost as heavily. About the middle of November, Turenne marched away with his army, and took up his winter quarters about Guisnes and Ardres and on the northern border of France. Three regiments of the English contingent accompanied Turenne ; and, though the hardships of the campaign were over, their ranks were still decimated by disease. According to the French the fault lay with the English themselves. D'Ormesson, a French official, writing to Bordeaux at the beginning of January, 1658, said that he had sent the English companies quartered hitherto at Guisnes to join those at Mardyke. ' In regard his Eminence hath charged me in all his letters to take special care of them, I have done what lay in my power to accommodate them with all things necessary. These troops were conducted by few officers and they seemed to me very feeble. I cannot impute this diminution to anything else but their officers, who are most of them absent, and the rest took no care at all of their sick men. I know they were well looked unto in their quarters, which were good ones, and exactly paid ; whilst the French soldiers were forced to camp in huts and without any pay.' D'Ormesson found that many of the companies, which should have been a hundred strong, were now reduced to fifty ; and he had received orders only to pay those officers and soldiers actually present with the colours.[1] When he tried to carry out his orders he met with unexpected difficulties. ' The officers,' he complained, ' would not suffer their men to

suspect his good faith, but thought he was deceived by his subordinates. *Clarendon State Papers*, iii. 380.
[1] Thurloe, vi. 709. Cf. *Clarendon State Papers*, iii. 386.

be mustered, which was desired a week ago to have CHAP.
paid them for the last month of December ; enraged, IX
they said, that some soldiers died at the end of the 1657
month to whom they had advanced pay for their subsistence, and that so this diminution would fall upon
them to their loss.' Mazarin complained to Lockhart
of the ' unreasonableness of the English muster rolls,'
saying that when his commissaries attempted to make
exact musters they were ' threatened with mutinies, and
deserting of all, and returning into England.' [1] The
result was that Mazarin, at Turenne's instigation, de- Jan.
manded that the six regiments forming the English $\frac{1}{11}$
contingent should be reduced to four. The first reason
he gave was that the English regiments were so weak
that there were only sufficient men for four regiments,
that is, 4000 instead of 6000. The second was the
deficiency in the number of officers. ' There is wanting
of officers, who are either dead or have absented themselves without leave, to the number of eighty or ninety.[2]
Some of the officers that are present are not so fit for
their commands as were to be wished, who by this
reducement might be purged out, and the body restored
to a better condition than formerly. And to the end he
might clear himself from having intentions to save
money, or infringe the treaty, he offered, that at the
same time his Highness shall consent to the aforesaid re-
ducements he will give ready money for 2000 new men
to be raised, and put into two new regiments, with
officers as his Highness shall think fit to give them ; and
added that the most essential motive that inclined him
to desire this favour from his Highness was, that all the
officers of that body might by this example be taught

[1] Thurloe, vi. 695, 725.
[2] Six regiments of infantry required 180 officers, therefore about one-half
were missing.

to expect their continuance in their charges in the future from the zeal they should express in keeping their companies complete; which he said will be no small advantage to the common interest; and blamed the officers for having been very careless in this point heretofore.' [1]

The fact that the regiments forming the English contingent were hastily put together, for this particular service, helps to explain the want of sympathy which apparently existed between the officers and their men. Besides this, many of the officers were undoubtedly men who had seen little service and were not accustomed to campaigning, or alive to the necessity of looking after their men. It is safe to assert that if Cromwell had sent over six of his old regiments their officers would not have afforded Turenne such occasion for unfavourable criticism, and the losses of the army during the winter would have been smaller.

Exposed to such hardships and such neglect, the English contingent rapidly melted away. By the end of the winter of 1657 it had lost half its numbers, and was reduced from 6000 to 3000 men.[2] Out of these 3000 a third were generally too sick to be fit for duty. In a letter to Turenne (written just before he sailed for England), Reynolds declared that at that moment there were not more than 1000 English foot fit to do service in the garrison of Mardyke. According

---

[1] Thurloe, vi. 726; *Lettres de Mazarin*, viii. 310. Lockhart to some extent admits the justice of these complaints. *Clarendon State Papers*, iii. 386.

[2] *Clarke Papers*, iii. 135. According to a French estimate, 2000 English died at Mardyke before the end of the winter. In November, according to a French official report, the English contingent consisted still of 3733 men in France and Flanders; so it is probable that Reynolds somewhat exaggerated. As to the garrison of Mardyke, about the end of December a French report states that the English part of it consisted of 1060 privates and non-commissioned officers, 36 dragoons and 52 officers, besides 240 sick. The French part consisted of 307 soldiers and 38 officers.—Bourelly, pp. 41, 52.

to his estimate the total number of 'able serviceable CHAP.
men' in the whole English contingent, both in France IX
and Flanders, was not more than 1800. He wound up 1657
by pressing Turenne to send back to Mardyke, in order Dec.
to reinforce it, the three regiments then quartered in $\frac{5}{15}$
Northern France.[1]

Turenne had refused the request when Reynolds
had made it before. He thought Mardyke sufficiently
garrisoned as it was, and in no immediate danger of
attack. If it was threatened, the best way would be to
reinforce it by sea. He asked the Protector to keep
four or five hundred soldiers permanently on shipboard,
so that they might be thrown into the place at a moment's
notice. They might be drawn, he suggested, from one
of the Protector's old regiments, that is, from the standing army.[2] The English government rejected the plan.
It was not possible, wrote Thurloe to Lockhart, to
keep any men on shipboard, as Turenne proposed.
Neither could fresh men be recruited to fill the ranks of
the regiments at Mardyke, owing to the ill treatment of
those now in the French service. ' I think it,' he said,
' almost as possible to persuade them to leap into the
sea as to go to Flanders in the French king's service.'
However, the Protector ordered two regiments of infantry to be drawn down to the coast, one at Dover, the
other at Yarmouth, to be ready for embarkation at a
moment's notice.[3]

Reynolds was not satisfied with this solution. Instead of that, he proposed that the English regiments at
Mardyke should be relieved from time to time as the

---

[1] Thurloe, vi. 658.
[2] Ib. vi. 579.
[3] Ib. vi. 614; cf. *Clarendon State Papers*, iii. 377. Apparently the
regiments in question were those of Colonel Salmon and Biscoe (*Clarke
Papers*, iii. 127, 129). In the end, the regiment of Colonel Gibbon was sent
nstead of Biscoe's (Thurloe, vi. 676).

CHAP. French were. Let the thousand sick men at Mardyke
IX be sent home to England to be cured, and 500 fresh
1657 men sent to take their place. 'I have no hopes,' he
said, ' of finding another expedient for the preservation
of our soldiers or safety of this place.'[1] He determined
to go to London and to press his views upon the government in person. For some time he had been desirous of
going home on private grounds, and his father-in-law,
Sir Francis Russell, had obtained the Protector's leave
for a short visit to England.[2] Rumour afterwards
asserted that Reynolds really wished to clear his character from the suspicions which his own indiscretion
had aroused. Dunkirk and Mardyke were so close
that parties of the two garrisons often came into contact
with each other, and informal parleys were frequent.
The Duke of York, who was serving at Dunkirk, often
came across French officers whom he had known when
he was in the French army ; they talked together and
interchanged civilities. Hearing of this, Reynolds, perhaps out of curiosity to see a young soldier of growing
fame, perhaps thinking that the wheel of fortune might
some day turn, desired to see the Duke, and an ostensibly
accidental interview took place among the sandhills
between Mardyke and Dunkirk. Reynolds behaved
with great deference to the Duke, addressed him by the
title of Highness, and desired that he would not look
upon him as one sent over by Cromwell, but as one
serving the King of France, who was as ready as any
of the French to pay him due respect. Nothing passed
but compliments. James thought, from the manner of
Reynolds, that he wished to say something important,
but was prevented from saying it by the presence of
one of his attendants. All Reynolds did was 'to let
fall some dark expressions,' implying that he hoped a time

[1] Thurloe, vi. 653.   [2] Ib. vi. 630.

would come when he would be able to be of service to CHAP.
IX the Duke.[1] This interview, and other civilities [2] to the Stuart princes, not unnaturally roused the suspicion of 1657 some of the officers at Mardyke; and they sent the Protector notice of what had passed. It is said that Lieutenant-Colonel Francis White, who was temporarily employed as Governor of Mardyke, was one of these informers, and set out for England to accuse Reynolds. Reynolds, resolving that White should not get the start of him, embarked for England on the same ship. Dec. The ship was small and not very seaworthy; a $\frac{5}{15}$ storm arose, it was wrecked on the Goodwin Sands, and both Reynolds and White perished.[3]

Henry Cromwell lamented deeply over the loss of ' that worthy person, Sir John Reynolds,' and Fleetwood styled it ' a sad and sore rebuke ' from the Lord. ' He was a very gallant person, and well beloved in our army,' wrote a French commander. However, when the news of his interview with the Duke of York became known, all men concluded that he was ' either false or

---

[1] *Life of James II*, i. 318, 326. The interview took place about the middle of November; it was known in England by November 25 (*Clarke Papers*, iii. 127). Lockhart heard of it in Paris early in January. ' It 's given out,' he writes, ' by some of Charles Stuart's faction here, that something passed at that meeting that I know he could not be capable of ; neither do I believe that any such meeting was ' (Thurloe, vi. 687, 731).

[2] ' Besides the order he gave to the ships in the Splinter not to shoot when either of us were aboard on that side (which was punctually observed), he sent several presents of wine to my lord Newburgh, desiring him to dispose of them to those for whom my lord knew he had a great respect.'—*Life of James II*, i. 327.

[3] The story that White was the person who accused Reynolds rests on the authority of the Duke of York.

White, who was lieutenant-colonel of the Protector's regiment of foot, was sent over to Mardyke about October 10 to replace Colonel Clarke as governor (*Clarke Papers*, iii. 122 ; *Cal. State Papers Dom.*, 1657-8, p. 123). The government provided for his wife and family, and for those of other officers wrecked with them (ib. p. 335 ; Thurloe, vi. 735). On the circumstances of their shipwreck, see Thurloe, vi. 668, 676, 686 ; *Cal. State Papers Dom.*, 1657-8, pp. 202, 213 ; *Mercurius Politicus*, December 10–17. p. 174.

CHAP.
IX
1657

Dec.
10
20

more light-headed than was requisite for a man in such a charge.'[1]

Simultaneously with the news of the death of Reynolds came the warning of an intended Spanish assault on Mardyke.[2] Then the advantage of the late preparations was seen. The Protector at once ordered twelve companies to be embarked, and within a couple of days 500 men of Colonel Gibbon's regiment landed at Mardyke.[3] Major-General Morgan, whose incorruptible fidelity and unwearied vigilance could be relied upon, became governor, while the Cardinal sent Marshal D'Aumont to superintend the completion of the fortifications, and some fresh companies of Swiss to relieve the French detachments stationed there. The garrison was made up to at least 2500 men, enough to defend Mardyke from any sudden assault, and more than it could comfortably hold. The Spaniards continued to make preparations for a formal siege; but the opinion was that a sudden attack was more to be expected, and Lockhart feared traitors in the garrison itself more than any other danger. In his opinion it was unnecessary to cram Mardyke with great numbers of men; with proper vigilance it was safe against a sudden assault, and in case of a regular siege it could easily be relieved from England. He urged the Protector to send no more men, and thought the last 500 might be withdrawn.[4]

[1] Thurloe, vi. 680, 681, 688.   [2] Ib. vi. 676, 679.

[3] Ib. vi. 676, 677, 695, 717, 735, 743. 'Major-General Morgan,' says Lockhart on December $\frac{19}{29}$, 'wrote by his last that, before Colonel Gibbon's four companies arrived, they had 1400 of the English foot that served all this campaign, 300 French foot, 200 officers, and 250 horse, which can be no inconsiderable garrison for such a place.'

[4] The four companies of Gibbon's regiment were recalled in January (Cal. State Papers Dom., 1657-8, p. 254). About this time the garrison seems to have been reinforced by three battalions from Guisnes, which had gone into winter quarters with Turenne's army (Thurloe, vi. 709).

Lockhart judged rightly. A smaller garrison properly supplied, and regularly relieved from England,
would have been far more efficient, and by such an
arrangement many lives would have been saved. The
English government hardly used to the full the advantage which the command of the sea gave it, though it
is safe to say that, without that advantage, Mardyke
could not have been held during the hard winter of
1657-8. Ever since the spring of 1657 Dunkirk and
Ostend had been blockaded by small English squadrons, who kept the Flemish privateers from coming
out to prey upon English trade, and prevented supplies
for the Spanish garrisons from going in.[1] A contrary
wind kept the fleet from taking part in the capture of
Mardyke; but as soon as it was taken, a squadron
under Vice-Admiral William Goodson was stationed
off the place. Seamen were sent on shore to assist
in extending the fortifications, and some brass guns
were lent by the fleet to mount upon the works. The
fire of the frigates that lay in the Splinter helped to
frustrate the Spanish attack on November 1.[2] Above
all, the very existence of the garrison depended on the
supply of provisions, wood for palisades, powder, hay
for horses, and other requisites which were almost
entirely drawn from England and brought in English
ships, though they were to some extent provided at
the expense of France.[3] All these things were more
easily and safely to be supplied from England by sea
than brought by land from Northern France.

Captain Thomas Sparling, who succeeded Goodson
early in November, 1657, reported that unless the ships
could be forced out of the road before Mardyke, and the

---

[1] *Cal. State Papers Dom.*, 1656–7, pp. 281, 337, 348, 353, 368, 383, 386.

[2] Ib. 1657–8, pp. 138, 143, 275, 277 ; *Clarke Papers*, iii. 122.

[3] See Thurloe, vi. 579, 618, 637 ; *Lettres de Mazarin*, viii. 242.

victuals of the garrison cut off, 20,000 men would find it difficult to retake the place.[1] At the end of January Sparling's frigates were forced off the coast by ' a sharp and violent north-east wind' and by 'the continual flowing in of the ice which came from the eastward.' Some of his smaller ships were frozen up in the harbour of Mardyke, and the garrison there had to break the ice in their moats twice a day.[2] As the Spanish army had retired into its winter quarters at the end of December,[3] there was no danger of a siege, but there was some fear that the Spaniards would seize the opportunity to effect the long threatened landing in England which was to be the signal for the rising of the Royalists. Winter had always been the time selected for the expedition, for the very reason that the English blockade could not be permanently maintained during that season. In November Cardinal Mazarin had sent Lockhart a memoir written with his own hand, saying that he had learnt, 'by intelligence which never yet failed him,' that the Spaniard intended to send into England, towards the latter end of January or the beginning of February, 3000 foot and 1000 horse under Charles II or the Duke of York, provided with artillery and with arms sufficient to equip 12,000 men. In an interview two or three weeks later the Cardinal added some further particulars. He said that hitherto ' the project had been to carry Mardyke first, and then to ship at Dunkirk, but there now being little hopes of carrying Mardyke, he believed their disappointment in that would go near to break their whole design, for those of Flanders would be loath to part with any forces so long as that thorn stuck in their sides.' [4]

---

[1] *Cal. State Papers Dom.*, 1657–8, pp. 160, 201.

[2] Ib. 1657–8, pp. 279, 283, 292 ; *Clarke Papers*, iii. 135 ; *Mercurius Politicus*, February 11–18, 1658, p. 318.

[3] Thurloe, vi. 705, 707, 729.   [4] *Clarendon State Papers*, iii. 377, 380.

The Cardinal's reasoning was sound, but now the
situation was altered. In the absence of the English fleet the Flemish privateers came out of Dunkirk, Ostend was free to serve as a place of embarkation, and the Spanish forces began to draw down to the coast as if they meant something.[1]

[1] Thurloe, vi. 803, 806, 817.

CHAPTER X

THE NORTHERN WAR

SIDE by side with the struggle between France and
Spain in Western Europe, there was another struggle
in progress in North-Eastern Europe between Sweden
and Poland. England was taking a decisive part in
the first war; the question was whether she should
intervene in the second. Through her fleet she might
exercise as great an influence in the Baltic and the
North Sea as she was doing in the Mediterranean and the
Atlantic. At the beginning of the Northern war England held entirely aloof; but as it was prolonged one
state after another was drawn in, and the theatre of
the war widened. English interests became involved,
and at last it seemed probable that England would be
drawn into this second struggle as well as the first.

In 1654 Queen Christina of Sweden abdicated and
was succeeded by her cousin Charles X. Eager to
emulate the fame of his uncle, Gustavus Adolphus,
and to extend the possessions of Sweden in the
Eastern Baltic, he availed himself of an old quarrel to
attack Poland.[1] His success was immediate and complete. The Swedish forces crossed the Polish frontier
on July 11, 1655. Warsaw was occupied on August 30,
Cracow surrendered on October 8. John Casimir fled
from Poland, and the Polish nobles welcomed Charles X
as their lawful sovereign. The great trading towns on

[1] See Gardiner, iii. 425.

the Vistula, the special object of Charles X's covetous- CHAP.
ness, held out longer; but Thorn and Elbing yielded on X
November 24, and only Dantzic stubbornly refused to 1655-6
accept the King of Sweden as its master.

At the end of 1655 Poland was at the feet of Charles
X, but during the next year the tide of war turned
against him. Brilliant as the successes were which he
had gained during the campaign, their results were
extremely unsubstantial. For the military genius of
Charles X, unlike that of Gustavus Adolphus, was not
matched by his political foresight, and he had failed to
forecast the consequences of his policy. ' I am apt to
believe,' said an English diplomatic agent who accom- Dec.31
panied Charles X, ' that the King of Sweden may have 1655
greater trouble to keep what he hath got, than he had
in getting it.' [1] So it proved. Before the winter of
1655 ended, the Polish magnates, who had flocked to
the Swedish camp, began to draw away from the foreign
invader whom they had welcomed six months earlier.
The patriotism of the Polish nation flamed up, and it
was fanned to fury by the exhortations of the Catholic
clergy to shake off the yoke of the Lutheran heretics.
Moreover, as the Swedish army had no financial re-
sources of its own and lived upon the conquered country,
national feeling and religious hatred were stimulated by
extortion and oppression. A general rising against the
Swedes took place; and with but 30,000 men at his back
Charles X had to fight not only the Poles, but the
Tartars, the Cossacks, and the Russians, who now
intervened on their side. In the spring of 1656
he marched against the enemies who were gathering
in Southern Poland, and won a great victory at Feb.
Golumbo. But in spite of victory he found his $\frac{8}{18}$

---

[1] Thurloe, iv. 361.

forces melting away from hardship and disease, while crowds of light horsemen hovered round his track, cutting off stragglers, intercepting convoys, and reducing his army to starvation.   He was obliged to retreat, and when he re-entered Warsaw in April, 1656, he brought but 4000 men with him.   Three months later, on July 1, Warsaw itself was retaken by John Casimir and the Poles.

Finding his own strength insufficient to maintain his conquests, Charles X looked round for an ally, and found one to his hand in the Elector of Brandenburg. Frederick William, the Great Elector, had a difficult game to play.   On the one hand, as duke of Eastern Prussia, he was a vassal of the Polish crown and bound by duty to support Poland against Sweden.   On the other hand, he was extremely eager to convert the feudal tenure by which he held his Prussian duchy into absolute sovereignty.   In the second place, the growth of Swedish power in Northern Germany, and the policy which Charles X was at present pursuing, were both in the highest degree detrimental to the state which, out of many scattered territories, the Elector was striving to build up.   By the treaty of Westphalia Sweden had obtained the western half of Pomerania, which properly belonged to Brandenburg.   Now the King of Sweden was bent on seizing West Prussia from the Poles and making it his own, thus cutting off East Prussia from the rest of the Elector's dominions.   It was not to his advantage that a strong military monarchy, like that of Sweden, should replace the weak Polish kingdom on his borders.

Nevertheless, as he was not strong enough to stand against Sweden alone, the Elector had been forced to temporise and to accept the terms offered him.   By the treaty of Königsberg in January, 1656, he agreed to become the vassal of Charles X for East Prussia, to pay CHAP. X Sweden half of the tolls levied in the Prussian ports of 1656 Memel and Pillau, and to admit Swedish men-of-war into his harbours.[1] He received, however, a certain accession of territory, at the expense of Poland, in the shape of the district of Ermeland. In the six months which had passed since the treaty, the fortune of war had been against the Swedish King; and he was forced to purchase the support of the Elector by large concessions. By the treaty of Marienburg in June, 1656, Frederick William obtained as the price of his assistance four Polish palatinates in full sovereignty, and promised that his whole army should co-operate with the Swedes in the next campaign. The immediate result of the treaty was a three days' battle under the walls of Warsaw, in which 18,000 Swedes and Brandenburgers defeated 60,000 or 70,000 Poles and Tartars. The Polish capital was recaptured by the victors, but the victory of Charles X was more glorious than fruitful. The scattered Polish forces gathered once more, and new adversaries appeared against the Swedes.

In the summer of 1656 the Russians overran Livonia, captured Dorpat, and laid siege to Riga. Still more threatening was the intervention of the Dutch in the struggle. Charles X did not greatly care what he gained or lost in the interior of Poland so long as he acquired Polish Prussia and its great seaports. The dominion of the Baltic was his chief aim, and for that the possession of this province was indispensable. For more than six months Dantzic had held out against all the efforts of the Swedish forces to subdue it. 'If he masters this place,' said Secretary Thurloe, 'it will be more worth to him than all his kingdom of

[1] Gardiner, iii. 444.

CHAP. Sweden.'[1] But the great trading city was a self-
X governed little commonwealth under the nominal suzer-
1656 ainty of Poland, and had no mind to accept a new and
exacting sovereign. It looked to Holland for help, and
with good reason. The United Provinces could not
grow enough food for their own consumption, and
Dantzic was the granary and the emporium from which
they drew their wheat.[2] Moreover, the Baltic trade was
the most important part of the foreign commerce of
the Dutch. In Amsterdam it was said, ' there be
whole streets that do live, flourish, and subsist by this
Baltic commerce.'[3] The whole mercantile navy of
Holland was estimated to consist of about 15,000 ships
(more exactly 14,850), and of those 6000 were employed
in the Baltic trade, whilst but 1500 sufficed for the
Dutch trade with England and France. And the average
burden of the ships employed in the Baltic trade was
so much greater than the others, that it amounted to
more than one-half of the total tonnage of the Dutch
mercantile marine.[4]

Dutch statesmen were never backward in pro-
tecting their trade, and the appeal of Dantzic was not
neglected. In July forty-eight Dutch men-of-war, under
Opdam, appeared off the mouth of the Vistula, and
brought the Swedish blockade to an end without firing
a shot. On September 11, 1656, a treaty was signed at
Elbing, between the ambassadors of the United Provinces and the Swedish chancellor, which assured the
citizens of Dantzic the free exercise of their trade, and
promised the Dutch the treatment of the most favoured
nation in regard to tolls and customs.[5] The sea-power

---

[1] Thurloe, iii. 440.
[2] Wicquefort, ii. 425 ; Philippson, *Der Grosse Kurfürst*, 1897, i. 239.
[3] Thurloe, iv. 654.   [4] Philippson, i. 197.
[5] Carlson, *Geschichte Schwedens*, i. 161 (forming vol. iv. of the *History of Sweden* in Heeren and Ukert's *Geschichte der Europaischen Staaten*).

of the Dutch had frustrated the attempt of Charles X CHAP.
to incorporate the greatest of the Baltic ports in his
dominions, and frustrated the King's scheme for securing 1655-6
the dominion of the Baltic.

During this period of the Northern war, England
remained perfectly neutral, though the sympathies of the
Protector and the nation in general were notoriously on
the side of Sweden.   There were, it is true, some Puritans
who thought Sweden's attack on Poland unprovoked,
and believed that its success would be detrimental to
the common interests of European states.   The Poles,
wrote Robert Baillie, were a sinful, popish people, and
yet 'they were a good bar for Christendom on that
side against the Turks' and Tartars' encroachments;
and if they be ruined a great gap will be opened for
these Scythian barbarians to fall on us all.'[1]   To most
Puritans, however, the mere fact that the Swedes were
Protestants and the Poles Catholics was sufficient
to decide the question in favour of the former.   Cromwell's admiration for Gustavus Adolphus predisposed
him in favour of the new King; and he thought to find
in Charles X a leader who would tread in the steps of
Gustavus and carry out the work which the Protestant
hero had left unfinished.   Abroad, report exaggerated
the closeness of the connexion between the two rulers
of Sweden and England.   'The Protector,' reported
Longland, the English agent at Leghorn, 'is generally
looked upon as an intimate colleague, if not the con-
triver, of the King of Sweden's expedition for Poland.'[2]
As a matter of fact, Charles X had not consulted the
Protector before undertaking the war.[3]   What gave

[1] Baillie, *Letters*, iii. 293.

[2] Thurloe, iv. 92 ; October 29, 1655. See also J. N. Bowman, *The Protestant
Interest in Cromwell's Foreign Relations* (Heidelberg, 1900), pp. 46–76; and
Guernsey Jones, *The Diplomatic Relations between Cromwell and Charles X*
(Lincoln, Nebraska, 1897).

[3] See Thurloe's words, Bischoffshausen, p. 213.

some colour to the popular belief was the negotiations
which followed the war and continued throughout a
large part of 1656.   In March, 1655, Coyet, an agent of
Charles X, came to England, charged to elaborate the
details of a commercial treaty and to pave the way for
a closer political connexion between the two countries.
In July followed a second Swedish ambassador, Christer
Bonde, whose business was to negotiate an alliance.[1]   In
August the Protector dispatched his kinsman, Edward
Rolt, to the camp of the Swedish King, and he accompanied Charles X during part of his campaign in Poland
in the autumn of 1655.   Rolt's mission, however, was
merely to carry the ratification of the commercial
treaty which the late Queen had concluded with the
Protector, and he was not empowered to negotiate.[2]
Bonde's negotiations in London ended, so far as the
scheme for a political alliance was concerned, in complete failure.   It was impossible for Charles X and the
Protector to arrive at an understanding ; their objects
were too dissimilar.   Cromwell wished to direct the
arms of Charles X against the House of Austria, and
proposed the formation of a general league of Protestant
powers for that purpose.[3]   All that Charles offered in
reply was a defensive alliance directed on the one hand
against all the enemies of either party, and on the other
against all who infringed the treaty of Osnabrück.[4]
Besides this, while the Protector was anxious to include
the Dutch in his general Protestant league and in any
particular arrangement with Sweden, Charles X asked
for the support of a squadron of twenty English ships
in the Baltic against the Dutch, and the defensive

[1] See Gardiner, *Commonwealth and Protectorate*, iii. 430–7 ; Pufendorff, *De
Rebus a Carolo Gustavo Sueciae Rege gestes*, ed. 1696, i. 9 ; ii. 86–92.

[2] Thurloe, iii. 418, 709 ; iv. 182, 275, 361, 363, 482, 539.

[3] Ib. iv. 486 ; Pufendorff, iii. 76.

[4] Ib. iv. 623 ; cf. Whitelocke, *Memorials*, iv. 238.

alliance he proposed to England would probably have CHAP.
X
1656 involved hostilities with Holland.[1] These negotiations, therefore, led to no result. The Protector confined his positive action to attempts to mediate between Sweden and Brandenburg and Sweden and Holland : to unite the Protestant powers remained throughout his chief object.[2] His attitude was defined in his own words to the Dutch ambassador in January, 1656.

' He must acknowledge ' (he said) ' that he had found no difficulty in the progress of the Swedes against the popish Polanders, nor in taking of Warsaw, Cracow, and other places in the upper parts ; and though the King had thought fit to pursue his conquests as far as Constantinople, he should have wished him from his heart good success ; or if he had struck in towards those parts where there are great store of Protestants, where they have suffered for some years great persecutions, that for his part he could very well have endured it ; but that at present he did confess, that it was not so pleasing to him, that those parts should be assaulted which do belong to Protestant princes ; though he doth find himself highly obliged in his conscience to endeavour, in this constitution of time, not only to prevent a rupture between the Protestant princes and states, but also to unite the same more closely in a common league of mutual defence against the inhuman cruelties of Popery ; that he had earnestly signified his mind to the present extraordinary Swedish ambassador in this city, and that he had formerly assured me, that he would not

[1] Gardiner, iii. 437; Pufendorff, ii. 88.

[2] Fleetwood, writing to Henry Cromwell on December 11, 1655, says : ' The great success that still it pleaseth God to give the King of Sweden doth very much alarum forrayne states. I am not without hope but that the Lord may make my lord Protector an instrument of great good upon this occasion to the whole Protestant interest ; he hath I am persuaded a very large heart above any for such a worke.'—*Lansdowne MS.*, 822, f. 226. See also, on the Protector's efforts to mediate, Thurloe, iv. 343, 505.

only accept no offer in prejudice of the United Netherlands; but also that he could now tell me in the presence
of these lords, that he hoped it would never enter into
their hearts to receive anything distinctly and not in
common with the United Netherlands, in regard of any
privileges, liberties, or otherwise in the commerce and
navigation in the East Sea and those parts adjacent;
that they had not yet judged it necessary to send an
embassy thither, believing that they shall suddenly see
which way the business will go, and that we should find
that they had not sat still, and that he hoped that it
will yet come in its time.' [1]

These last words were important, for they embodied
a declaration of Cromwell's commercial policy. The
conquests of the King of Sweden threatened the trade
of England and Holland alike. If Charles X obtained
possession of all the Polish ports, he might, for the sake
of raising a large revenue, impose such heavy customs
duties on all imports from foreign countries that their
manufactures would be unable to compete with native
products. This he did begin to do, to the detriment of
the trade of both English and Dutch. 'The state of
England,' wrote a merchant to Thurloe, 'for political
causes, may seem to connive at the Swedish progress,
yet the trade of England will find a great change to
the much decay of the same.' [2] The government was
warned that, if the Swedes were allowed to impose heavy
duties upon English cloth, it would be supplanted by
Silesian or Polish cloth which was not similarly burdened.
As it was, the English cloth trade was already declining in Germany and Poland. 'Truly,' wrote Richard
Bradshaw, 'if some speedy course be not taken that all
woollen manufactures may come as cheap and as well

[1] Thurloe, iv. 389; cf. iv. 684.
[2] Ib. iv. 119.

made to the strangers as they can make them, they will
soon out England of that trade in these parts.' [1]

Holland, which was threatened in the same way as
England, met the danger, as we have seen, by dispatching Opdam's fleet to the Baltic and wringing from
Charles X the treaty of Elbing. England, which was
on better terms with Sweden, was able to conclude an
advantageous commercial treaty without any such display of force. The treaty signed on July 17, 1656, was
the sole result of the mission of Bonde and Coyet to
England.[2] By it the long discussed political alliance
was reduced to a mere permission to the King of Sweden
to raise a certain number of volunteers for his army in
England.[3] A form of certificate was also agreed upon
which would free merchant ships of either nation from
molestation by the cruisers of the other, excepting in
the case of goods which were contraband of war. But
the most important provision was one stipulating that
the tolls levied in such parts of Poland and Prussia as had
fallen under the power of the Swedish King were not to
be raised higher than the point reached in 1650, and were
to be lowered still further if they were lowered in favour
of any other nation.[4] In its essence, therefore, this treaty
closely resembled the treaty between Sweden and
Holland signed at Elbing a couple of months later; and
as the Elbing treaty included the English, Danes,
French, and Brandenburgers as well as the Dutch, all
these nations were placed upon the same footing. The

---

[1] Thurloe, iv. 86, 296, 404 ; v. 126.

[2] A long account of the negotiations is given in Whitelocke's *Memorials*,
iv. 219–71, ed. 1853.

[3] The Protector had already given leave for 1000 men to be raised in Scotland, under the command of Lord Cranston (Gardiner, iii. 431, 439). Now leave
was given to Sir William Vavasour to raise 2000 more (Carlboom, p. 146). See
also Thurloe, iv. 561 ; Whitelocke, *Memorials*, iv. 232.

[4] Treaty between the Protector and Charles X, July 17. Pufendorf, *De
Rebus a Carolo Gustavo gestis*, Appendix, pp. 3–10, ed. 1696.

CHAP. commercial question, so far as concerned access to the
X ports of Polish Prussia, was settled upon the basis of
1656 equal rights for the trade of all, or, to use a modern
phrase, by the adoption of the principle of ' the open
door.' On the other hand, this settlement only affected
the trade of a particular portion of the Baltic ; it was
limited and local in its application. It could not put
an end to the jealousy between England and Holland,
and it did not allay the fear with which the Dutch
regarded the extension of the Swedish dominion over
the Baltic and the Baltic lands. Only let the war
spread from the Eastern to the Western Baltic, and
fresh questions would arise ; new powers would be
drawn into the vortex, England might be forced to
take part in the struggle, and would perhaps be brought
into collision with other Protestant states. In 1657 it
seemed very probable that some such conflict would be
the inevitable result of the change which took place in
the character of the war.[1]

During the autumn and winter of 1656, fortune
turned still more against Charles X. It is true that in
October the vast Russian army which had besieged
Riga was forced, by the valiant defence of Magnus de la
Gardie and his small Swedish garrison, to raise the
siege. Englishmen exulted at the news of the Czar's
defeat. ' God seems to have put his hook into the
jaws of that scourge of the world,' wrote Richard
Bradshaw to Thurloe, and Monck also expressed his
gladness.[2] But when the Russian armies retired, they
left Livonia a plague-stricken desert behind them.
This military success of the Swedes was followed by a

---

[1] Thurloe, after mentioning the Danish declaration of war, adds : ' This
drew the King of Sweden out of Poland, and sett the war on a wholly new foot,
and most of the Princes and States in Europe found themselves concerned to
intermeddle in it.'—Bischoffshausen, p. 215.

[2] Thurloe, v. 505, 506.

diplomatic defeat of more lasting importance. In December, 1656, a treaty took place between Poland and
the Emperor in which Ferdinand III, while promising
to mediate between Sweden and Poland, also pledged
himself to furnish 4000 men to aid the Poles against the
Swedes. It was easy to foresee that this first timid
step on the part of Austria would be followed before
long by more decisive action. To meet that danger
Charles X, whose army was now reduced to 12,000 men,
was obliged to draw closer the tie between himself
and the Elector of Brandenburg. On November 20,
1656, took place the treaty of Labiau, by which
Sweden recognised the sovereignty of the Elector over
Ducal Prussia and Ermeland, and renounced the claim
to share the proceeds of the tolls in Prussian ports.[1]
Thus, so far as Sweden was concerned, the feudal tie
between Prussia and Poland was broken.

Meanwhile in Poland itself the confusion grew wilder
still. In January, 1657, George Rakoczy, the Prince of
Transylvania, invaded the unhappy country, leaguing
himself with the Swedes and the Cossacks. ' Poland,'
said an Englishman, ' is the stage whereupon the sad
tragedy of the north-east part of the world is acted, the
persons are the Swedes, Poles, Muscovites, Tartars,
Cossacks, Brandenburgers, Danes, and Hollanders.' [2]
It seemed as if nothing could avert the complete ruin of
that unhappy nation, and as if the ' Finis Poloniæ ' of
the Polish patriot might have been uttered in 1657
instead of 1795. But three events took place in the
course of the year which totally changed the nature of
the struggle, altered the whole character of the northern
question, and transferred the seat of the war from
Poland to the Western Baltic. On April 2, 1657, the

[1] Philippson, i. 253 ; Waddington, *Le Grand Electeur*, i. 373.
[2] Thurloe, v. 409.

Emperor Ferdinand III died. His eldest son, Ferdinand King of the Romans, had died on July 9, 1654 ; and the claims of the House of Hapsburg to the imperial crown now devolved upon his second son, the Archduke Leopold. It might have been expected that Leopold, as a candidate for the empire, would have refrained from helping Poland, in order to secure the votes of Sweden and Brandenburg in the coming election. He took the opposite course, and definitely placed himself on the side of Poland against Rakoczy and Charles X. By the Austro-Polish treaty of May 27, 1657, 12,000 Austrian troops were to be sent to the help of Poland ; and the first result of their intervention was the regaining of Cracow from the Swedes and the total frustration of Rakoczy's campaign.[1]

In the same month of May, 1657, took place also the second of the three events which saved Poland. Frederick III of Denmark, encouraged by the intervention of Austria and the ill-success of the Swedes, at last plucked up courage to declare war against Sweden. Denmark had many grievances against its ancient rival, and it seemed a favourable opportunity to recover the territory lost by the disadvantageous treaty of 1645. Three Danish armies were designed to take the field at once : one was to attack Bremen and drive the Swedes out of Western Germany ; the second was to attack, from Scania, the southernmost provinces of Sweden in the Scandinavian peninsula ; the third, from Norway, was to penetrate into the western provinces of Sweden.[2]

When these new enemies thus suddenly arrayed themselves against him, Charles X was obliged to change completely his plan of action. His resolution

[1] Philippson, i. 264.
[2] Carlson, i. 233.

was rapidly taken. For a moment he thought of adopting the plan which Mazarin and Cromwell continually
pressed upon him, and turning his arms against Silesia
and the hereditary possessions of the House of Austria.
But it was only for a moment that this plan attracted
him ; then, for the present, he definitely abandoned it.
The opportunity of turning his back upon the Polish
chaos was too tempting to be neglected. ' Nothing, said
the King, can be done with these barbarians, beat them
as much as you like.'.[1] Even the acquisition of West
Prussia, hitherto the main object of Swedish policy and
pursued by Charles with invincible tenacity, became
more and more an open question with him. He talked
of giving up his claim to that province to the Elector of
Brandenburg in exchange for East Pomerania. For he
had made up his mind at any cost to get out of Poland.

War with Denmark was far more attractive to him
than war with Poland, for the military inferiority of
the Danes to the Swedes had been proved in the last
struggle, and he knew the internal weakness of the
Danish state. Conquests were to be made there of far
greater value than anything that could be got from the
Poles. The dream of Swedish statesmen was to extend
Sweden to its natural boundaries, and if the Danes were
beaten it might now be realised. The Danish provinces
in the south of the Scandinavian peninsula—Scania,
Blekinge, Halland—would be the prize of victory. For
the establishment of the Swedish dominion in the
Baltic these coastlands were far more important than
those of Polish Prussia. By gaining them Sweden
would have the Sound in her grip. Besides this, Charles
was obliged to withdraw his forces from Poland in order
to protect his own dominions. It was necessary to
defend Sweden itself from the Danish armies which were

[1] Philippson, i. 264.

CHAP.
X
1657
directed against it. It was still more necessary to defend Bremen and the Swedish territories between the Elbe and Weser; for in Western Germany the Swedish power was neither solid nor deeply rooted.

These were very sound reasons for transferring the seat of the war from Poland to Denmark. Charles therefore resolved to turn his forces against the Danes; but he left Poland with the confidence of a conqueror hurrying to fresh triumphs. He believed that his task would be easy. In a few months, he intimated to the Elector of Brandenburg, he would return to Prussia and force the Polish war to a decisive issue. He felt sure now of the alliance of France and England; and a final struggle with the House of Austria to which those powers urged him was still the ultimate object of his schemes, though in the immediate present he had other antagonists to overcome. The Elector of Brandenburg was promised Silesia and large acquisitions on the Rhine if he would take part in this intended league against Austria. Meanwhile Charles left his ally to maintain himself against Poles and Austrians as best he could.[1]

The King of Sweden lost no time in putting this new scheme of strategy into execution. During May and June, 1657, he collected upon the Vistula the troops which he withdrew from Poland, and by the end of July he was on the Elbe with his army. In a campaign that lasted but fourteen days, he drove the Danes out of the territories of Bremen; and then pushed through Holstein into the enemy's country, driving the Danish forces in disorder before him. Six thousand Danes garrisoned the strong fortress of Fredriksodde, which stood on the eastern coast of Jutland opposite the island of Funen. On November 3, 1657, it was stormed by 4000 Swedes; some 3000 prisoners were

[1] Philippson, i. 265.

taken, and 1500 of the garrison lost their lives in the CHAP.
assault, while only some 70 of the assailants fell.[1] X
This splendid feat of arms made the Swedes lords of 1657
all Jutland. Nor was that all; it enabled them
to attempt with some chance of success the passage
from Jutland to the islands of Funen and Zealand, and
so to attack Copenhagen itself. What protected the
Danish capital was not the Danish army, but the Danish
fleet. Superior in force and numbers to the Swedish
fleet, and strengthened by some Dutch ships, it
prevented Charles X and his army from passing the
Little Belt, which separated Jutland from Funen,
and the Great Belt which separated Funen from Zealand. Denmark had been thoroughly beaten in the
field, but it was not yet crushed.

On the other hand, Charles X and Sweden now stood
alone. The withdrawal of the Swedish troops from
Poland had been followed by the defection of the
Elector of Brandenburg. He saw himself exposed, by
the deliberate policy of his ally, to the united arms of
Poland and Austria, and naturally made the best terms
he could for himself and his people. In August, 1657,
when the Swedes were entering Jutland, he made a
truce with the Poles. This was followed on September
19, 1657, by the treaty of Wehlau. The Elector gave
up Ermeland and four Polish districts which he had
acquired in the course of the war; but received full
sovereignty over his Prussian dukedom, and became
absolutely independent of Poland. He had thus succeeded in obtaining one of the chief aims of his policy,
and in return he pledged himself to join the coalition
against Sweden with at least 6000 men.[2]

---

[1] Carlson, i. 252; Thurloe, vi. 604.

[2] Philippson, i. 275 ; Waddington, *Le Grand Electeur*, i. 391 ; E. Salzer,
Der Ubertritt des Grossen Kurfürsten (Heidelberg, 1904).

CHAP.
X
1657

There was a prospect that the coalition against Sweden would be strengthened by a still more important accession. The Dutch feared the predominance of Sweden in the Baltic on account of their trade ; their ambassador in Denmark, Conrad von Beuninghen, had been the chief agent in persuading the Danish king to attack Sweden. The appearance of a Dutch squadron in the Baltic, charged to save Denmark from complete subjugation and to wrest from the Swedes the fruit of their victories, seemed only a matter of weeks.

In this hour of need Charles X turned to England for assistance : for money to pay his troops, and for ships to counterbalance the Dutch fleet. Throughout 1657 active negotiations went on between England and Sweden. In January Charles X, through George Fleetwood (the brother of Cromwell's son-in-law Charles Fleetwood), applied to the Protector for a substantial loan. The Protector answered the request by demanding the cession of Bremen as security for the money. This demand was seriously meant. In all later negotiations it was repeated ; and Swedish diplomatists were convinced that Cromwell aimed at obtaining a foothold in Germany, and was not merely seeking a plausible pretext for refusing the loan. Charles X as stubbornly refused the cession of Bremen ; merely as a recruiting ground for his armies it was absolutely necessary to him.[1] However, he proposed that the Protector should possess himself of Oldenburg or East Friesland, neither of which districts belonged to Sweden. The Protector rejected these offers. If he was to ask Parliament to support him in a new

---

[1] Erdmannsdörffer, *Deutsche Geschichte vom Westphalischen Frieden*, &c., i. 284 ; Carlson, *Geschichte Schwedens*, i. 242 ; Carlboom, *Sverige och England*, 1655–7 (Gothenburg, 1900), pp. 133–6. Fleetwood's letter of January 23, 1657, gives a full account of Cromwell's demand for Bremen, and his reasons. It is printed in Wolfgang Michael's *Cromwell* (Berlin, 1907), ii. 169, 223.

foreign enterprise, and that one on a great scale, he CHAP.
must be able to show Parliament some profitable X
acquisition, such as Bremen would be. In any case, 1657
England must have some strong military basis at her
disposal before he could entertain an offensive league,
or send troops to the new field of action.[1]

In spite of Cromwell's refusal, Charles X renewed the
attempt. In August, 1657, he sent a new ambassador,
Friesendorff, to London, charged to offer Cromwell the
choice between a series of alternatives. He was again
offered Oldenburg, or rather invited to conquer and
make it his own ; the King was willing to cede Cromwell also his own hereditary claim to the county of
Delmenhorst, to let him take East Friesland if he chose,
and to allow him to garrison the Bishopric of Munster
and other parts of the Westphalian circle. If Cromwell
wished also to obtain a footing in the Eastern Baltic,
Charles was willing to cede him the fort of Weichselhaupt
at the mouth of the Vistula, and part of Pomerellen.
But the alternative which Charles himself preferred
was that Cromwell should take part in the King's
Danish conquests, and he offered him North Jutland
and certain islands as his share in the partition of
Denmark, to which he was willing to add part of Ditt-
marsh and the city of Gluckstadt. Finally, though he
trusted that Cromwell would content himself either
with a footing upon the Weser, such as the first alternative offered, or with one upon the Elbe, as the second
offered, the ambassador was empowered if he found
that the Protector wished to have his foot upon both
rivers, and that there was no other means to persuade
him to break with Denmark and give substantial
assistance against it, to consent even to that.[2]

[1] Carlboom, pp. 141-5 ; Pufendorff, iv. 79-81.
[2] Erdmannsdörffer, i. 285 ; Guernsey Jones, p. 55 ; Pufendorff, iv. 82.

Cromwell did not accept any one of these alternatives. Perhaps he would even then have allied
himself with Sweden, if Charles X had promised
Bremen. But fortunately for both Germany and
England, the Swedish king did not make up his mind
to the sacrifice until it was too late. On October 12,
and again on November 5, 1657, he empowered
Friesendorff to offer Bremen.[1] By that time the
Protector had too much on his hands in Flanders to
engage in a fresh enterprise of such magnitude.
Moreover, the offer was coupled with an unacceptable
condition. Cromwell's mind was filled with the idea of
a great struggle against Rome and the House of Hapsburg. The acquisition of Bremen had seemed desirable
because its possession would enable him to influence
the States of North Germany and to further the
formation of a Protestant league. The vacancy of
the empire made the present moment a favourable
opportunity for an attack on the Austrian power, and
schemes for the transference of the imperial dignity
to the King of Sweden or some other Protestant prince
were already on foot.[2]

Charles X also talked of a crusade against the House
of Hapsburg. He professed his Protestant zeal, and
his desire to promote a general league of the Protestant states, and proposed a regular scheme for that
purpose through Friesendorff in the autumn of 1657.[3]
But this league was a secondary object in his mind.
With him the traditional policy of Sweden always
came first, namely to establish its dominion over the
Baltic Sea and its coasts. If the Protector wanted
him to attack Austria he must first help him to

[1] Michael, ii. 169–71.
[2] Ib. ii. 145, 161, 217. See also Schlezer's report on his interview with
Cromwell on May 14, 1657. Urkunden und Actenstücke, vii. 766.
[3] Guernsey Jones, p. 58 ; cf. Pufendorf, iv. 84–86.

crush Denmark. In short, he stipulated that Cromwell should become his accomplice in partitioning
Denmark as the price of Bremen.

Cromwell was not disposed to do this. He had too
keen an appreciation of English interests. As Thurloe
justly observes : the Protector, 'though he wished in
general the prosperity of the Swede his ally, hoping
that at last his arms might be directed the right way,
yet did not like that the Swede should conquer the
Dane and possess all those countries, believing he, being
thereby become so powerful a prince, might engross the
whole trade of the Baltic sea wherein England is so
much concerned.'[1]

But it was equally contrary to English interests that
Sweden should be overthrown by the coalition against
it. 'To me it is evident,' wrote Baillie in 1656, 'that
the ruin of the King of Sweden is the ruin of all the
Protestants round about.'[2] The result of the withdrawal of the Swedish forces from Poland had been to
expose the Polish Protestants to severe persecution;
and if Sweden was expelled from its possessions in
Germany a similar persecution might follow there.[3]
Besides this, if by the assistance of the Dutch the
Danes overcame Sweden the Dutch would secure, as the
reward of their assistance, commercial privileges in the
Baltic which would render it impossible for the English
to compete with them. The Protector, therefore, in
Thurloe's words, 'in this whole business laid this for a
foundation, that it was not for the interest of this nation
that either the Swede or the Dane should be ruined.'[4]
Accordingly he sought to mediate between Sweden and

[1] Bischoffshausen, p. 215. See also G. L. Beer, *Cromwell's Policy in its Economic Aspects*, p. 40 (Boston, 1902).
[2] Baillie, *Letters*, iii. 321.
[3] See Carlyle's *Cromwell*, Speech xvii; and Thurloe, iv. 120.
[4] Bischoffshausen, p. 217.

CHAP.
X
1657
Denmark, to detach Brandenburg, and if possible Russia from the coalition against Sweden, and to prevent the Dutch from openly intervening on behalf of Denmark.[1]

In the latter part of 1657, English diplomacy was extremely busy at these tasks. As early as March 10, 1657, Thurloe wrote to Henry Cromwell, saying: ' His Highness is sending two agents, one to the Dane and the other to the Muscovite, to incline them towards Sweden.'[2]

The agent destined for Russia was Richard Bradshaw, a kinsman of the regicide, John Bradshaw, who held the post of English resident at Hamburg. His instructions directed him to represent to the Grand Duke of Muscovy the advantages which would accrue to him from making peace with Sweden, and to offer the Protector's good offices for effecting it. He was further to negotiate for the restoration to the English merchants of those commercial privileges which they had lost in consequence of the Czar's anger at the execution of Charles I. Bradshaw set out about the middle of May, reached Riga, where he was received with great honour by Magnus de la Gardie, the Swedish governor, and proceeded thence at the invitation of the Duke of Courland to Mittau. But his progress was retarded by the plague which raged in those countries, and by the obstacles which the Russian authorities threw in his way. He waited there many months in expectation of an answer to his demand for a safe-

March, 1658 conduct, and as no answer came returned to Hamburg without entering Russia. It was clear that the Russian government was either unwilling to accept the offered

---

[1] ' The Protector in all these cases governs himself by the Protestant cause,' wrote Thurloe on October 2, 1657, ' and he thinks a peace between the two northern crowns is the best for that, if it may be had.'—Thurloe, vi. 547.

[2] Ib. vi. 107.

mediation, or wanted to see how the fortune of war would
turn before it came to terms with Sweden.[1]

The agent sent to Denmark was Philip Meadowe, who had been for some time English agent at Lisbon, and was a man of very considerable diplomatic capacity. Though it was intended to dispatch him in March, he did not actually sail till September 3. No doubt the reason was that the negotiations going on between the Protector and Sweden rendered delay advisable until the situation became clearer. His instructions ordered him to offer the King of Denmark the mediation of Cromwell to compose his quarrel with Sweden. He was to represent the regret with which the Protector had received the news of the war between the two states, ' whose power and force being conjoined might have been a terror to the common enemy and of great advantage to the Protestant interest; but being turned one against the other, besides the effusion of much Christian blood and the weakening of themselves, it must needs be of great prejudice and hazard to the Protestant cause, especially at this time when the Pope's party do with one consent arm against the professors thereof in all parts of the world; and it is certain that nothing could have fallen out more for the advantage of Spain, who is at open war with us, and for the good of the King of Hungary and that Austrian family, the head and chief pillar of the Popish state, than this rupture at this time.' The Protector pledged himself to carry out his mediation with all impartiality; and affirmed his desire to preserve the integrity and independence of Denmark, of which the King was to be personally assured. ' You shall assure him,' ran the words, ' of our true and sincere affection towards him and his affairs; and that we do

[1] Thurloe, vi. 155, 278, 309, 331, 349, 407, 521, 602, 617, 635, 655, 716, 807, 855. *Urkunden und Actenstücke*, vii. 778.

not judge it the interest of the commonwealth under our government that he should be opprest by any of his neighbours whatsoever, or that any part of his dominions, territories, or privileges should be wrested from him, or put in danger to be so hereafter in any time to come.' [1]

The King of Denmark at once accepted the Protector's mediation (September 25), and the King of Sweden professed his willingness to do the same (October 19). But difficulties arose as soon as it came to settling the details of the intended negotiation. The King of Denmark proposed that Lübeck should be the place of treaty, to which the King of Sweden objected.[2] Charles X proposed that France should be one of the mediators, and Frederick III wished that the States General also should be invited to mediate. To this the Swedish sovereign objected, because the States General had not yet ratified the treaty of Elbing. But the great difficulty was the demand of the Danes that their allies, the King of Poland and the Elector of Brandenburg, should be comprehended in the peace. Instead of a separate treaty between Denmark and Sweden they proposed a general treaty and a kind of congress. This change in the policy of the Danish King, which for the moment proved fatal to the plan of mediation, was due to the influence of the Dutch ambassador. The Danes were persuaded that, if they consented to treat separately, the King of Sweden would have the game in his own hands. ' The very knot of the difficulty is this : should the Dane desert

---

[1] ' Instructions unto Philip Meadowe Esq. upon his repaire to the King of Denmark.' *Foreign State Papers, Denmark*, xvi. 243. The MS. is not dated, but from internal evidence it appears to belong to the summer of 1657. Cf. Guernsey Jones, p. 52 ; and Meadowe, *A Narrative of the Principal Actions occurring in the War betwixt Sweden and Denmark*, p. 17.

[2] Thurloe, vi. 515, 533.

the Pole, and make offer to the King of Sweden to treat CHAP.
with him apart from the other, his fear is that the King X
of Sweden will make use of this advantage against him, 1657
to conclude a peace underhand with the Pole; which
the Pole will be easily induced to do, receiving this dis-
obligation from the Dane; and then the war will lie
heavy on Denmark; for neither of these princes divided
is able to maintain the war against Sweden. If therefore they separate their interests, then happy he that
prevents the other, by making his peace first; at least-
wise the King of Sweden, having thus disunited them,
will at the same time begin a public treaty with Denmark
and a private one with Poland, and force Denmark
into dishonourable conditions, by the jealousy of a
peace to be made with Poland; and so *vice versâ*; and
at last, where he sees most advantageous conditions
offered, clap up a peace there, and prosecute the war
against the other.'[1] *Divide et impera*, said Meadowe,
would be the motto of the Swede; and the King of
Denmark used the same adage to the English ambassador
in explaining his own view of the situation.

There were only two ways of getting the Danes to
consent to treat separately. One was a definite certainty
that the Lord Protector would interpose to procure
them 'equal and honourable terms' from the King
of Sweden. The other was some assurance as to the
nature of the terms upon which the King of Sweden
was prepared to make peace. If those terms were such
as they could reasonably comply with, 'as a foundation
of a just settlement,' they would accept them at once.
In such a case the question of the inclusion of Brandenburg and Poland would not be allowed to stand in the
way.[2]

---

[1] Meadowe to Thurloe, November 22, 1657. Thurloe. vi. 626.
[2] Thurloe, vi. 626, 640.

However, it proved impossible to draw from the King of Sweden any such intimation of the nature of the terms he meant to ask. It was clear, too, that he meant to ask more than the Danes felt inclined to concede. Their idea was a restitution of conquests and a return to the *status quo ante bellum*. He demanded some satisfaction for the attack made upon him, some compensation for the expense which the war had cost him, and the damage it had done to his affairs. ' In his jolly way of expression, since the Dane had led him so long a dance from Poland to Jutland he was resolved at least to make him pay the fiddlers.' [1]

Oct.
24
Nov.
3
Under such conditions little could be hoped from the side of Denmark. Until the capture of Fredriksodde the Danes did not despair of successful resistance in the field; after that event they relied upon their allies to come to their assistance in time to save them. They did not realise the weakness of their military position.

The hopes of successful mediation, therefore, rested mainly on the result of the mission to the King of Sweden. The envoy sent by the Protector to Charles X was Major-General William Jephson, a soldier who had fought in the Irish wars, and a member of Parliament, but a man with no diplomatic experience and of small aptitude.[2] The letter accrediting Jephson expressed the trouble and grief with which Cromwell had received the news of the war between Denmark and Sweden, and his passionate desire to do all the good offices in his power for the healing of the breach.[3] On October 12, at Wismar, Jephson had

---

[1] Meadowe, p. 33.

[2] Compare Schlezer's remarks on his qualifications. *Urkunden und Actenstücke*, vii. 782.

[3] Masson, *Life of Milton*, v. 370. The printed instructions to Jephson (which seem to have been drawn up before the war with Denmark began) refer

audience of Charles X and found him well disposed to CHAP.
X
accept the Protector's mediation.   The ambassador had
been instructed to say that the Protector was not in a 1657
condition to contribute money, ' our late civil wars at
home, and since that our wars with the Low Countries,
and now with Spain, having exhausted this nation,'
but he was willing if possible to give Sweden some
assistance.[1] The King received this well. ' He is very
sensible,' said Jephson, ' of the great expense and
difficulty incident to the war with Spain, and gives great
expressions of rejoicing at the great successes God hath
given his Highness against that potent enemy. He
very much approves of his Highness's pious intentions
endeavouring a general peace amongst the Protestant
party.   As to that betwixt the Dane and him, he hath
already expressed his consent to treat with him upon
honourable terms.' The difficulty was that Charles X
thought the King of Denmark only wished to gain
time, and he feared lest this treaty should retard the
final agreement between himself and the Protector.[2]
Jephson held that the King of Sweden was really
desirous of peace with Denmark. He ' hath at present
so many enemies to deal with that, unless he make
peace with some of them, it seems almost impossible he
should be able to preserve his interest in Sweden and
Germany.' [3] But it seemed more doubtful whether the
King of Denmark sincerely wished for peace. Jephson
came to the conclusion that it would be necessary
for England to put some pressure upon Frederick III
to make him accept reasonable terms. ' I suppose,' he

entirely to the proposed alliance between England and Sweden which George
Fleetwood had endeavoured to negotiate during the latter part of 1656. But
they allude to other instructions not now extant.—Thurloe, vi. 478, 479.

[1] Thurloe, vi. 478; see also Pufendorff, iv. 85.
[2] Ib. vi. 559, 567.
[3] Ib. vi. 574.

told Thurloe, 'nothing will more provoke him to it than some apparent testimony of his Highness's conjunction with the King of Sweden, which is earnestly expected here to be effected by the King of Sweden's ministers in England.' . . . 'I do believe nothing will more tend to the settlement of affairs here than if you would be pleased, if it may be done with conveniency, that some few of your frigates did appear toward the Baltic sea.' [1]

When Jephson wrote this there was some probability that the Protector would support his mediation by such a show of force. Fleetwood and Friesendorff pressed the English government hard, and obtained at last a promise, if not of active intervention in favour of Sweden, at least of an armed demonstration. On October 3, 1657, orders were issued to prepare a fleet of twenty men-of-war for the Baltic, which was to be commanded by Admiral Montagu. 'The design for the twenty ships,' wrote Thurloe to Montagu, 'is to give countenance to Sweden whose affairs are in a most dangerous condition, being left alone in the midst of very many powerful enemies, as the Pole, the King of Hungary, the Muscovite and the Dane; and fears also the Dutch, who give money, and if need be will send to the Danes the eighteen ships which were appointed to be upon the Dogger Bank. The ministers of the King of Sweden are of opinion that if twenty ships were sent that way to wait upon the motions of the Dutch, though no act of unkindness passed, yet it would keep the Dutch from him.' [2] As the Dutch did not dispatch their eighteen ships to the Baltic, Montagu's squadron was never sent, and the Protector confined himself to diplomatic pressure.

[1] Jephson to Thurloe, October 24 and October 26, 1657.   Thurloe, vi. 574, 577.

[2] *Cal. State Papers Dom.*, 1657–8, pp. 431, 432; Thurloe, vi. 582; *Carte MSS.*, lxxiii. 132, 138 ; Guernsey Jones, p. 61 ; Pufendorff, iv. 84.

The King of Sweden was greatly annoyed by this CHAP.
X
1657 disappointment. When Jephson explained to him the reasons why this English squadron had not appeared in the Baltic, he answered 'that he wished either that had been done, or that so much occasion had not been given to expect it.' However, he admitted that it was not Jephson's fault; the intelligence which gave him that hope came from the Swedish envoys in England. Charles wound up by saying, that if the Protector 'had as much cause to know the King of Denmark and the rest of the Protestant princes in Germany as he himself hath had (who he saith for the most part do very little care for the obligation of a promise, but submit still to the greater power), he would have thought it the likeliest way to have brought Denmark to a peace by making him afraid.' [1]

As the Protector put no pressure upon the King of Denmark, Frederick refused to cede any territory, even after the capture of Fredriksodde. When the news reached Jephson from Meadowe, he saw that peace was impossible, for it was absurd to expect the King of Sweden to surrender all he had conquered without any compensation. 'I cannot find,' said he, 'that 'tis very probable that the King of Sweden, who imputes the loss of all Poland and the endangering of the loss of all he hath on this side of the Baltic sea to the King of Denmark's unjust breach of the peace with him, will put himself in the same condition he was, and leave himself liable to the same inconveniences, without any further security, now he hath by arms made himself master of near a third part of Denmark.' [2]

<hr>

[1] Thurloe, vi. 629, 643.

[2] Ib. vi. 640, 674; compare the opinion of Meadowe on the terms expected by the Danish King, vi. 662.

Since it was clear that the Protector's attempt at mediation would end in failure, the second object of Jephson's mission came into prominence. He had no particular proposition to make, but general instructions to treat of the terms upon which assistance might be granted, if any should be demanded from England, either of money, ships, or men.[1]

The fact that the King of Sweden's ambassadors were negotiating on these very same questions with the Protector himself prevented at first any discussion of these points with Jephson. The ambassador told the King at the beginning that he ' was ready to treat with his Majesty, or whom he should please to appoint upon any proposition for a strict conjunction of arms and counsels,' but the King made no answer, ' by reason of his expectation of the success of his negotiations now on foot in England.' [2] The negotiations of Fleetwood and Friesendorff were, however, a failure. They had failed to get the Protector to send an English squadron to the Baltic, though they had confidently assured their master that it was coming. They could not succeed in obtaining a loan. In November, 1657, the Protector was so far influenced by their representations that he promised to furnish the King of Sweden with £30,000 in three monthly instalments. But when December came, the English government was unable to pay the first instalment. In the interval part of the fleet had come home from the Mediterranean ; ready money was needed to pay off the crews, and little was to be got for that purpose, and nothing for any other. The language of the Swedish ambassador at this disappointment was painfully free, and Secretary Thurloe was greatly hurt by it.[3]

---

[1] Thurloe, vi. 674.

[2] Ib. vi. 567, 574.

[3] *English Historical Review*, vii. 727 ; Thurloe, vi. 652 ; Guernsey Jones, p. 63 ; Pufendorff, iv. 84.

On this second disappointment Charles X seems to
have turned to the English envoy. Jephson received a message that if he had any proposal to make to the King he should make it at once. As we have seen, he had not been instructed to make any definite proposal. All he could do, in his own words, was to let the King know ' that it will be impossible for his Highness to give him any considerable assistance without the Parliament's help in point of money, who will at least expect that some places of strength be put in his hands for safety of our men and frigates while they shall be in the service, and for security for the payment of the money that shall necessarily be disbursed for their maintenance.' [1]

About the beginning of January, 1658, Jephson had an interview with Charles X himself. He reported it to Thurloe as follows : ' I discoursed largely to him the reasons which hindered you from giving that present supply of money which was promised and he very earnestly expected. He could not (or at least would not) seem to be unsatisfied with them ; but I found he was very much troubled that the thing was not done.' Jephson himself urged that it should be done, and that with all possible speed. Not doing so might prove even more prejudicial to the Protector's interest than the difficulty of raising so much money possibly could be. Money was the only form of supply which could be given the King at this time of year; and unless he received some proof that England really meant to give him serious help he might be forced to make peace with Austria and Poland, as he could not have a peace with Denmark.[2]

As to the proposed assistance, the King's demands

[1] Jephson to Thurloe, December 14, 1657. Thurloe, vi. 674.
[2] Thurloe, vi. 727.

were summed up under three heads. ' Though the King of Sweden be supplied with men yet it will be impossible for him to go on with so great a war without some supply of money; which you may please to consider in what proportion and on what terms it may be done. Then he says that, if the King of Denmark will not consent to a peace, 'twill not be possible for him to carry on his war, unless the Protector join with him against the other; and therefore desires order may be given to the envoy in Denmark to declare to the King of Denmark that, unless he will assent to peace on equitable terms, you will help Sweden against him. Lastly he desires that, in the meantime, you would give order to your public minister in Holland to press the States General not to assist the King of Denmark.' [1]

These demands were not excessive, but they were more than the Protector, at the moment, was inclined to accede to. Without some supply from Parliament he could not find money to subsidise the King of Sweden, and Parliament was to meet again on January 20. The question must wait till it met. As to the second, Cromwell had already declined to employ threats or force against Denmark. He was not prepared to declare openly on behalf of Sweden against another Protestant power, nor did he despair of the success of diplomatic measures. As to the third, the Protector had already determined to put what diplomatic pressure he could upon the Dutch, and to do so in concert with France. ' Mr. Downing,' wrote Thurloe to Meadowe on December 18, ' embarks the next Monday for Holland, instructed to incline the States General to a treaty endeavouring to make a peace between the Swedes and Danes separately; [2] and I think it is their interest to do

[1] Thurloe, vi. 729.
[2] *English Historical Review*, vii. 725; cf. Thurloe, vi. 676; *Urkunden und Actenstücke*, vii. 787.

so, and I am sure it is that of the Protestant interest,
and I very much wonder that the Dutch with you
should promote the contrary counsels.'

The question of the attitude of the Dutch was the
key of the whole. The success of Cromwell's attempted
mediation between Denmark and Sweden, and the
success of those larger designs to which peace between
those two powers was a necessary preliminary, depended
in each case upon the Dutch. In all his plans of foreign
policy the Protector found the Dutch obstructing his
way; and during the latter part of 1657 the relations of
England and the United Provinces grew more and more
strained. The two states were admittedly on the brink
of war. ' Merchants,' said the English agent at Leghorn
in a letter dated December 30, 1657, ' write generally,
both from England and Holland, that a breach will
suddenly follow betwixt them.' [1]

To begin with, there was the old quarrel about the
right of search. The maritime treaty which Nieupoort,
the Dutch ambassador in England, had for many
months been striving to conclude had come to nothing.
' The Dutch will be able to procure none of those points
they insist upon,' wrote Thurloe on October 2, 1657.
' They here say what is just shall be observed, but they
will not have novelties put upon them.' [2]   The English
negotiators were determined to maintain all the traditional rights of belligerents over the commerce of
neutrals, refusing to admit the Dutch maxim that free
ships made free goods, or to limit the definition of contraband of war as the Dutch desired. [3]   The impossibility
of arriving at an agreement in commercial questions prevented any agreement in questions of European politics.

[1] Thurloe, vi. 697.
[2] Ib. vi. 547.
[3] See Thurloe's ' Review of the Several Negotiations between England and
the United Provinces.' *English Historical Review*, xxi. 319.

To use Thurloe's language, all proposals of ' alliances of common and mutual defence, wherein provision was to be made for the good of the Protestant religion and the professors thereof against the growing interest of Popery,' failed for one and the same reason : ' in respect the United Provinces always found it necessary for them to mingle therewith the considerations of trade.'

The war between England and Spain had increased the ill feeling between England and Holland. English Puritans, who regarded it as a kind of crusade, saw with indignation the apathy of the Dutch in a contest when the cause of Protestantism was at stake. 'His Highness,' complained Thurloe in June, 1656, ' hath great engagements upon him at present against the most potent and cruellest enemy in the world to the Church of Christ, which he is forced to be alone in, all other Protestants standing still without contributing any help at all. And the Hollanders had rather he should be alone in it than that they should lose a tun of sack or a frail of raisins.'[1]

As the war progressed, the danger of accepting the Dutch maxim that the flag covered the cargo plainly revealed itself. Even though it was not accepted by England, the Dutch helped the Spaniards, ' for by concealing the Spanish goods in their names and ships the Spaniards drove their trade in security.'[2] The attempt of the English government to prevent this by exercising the right of search led to continual friction.[3]

In the summer of 1657 rose a new cause of quarrel between the two nations. Portugal was the ally of England in the war with Spain, and the Dutch, in order

[1] Vaughan, i. 433.   [2] Thurloe, *Review*, &c.
[3] Ante, Vol. i. p. 45.

to enforce their claims upon Portugal with regard to Brazil, sent in September, 1657, Admiral Opdam and a squadron of fourteen ships to blockade Lisbon, where, it was said, he was to be joined by De Ruyter and sixteen others.[1] As Spain was at the same time attacking Portugal by land, the independent existence of Portugal seemed endangered. Moreover, as Lisbon was the English naval base in those waters, English as well as Portuguese interests were attacked. 'The blocking up of the port,' predicted Thurloe, 'if it take effect, will hazard the putting of that kingdom into the hands of Spain, at this time when they are so distracted by the war Spain makes upon them at land; and what the consequences will be to us if we lose that port, which is all we have in those parts, is easily seen. Their joining their fleets against us with Spain will not do us the prejudice that this will.'[2] In another letter he says: 'The Spaniard could have never had so great an advantage as this but from the Dutch; and I am persuaded that God will judge them for it at one time or another.'[3] It was in vain that the English government endeavoured by diplomatic means to persuade the Dutch to suspend their operations against Portugal. War was declared by Holland on October 27, and some fifteen ships returning from Brazil were captured by De Ruyter. 'The Dutch war against Portugal,' wrote Thurloe to Henry Cromwell on November 10, 1657, 'doth much trouble us in the war with Spain, and endangers the putting that country into the hands of Spain. Some discourses have been with the Dutch ambassador here, who seems deaf to anything but their own advantages of trade; and truly their carriage in this and in that business of

---

[1] Thurloe, vi. 519, 559. See Wicquefort, *Histoire des Provinces Unies,* ii. 478–83. Brandt, *Vie de Michel de Ruiter,* 1698, pp. 97–9.

[2] Thurloe, vi. 425.

[3] Ib. vi. 493.

CHAP.
X
1657

Sweden is such that shows no good will to this nation, or indeed to the Protestant cause, however they profess the contrary ; and without they do provoke this state above measure, little notice will be taken of their injuries, but endeavours will be used to continue in peace with them ; it being very dangerous to the whole profession, for the Protestants to fall out amongst themselves ; they are already too much embroiled in the eastern parts of the world, wherein the Dutch have the greatest hand.'[1]

Simultaneously with this threatened breach between England and Holland about the question of Portugal, came the growing hostility between the two powers caused by the war between Denmark and Sweden. The attack of Denmark upon Sweden had been encouraged by the Dutch, although they were nominally at peace with Sweden. Thurloe states their motive bluntly in one of his letters to Henry Cromwell. ' This war is of great consequence, especially because it's fomented by the Dutch, who favour the Dane, hoping by his means to get the trade and commerce of the East Sea.'[2]   Just as the Protector had allowed the King of Sweden to raise volunteers in England and Scotland, so the Dutch had allowed levies for Denmark to be freely made in the United Provinces.[3] This was not held a breach of neutrality; but the fact that English and Dutch were fighting as auxiliaries in opposite camps increased the ill-feeling between the two nations. Added to this, much money was raised in Holland for the service of the Danish King by the merchants of Amsterdam.[4] The merchants of Amsterdam also hired ships to the Danes for use in the war against Sweden. It was said that the Danes had obtained from this source twelve or

---

[1] Thurloe, vi. 609.   [2] Ib. vi. 425.
[3] Ib. vi. 509, 758.   [4] Ib. vi. 370, 394, 509, 758.

fifteen men-of-war and many seamen.[1] As the Danish and Swedish fleets were about equal in strength, this reinforcement might turn the scale in favour of the Danes.[2] Last of all, as we have seen, there was the possibility that the Dutch government might send a squadron to the Baltic to assist the Danes.[3]

It was widely believed in Europe that the Protector had actually threatened Denmark with war, and had declared that he would assist Sweden if the Dutch assisted the Danes.[4] But Cromwell's desire to keep the peace between England and Holland was the corner stone of his diplomacy. Before Meadowe set out for Denmark he informed the Dutch ambassador in England of the object of his mission, and told him that the Protector was not sending either men or money to the assistance of Sweden, and did not as yet intend to send any; ' but that he, as a good friend, did first try " viam concordiae." ' [5]

That was in August, 1657; in November, when the Dutch declaration of war against Portugal had made the situation still more threatening, the Protector, through Lockhart, suggested to Cardinal Mazarin the joint action of England and France to settle both the Portuguese and the Swedish question. The Swedish ambassadors, he told Lockhart, pressed hard for an offensive and defensive alliance against the House of Austria. Would France join a league ? Mazarin did not receive the suggestion favourably, nor did Lockhart press it, but joint diplomatic action on behalf of Portugal and Sweden was speedily resolved upon.[6]

When Downing was sent to the Hague he was instructed to act in concert with the French ambassador.

---

[1] Thurloe, vi. 250, 370. [2] Ib. vi. 513, 538, 551, 662.
[3] Ante, p. 318, 328. [4] Thurloe, vi. 327, 747.
[5] Ib. vi. 478.
[6] Ib. vi. 605, 619 ; Lettres de Mazarin, viii. 208, 227, 236, 274.

'The reasons of his going,' wrote Thurloe to Lockhart, 'are to negotiate in those affairs in the East Sea, and also of Portugal; and in case France will give orders to Mons. de Thou to speak with that vigour in those two businesses as the Cardinal expressed to you, it is very likely it may prove of very good effect.'[1] Downing arrived at the Hague in January, 1658, and the choice of an agent, able, bold, skilful in commercial matters, and notoriously disposed to carry out his instructions with the utmost vigour showed that the intervention of England must be taken seriously. The evidence his mission afforded of the good understanding between England and France made the United Provinces more conciliatory, and so rendered peace between England and Holland possible.

All the Protector's schemes for a general Protestant league had vanished into thin air. This alliance between England and France had taken their place—a practical policy had replaced a visionary one. Nevertheless the scheme of a great Protestant league against Austria and Spain still haunted the imagination of Cromwell's ambassador to the King of Sweden. Jephson believed Charles X was desirous to make peace with the King of Denmark as a prelude to projects more in harmony with the ideas of the Protector. 'I do not find him unapt to make peace,' said he, 'with him, the King of Poland, or the Muscovite, or all of them, that he might bend himself wholly against the House of Austria; for, if my observation deceive me not very much, his great design is the same as his uncle's was, on the Empire, which he might have put very fair for, had he not been diverted by the King of Denmark, and does not yet despair of, at least, as I believe, if he can make peace with some of his neighbours and be favoured by

---

[1] Thurloe, vi. 637, 639, 676, 720, 734, 748.

England and France.'[1] Such plans were only possible
if there was a general agreement among the Protestant states, that is, if Denmark, Brandenburg, and Holland were reconciled to the King of Sweden. The Protector and his ambassador both dreamt of a general Protestant congress in which all existing differences should be settled. ' I know nothing in my poor opinion,' said Jephson, ' were more worthy of his Highness (at this time when he hath ministers with all the most considerable Protestant princes and states) than to propose a general meeting for the advancement of the common interest of religion, and the civil interest, and reconciling of differences ; for, until both religion and the civil interest of every state be something secured, I fear particular treaties will not do the work.'[2] But in spite of the ardour with which Jephson advocated a Protestant league, some doubts of its feasibility crossed his mind. ' It may be said,' he lamented, ' with as much truth as it ought to be with grief, that religion amongst states is much oftener pretended for their own interests than really embraced for the honour of God ; yet methinks it were not labour ill spent to discover any that durst publicly avow that principle.'[3] The only Protestant ruler who seriously attempted to make religion the main motive of his policy was the Protector ;[4] and this tended to restrict his action and retard his decisions, because the dissensions of the Protestant powers made it impossible for him to intervene in the affairs of Northern Europe without fighting some of his co-religionists. Even in the Protector's case the com-

---

[1] Thurloe, vi. 643.

[2] Ib. vi. 604. Jephson to Thurloe, November 10, 1657.

[3] Thurloe, vi. 629. Jephson to Thurloe, November 24, 1657.

[4] See a curious conversation recorded by Schlezer in a letter dated April 18, 1656. This letter is not given in *Urkunden und Actenstücke*, but it is quoted by Professor Michael in his *Cromwell*, ii. 116.

mercial interests of his country and purely political considerations were never absent from his mind. Though his ultimate object might be the advancement of Protestantism, the practical steps he took to attain it for the most part directly advantaged England.

Cromwell's subjects did not hesitate to put national ends first. A debate which took place in Parliament on the day of the Protector's inauguration illustrated this. In the spring of 1657 John Dury returned to England with an account of the promising result of his three years' labours to reconcile Dutch, Swiss, and German Protestants. Fleetwood took up the question
and moved a resolution in favour of the reunion of the various Protestant churches, and further, for a public declaration that England would assist the eminent representatives of Protestantism who were at present engaged in war. Desborough and other officers backed Fleetwood's proposal, but Lambert objected to any express resolution for the protection of Protestantism, lest it should occasion a counter-league amongst the Catholics, and in particular a coalition against England. The opposition was so strong that the whole motion seemed likely to be lost, but in the end the House passed a vote asking the Protector 'to encourage Christian endeavours for uniting Protestant churches abroad.'

It was evident that the lawyers, country gentlemen, and merchants, who now formed the strength of the Protector's party, had little sympathy with the militant and aggressive Puritanism represented by the military leaders, and Cromwell had to take this into account in shaping his foreign policy. Even the moderate resolution which the House had finally passed was more than he could attempt to carry out. It had seemed to Dury 'to open a door for action,' and he complained of

Cromwell's lukewarmness, but had to confess that the CHAP.
war between Denmark and Sweden rendered the X
progress of his enterprise impossible.[1] 1657

[1] *Commons' Journal*, vii. 578 ; *Urkunden und Actenstücke*, vii. 772, 775;
A Summary Account of Mr. John Dury's former and latter Negotiation, 1657 ;
K. Brauer, *Die Unionstätigkeit John Duries unter dem Protektorat Cromwells*,
Marburg, 1907, pp. 192, 200 ; Vaughan, ii. 196, 210, 214.

END OF VOLUME I